Constructing the Self in a Digital World

It has become popular in recent years to talk about "identity" as an aspect of engagement with technology – in virtual environments, in games, in social media, and in our increasingly digital world. But what do we mean by identity, and how do our theories and assumptions about identity affect the kinds of questions we ask about its relationship to technology and learning? *Constructing the Self in a Digital World* takes up this question explicitly, bringing together authors working from different models of identity but all examining the role of technology in the learning and lives of children and youth.

Cynthia Carter Ching is Associate Professor of Learning and Mind Sciences at the University of California, Davis. Her research focuses on how people across the lifespan and within particular sociohistorical contexts make meaning with and about the technologies in their lives. In 2007 she won the American Educational Research Association's Division C Jan Hawkins Early Career Award for Humanistic Research and Scholarship in Learning Technologies for her study of digital photo journals in early childhood education. She has also served as an Associate Editor at *The Journal of the Learning Sciences*. Her work has appeared in *Teachers College Record, Urban Education, The Journal of the Learning Sciences, Computers & Education, Early Education and Development*, and *E-learning & Digital Media*. She has previously worked at the University of Illinois at Urbana-Champaign and received her PhD from UCLA.

Brian J. Foley is Associate Professor of Secondary Education at California State University, Northridge. His research focuses on the use of the Internet to support learning communities for students and teachers and the use of visualization in science education. This work includes studying communities of teachers as well as students. He explores how students in informal online environments such as Whyville.net create and define their community. Working with science teachers, Foley helped develop the Computer Supported Collaborative Science program, a model of teaching that takes advantage of cloud computing to enable a more collaborative science classroom. Foley completed his PhD at University of California, Berkeley, and has worked at the Caltech Precollege Science Initiative and University of California, Irvine.

LEARNING IN DOING: SOCIAL, COGNITIVE, AND COMPUTATIONAL PERSPECTIVES

SERIES EDITOR EMERITUS
John Seely Brown, Xerox Palo Alto Research Center

GENERAL EDITORS
Roy Pea, Professor of Education and the Learning Sciences and Director, Stanford Center for Innovations in Learning, Stanford University
Christian Heath, The Management Centre, King's College, London
Lucy A. Suchman, Centre for Science Studies and Department of Sociology, Lancaster University, United Kingdom

The Construction Zone: Working for Cognitive Change in School
Denis Newman, Peg Griffin, and Michael Cole

Situated Learning: Legitimate Peripheral Participation
Jean Lave and Etienne Wenger

Street Mathematics and School Mathematics
Terezinha Nunes, David William Carraher, and Analucia Dias Schliemann

Understanding Practice: Perspectives on Activity and Context
Seth Chaiklin and Jean Lave, Editors

Distributed Cognitions: Psychological and Educational Considerations
Gavriel Salomon, Editor

The Computer as Medium
Peter Bøgh Anderson, Berit Holmqvist, and Jens F. Jensen, Editors

Sociocultural Studies of Mind
James V. Wertsch, Pablo del Rio, and Amelia Alvarez, Editors

Sociocultural Psychology: Theory and Practice of Doing and Knowing
Laura Martin, Katherine Nelson, and Ethel Tobach, Editors

Mind and Social Practice: Selected Writings of Sylvia Scribner
Ethel Tobach et al., Editors

The list of books in the series continues after the index

Constructing the Self in a Digital World

Edited by

CYNTHIA CARTER CHING
University of California, Davis

BRIAN J. FOLEY
California State University, Northridge

CAMBRIDGE
UNIVERSITY PRESS

CAMBRIDGE UNIVERSITY PRESS
Cambridge, New York, Melbourne, Madrid, Cape Town,
Singapore, São Paulo, Delhi, Mexico City

Cambridge University Press
32 Avenue of the Americas, New York, NY 10013-2473, USA

www.cambridge.org
Information on this title: www.cambridge.org/9780521513326

First published 2012

Printed in the United States of America

A catalog record for this publication is available from the British Library.

Library of Congress Cataloging in Publication data
  Constructing the self in a digital world / [edited by] Cynthia Carter Ching,
  Brian J. Foley.
     p.   cm. – (Learning in doing: social, cognitive and computational
  perspectives)
  Includes bibliographical references and index.
  ISBN 978-0-521-51332-6 (hbk.)
  1. Educational technology – Social aspects.   2. Computer-assisted
  instruction – Social aspects.   3. Online identities.   4. Identity (Psychology)
  5. Self-culture.   6. Digital media–Social aspects.   7. Internet and teenagers.
  8. Learning.   I. Ching, Cynthia Carter.   II. Foley, Brian J.
  LB1028.5.C624   2012
  371.33–dc23   2012009111

ISBN 978-0-521-51332-6 Hardback

Contents

Contributors

Pamela Aschbacher is Director of Research at the California Pre-College Science Initiative at the California Institute of Technology in Pasadena, California.

Marina Bers is Associate Professor, Eliot Pearson Department of Child Development, and Adjunct Professor of Computer Science at Tufts University in Medford, Massachusetts.

Claire Charles is Lecturer in Education Studies at Deakin University in Geelong, Victoria, Australia.

Clement Chau is a doctoral candidate in the Eliot-Pearson Department of Child Development at Tufts University in Medford, Massachusetts.

Cynthia Carter Ching is Associate Professor of Learning and Mind Sciences in the School of Education at the University of California, Davis.

Alan Davis is Associate Professor of Educational Psychology at the University of Colorado, Denver.

Lisa Bouillion Diaz is Extension Specialist in Technology and Youth Development at the University of Illinois at Urbana-Champaign.

Alicia Doyle-Lynch is Lecturer in Urban and Environmental Policy and Planning at Tufts University in Medford, Massachusetts.

Deborah A. Fields is Post-Doctoral Researcher at the University of Pennsylvania in Philadelphia, Pennsylvania.

Brian J. Foley is Associate Professor of Secondary Education in the Michael D. Eisner College of Education at California State University, Northridge.

Melanie S. Jones is Associate Faculty Associate in the Psychology Department at the University of Wisconsin-Madison.

Yasmin B. Kafai is Professor of Learning Sciences in the Graduate School of Education at the University of Pennsylvania in Philadelphia, Pennsylvania.

Cameron McPhee is a psychometrician, statistician, and research analyst at the American Institutes for Research.

Caroline Pelletier is Lecturer in the Department of Children, Families, and Health in the Institute of Education at the University of London.

Carol Cuthbertson Thompson is Interim Coordinator Bantivoglio Honors Concentration, Associate Professor in Education at Rowan University in Glassboro, New Jersey.

X. Christine Wang is Associate Professor of Early Childhood Education at State University of New York at Buffalo.

Daniel Weinshenker is Rocky Mountain/Midwest Regional Director of the Center for Digital Storytelling in Denver, Colorado.

Natasha Whiteman is Lecturer in the Department of Media and Communications at the University of Leicester.

Series Foreword

This series for Cambridge University Press is widely known as an international forum for studies of situated learning and cognition. Innovative contributions are being made by anthropology; by cognitive, developmental, and cultural psychology; by computer science; by education; and by social theory. These contributions are providing the basis for new ways of understanding the social, historical, and contextual nature of learning, thinking, and practice that emerges from human activity. The empirical settings of these research inquiries range from the classroom to the workplace, to the high-technology office, and to learning in the streets and in other communities of practice. The situated nature of learning and remembering through activity is a central fact. It may appear obvious that human minds develop in social situations and extend their sphere of activity and communicative competencies. But cognitive theories of knowledge representation and learning alone have not provided sufficient insight into these relationships. This series was born of the conviction that new, exciting interdisciplinary syntheses are underway as scholars and practitioners from diverse fields seek to develop theory and empirical investigations adequate for characterizing the complex relations of social and mental life and for understanding successful learning wherever it occurs. The series invites contributions that advance our understanding of these seminal issues.

Roy Pea
Christian Heath
Lucy Suchman

Introduction

Connecting Conversations about Technology, Learning, and Identity

Cynthia Carter Ching and Brian J. Foley

In 1995, Sherry Turkle's *Life on the Screen* opened up a new field of research, that of interpretive and descriptive studies of human behavior in online environments. Her work exposed a multiplicity of virtual selves and posed provocative questions about the relationship between technology and identity. When asked to respond to rampant speculation at the turn of the millennium about the future of computing, Turkle asserted that "the question is not what will technology be like in the future, but rather, what will *we* be like, what are we becoming as we forge increasingly intimate relationships with our machines?" (2003, p. 1).

While Turkle was certainly not the first scholar to demand that attention be paid to the impact of our technological tools upon our physical and psychological selves (e.g., Haraway, 1985), her question of "What are we becoming?" reflected a growing concern. In fact, over the past two decades a substantial body of scholarly work has emerged to deal with this question from numerous academic fields. Authorities in media studies describe broad ways in which human activity and culture have changed, for good or for ill, due to an influx of technology (e.g., Postman, 1993; Rheingold, 2000; Trend, 2001). "New Literacy" scholars assert that because of changes in social media, multi-media, and writing tools, the very definition of what it means to be a literate person is evolving away from print-based communication (Cope & Kalantzis, 2004; Lankshear & Knoble, 2007; New London Group, 1996). Cultural studies and feminist psychology research detail the ways in which a "cyborg" mentality evolves from the intimate fusion of humans and machines (e.g., Haraway, 1985; Hayles, 1999). According to the cyborg model, the nature of human activity and psychology fundamentally changes as we incorporate more and more digital technology into our physical surroundings, our daily activities, and even our very bodies through medical and wearable technology (Haraway, 1991).

1

From an identity perspective, much of the scholarship on technology's influence in the vein of Turkle's prescient question seems to be describing a unidirectional model of impact: our communities and our selves, physical or virtual, are altered in accordance with the affordances or structures of the technologies we employ. Another specific example of this unidirectional model is the current concern over videogames and their effects on children's attention and health (e.g., Chan & Rabinowitz, 2006; Vandewater, Shim, & Caplovitz, 2004). In many versions of this conversation, particularly as research studies are taken up by media outlets, identity and agency take a backseat to mass effect, as if popular culture presents consumer technologies, and cognitive deficits and obesity automatically follow in their wake. Yet there is an alternative perspective suggesting that perhaps the power of technology lies in the human side of the equation – in the meanings we create, and in the ways we both welcome and resist technology's presence in our culture, our physical and social surroundings, and our personal lives.

While originally published in 1954, long before the word "technology" became synonymous with computing, Martin Heidegger's *The Question Concerning Technology* encapsulates this alternative philosophy. Heidegger asserts that "[T]he essence of technology is by no means anything technological. … We ask the question concerning technology when we ask what it is. Technology is a means to an end. … Technology is a human activity. These two definitions belong together" (1982, p. 4). Heidgegger suggests that perhaps there is only one side of the equation, the human side, and thus, the distinction between technology and its object is a false dichotomy, insofar as we develop and harness technologies to achieve human goals. In recent years, some research on gender and technology, largely from an ethnographic tradition, has painted quite a different picture than a unidirectional model (Gajjala, 2004; Margolis & Fisher, 2002; Selfe & Hawisher, 2004). According to this research, and in accordance with Heidegger, technology is situated within the meaningful histories of individuals and communities, and its impact is largely determined by the agency of those who manage to harness its expressive or exploratory potential.

The constellation of chapters in this book investigates, and perhaps complicates, the relationship between influence and agency in the emerging field of technology and identity. The research contained in these pages details how the use of technology creates possibilities and imposes constraints, how individuals make choices and are denied choices, and how identities both shape and are shaped by technology tools and experiences. The individuals and communities described are diverse: from young children to adults, from struggling inner-city youth to privileged and resource-rich schools, from a focused examination of a single ethnic group to multicultural communities in physical and virtual spaces. Throughout the different studies in the book, however, there remains one constant: an emphasis on *learning* as the context, or even the main point, of investigation in all our research.

A Learning Research Perspective

Why learning? The simple answer is that we are all educational researchers. Learning, broadly defined, is what we do. It is the thematic glue that binds us together, both professionally and personally, and it is a large part of our own identities. In fact, the genesis of our idea for this book occurred when some of the chapter authors presented together in a symposium on "Technology and Identity" at the annual meeting of the American Educational Research Association. When we began thinking seriously about the possibilities for a book, we considered what perspectives might be missing from our original conference cohort and what additional work should be represented. We sought out other colleagues to complete the comprehensive vision we had, and the whole book eventually took shape.

In a broader sense, though, our focus on identity would be incomplete if we did not include a focus on learning. The evolution of identity spreads across the entire lifespan (Case, 1985; Fivush & Buckner, 2003; Harter, 1999), and an awareness of self and the ability to critically examine self-representations are considered developmental milestones on the road to reflective adulthood (Erikson, 1968; Harter, 1990). From a developmental research perspective, learning about the self is one of the most important kinds of learning that humans do. Furthermore, identity, as instantiated via motivations or personal epistemologies, mediates all other kinds of learning in some way and can be viewed as an analytical lens for examining learning in general (Gee, 2001; Wortham, 2006). If we take the perspective that learning is situated within communities, then learning and community identification are fundamentally connected (Lave & Wenger, 1991; Wenger, 1998). As researchers studying identity, therefore, we must examine not only individuals and their learning but also the social and cultural contexts, practices, and technologies, digital or otherwise, that shape and are shaped by the development of selves (Goffman, 1959; Holland, Lachiotte, Skinner, & Cain, 2001).

Thus, we focus not just on technology and identity, but also on the intersection of learning, technology, and identity. This intersection is an underdeveloped area in the fields of educational research and educational technology. It is high time that basic conversations about learning and technology explicitly include questions of identity as an integral part of the discussion. Beginning over three decades ago, authors like Seymour Papert (1980), Jan Hawkins (1985), Idit Harel (1990), and Yasmin Kafai (1995) revealed the human face of educational technology research and called for empowering computer applications and other technology developments that would lend themselves to learners' personal expression and exploration. Yet the vast majority of research on educational technology in formal or informal learning environments has relied primarily on instrumental, cost-benefit analyses, and standardized knowledge assessments (see reviews by Culp, Honey, & Mandinach, 2005; Means & Olson, 1997).

This instrumentalist perspective has several unfortunate consequences. First, a focus on standardized knowledge assessment limits our examination of the role of technology in learning to strictly cognitive effects, rather than a broader investigation of technology's potential relationships to social and emotional development. Second, cost-benefit analyses are often short-term in scope, and thus do not account for the emergent and shifting roles of various technologies in learning across the lifespan. Finally, an instrumentalist view of technology and learning encourages a preoccupation with the *effects of* technology rather than *engagements with* technology, and it certainly does not afford the possibility of abandoning a focus on effects altogether and dealing instead with complex activity systems of individuals, communities, cultures, and technologies (Barab, Schatz, & Scheckler, 2004).

Nevertheless, some scholars have taken up the effort of investigating technology designs and learning environments with a focus on individual and collective identities (e.g., Bers, 2001; Goldman-Segall, 1998; Pinkard, 2005; Steinkuehler & Williams, 2006). Many of them, but by no means all, are represented in this volume. Our approaches vary widely, however, and that is another reason for this book: to expose and make explicit the different methods, theoretical backbones, and researcher stances toward technology and identity that exist in this emerging field.

Developmental and Sociocultural Approaches to Identity

The challenge of reconciling differing approaches is present throughout the broader area of identity research. Different fields describe identity in widely diverging ways, and approaching identity development from a holistic perspective typically requires drawing on research traditions in multiple fields (Buckingham, 2008; Nasir & Cooks, 2009).

A traditional psychological model depicts a healthy adult identity as a coherent set of traits, dispositions, values, and beliefs about the self that can remain relatively unchanged across a wide variety of situations and contexts (Harter, 1997; Marsh & Hattie, 1996). Although developmental psychologists describe childhood through adolescence as being occupied with the process of developing a consistent self-concept (Harter, 1999; Kroger, 2007; Marcia, 2002), in a traditional developmental model, the intensive period of identity development then mostly halts, and adulthood becomes largely concerned with ensuring that the resulting self-concept is integrated, internalized, and realized through life choices (Erikson, 1968; Higgins, 1996). Individuals can choose to represent the self in different ways depending on social cues and contexts (Markus & Nurius, 1987; Schlenker, 2003), but ideas about the self are not necessarily changed through this process. From a psychological perspective, identities may evolve over the lifespan and in response to consistent social messages, but a core concept of self should be sustainable, resilient, and resistant to temporary external influences.

A sociocultural or anthropological model, however, looks very different. Identities are often described as flexible enactments, which only become visible via individual or joint practices displaying and realigning varying aspects of our selves (Goffman, 1959; Wenger, 1998). Identities are not viewed as static clusters of traits, but rather they constantly shift and are repositioned in conjunction with social influences: a mutual refiguring of the individual and his or her cultural world (Holland et al., 2001; Lave & Wenger, 1991). Furthermore, some researchers argue that the very nature of the self is inherently in flux, such that identities are narratively constructed, deconstructed, and reconstructed throughout the entire lifespan in the ongoing and everyday process of telling and retelling stories about ourselves to different audiences (Connelly & Clandinin, 1990; Ochs & Capps, 1996).

Given these two diverging approaches, it seems that identity can be figured as both a developmental construct and a fluid ongoing process. Not coincidentally, research on technology and identity often falls out along some parallel lines. One approach is to assert that identity development is a critical function of childhood, adolescence, and early adulthood, and to investigate the ways that technology can participate in that developmental process. In this model of inquiry, the self that develops and is expressed is not limited to the technological environment; rather, technology functions as a tool for the development of selves (or aspects of selves) that are more consistent across environments and that drive future identity development going forward. A different approach, and one that has become more common in recent years with the rise of digital authoring technologies and immersive online environments, is to frame technology as a tool for identity exploration and experimentation. According to this approach, so-called identity play takes place in various contexts and throughout the lifespan. This work is more informed by a fluid model of identity and examines how representations of the self or ideas about the self are constructed through use of online environments or other digital media. We have organized our volume into two parts in accordance with this broad distinction.

Overview of the Book

Part I contains research that investigates relationships among technology, learning, and identity from a developmental perspective. While much identity research focuses on adolescents, Chapter 1 by Cynthia Carter Ching and X. Christine Wang starts off the book at an earlier point in the developmental spectrum. The chapter describes a study in which a classroom of kindergarten and first-grade students create digital photo journals about their lives and emerging academic identities at school. Ching and Wang analyze children's journals to determine the kinds of self-representations children construct and what kinds of stories children tell about themselves in school through their photos and captions. Borrowing from Foucault, Ching and Wang investigate the potential for the digital journal activity to function as a type of "technology of the self" for young children. The authors find that although children demonstrate significant self-awareness and agency in their journals, it is also the case that Foucault's concerns regarding self and power are both visible and important in the perhaps unlikely context of early childhood education.

Chapter 2 by Alan Davis and Daniel Weinshenker takes a close look at the process of constructing the self through narrative by tracing the evolution of personal stories through the phases of conception, production, presentation, and post-reflection. Through two case studies, Davis and Weinshenker articulate how urban youth can create digital narratives about themselves and thus embrace a sense of agency and imagined futures. One function of Chapter 2 is to describe the affordances of an after-school setting focused on digital video production and digital storytelling for urban youth to engage in self-representation and self-reflection. But beyond the description of the project itself, the chapter also takes a longitudinal developmental approach and follows up with the two case participants five years after the initial project, to investigate the long-term impact of the digital storytelling process. Looking across both of the first two chapters, we find that they are similar, in that the authors examine the potential of digital media and digital authoring to function as focal points for critical periods of identity development, and both chapters approach this work from the perspective of constructing the self through storytelling.

In Chapter 3 by Carol Cuthbertson Thompson and Lisa Boullion Diaz, the book moves from learners constructing digital stories about their own identities, to youth creating digital media about published urban-fiction stories and co-constructing identity and agency in the process. Thompson and Bouillion Diaz investigate the relationship between the identities of inner-city youth and the organization and constituent practices of a community technology center in which they participate. The chapter describes the collaboration among a technology center and its adult mentors, community youth, and an urban fiction author. While the explicit goal of the activity is for youth to design Web sites about popular novels, Thompson and Bouillion Diaz examine how the prospects and identities of these youth are altered by their increasing engagement and technology skill development, how their emerging web pages mediate youth-adult negotiation of design sensibility and authority, and also how the voices of the participating youth affect center staff and researcher conceptions of technology-supported learning.

No assemblage of research on identity and development would be complete without a diagnostic assessment, and Chapter 4 by Marina Bers, Alicia Doyle-Lynch, and Clement Chau provides just that as the final contribution to Part I. The chapter describes the development, testing, refinement, and application of an instrument for measuring "positive technological development" (PTD). This is diagnostic assessment with a twist, however, in that, while many developmental instruments are designed to identify deficits or delayed function as compared to some normative standard, Bers and colleagues take as a starting point the assumption that many youth are already using technology in powerful and positive ways. Building on the positive youth development movement, the authors articulate a developmental trajectory from baseline technology use toward an exceptional youth technology stance that focuses on caring, competence, confidence, connection, character, and contribution. The chapter describes the diagnostic instrument itself and also provides a rich description of youth constructing a virtual city as an example of how PTD constructs are embodied in youth technology practices.

Part II of the book focuses on research that examines the continuous construction and exploration of identities via technology and within technology-rich environments. Participants in the studies described in this part of the book jump back and forth between multiple identities across environments, or even display different identities simultaneously or on a moment-to-moment basis. Whether participants are seemingly unaware of these shifts or explicitly engaging in identity play, these studies of selves-in-flux demonstrate the profound complexity of interactions among person, place, and social world.

Chapter 5 by Brian Foley, Melanie S. Jones, Pamela Aschbacher, and Cameron McPhee introduces Whyville.net, an interactive science-learning community where teen and "tween" users interact via avatars they design themselves as visual representations of their Whyville identities – literally *constructing* their online selves. The authors use surveys and focus groups to investigate relationships among users' real-life identities, real-life appearances, and their Whyville avatars and find that, when it comes to identity experimentation or identity representation, many youth do both; that is, they create multiple identities on the site over time, such that some avatars are reflective of their own physical appearance and demographics, and some are not. Young users' reflections on their identity experimentation, in particular the activity of creating and using avatars that are of a different gender and/or race, can lead to powerful insights about racial and gender bias, including the conclusion that "you can make friends easier on a boy face."

In Chapter 6, Claire Charles unpacks the tensions involved in "young femininity" through an examination of performative gender within technology-rich curricula across two settings: a privileged girls' school and a public co-educational middle school. Charles finds that the girls at both sites in her study inhabit a world of contradictions. They display powerful agency and skill through their mastery of a wide variety of technologies, yet they cannot seem to escape a sense of objectification. In one case the idea of female-as-object is internalized, as the girls themselves ruthlessly evaluate feminine physical appearance. But in another case male gaze is explicitly enacted, normalized, and accepted in the classroom, as boys at the co-educational school use a simulation game to create a female victim. Through the examination of both cases, Charles reminds us that technology does not itself create or deny opportunities for agency or objectification, but rather that technology activities and technology users are situated within complex webs of gendered meanings, contexts, and relationships.

Chapter 7 by Caroline Pelletier and Natasha Whiteman examines the construction and negotiation of fan identity in two contexts: an online fan site for discussion of a particular videogame, and a videogame-making project in an after-school club. The authors examine how participants in both contexts use talk, activity, and artifact construction to position themselves in relation to videogames, to one another, to fandom in general, to fans of other videogames, and to a larger community of game players and non-players. While enacting fan identities occurred in both the game-making and fan site contexts, students in the afterschool program discovered, in true constructionist fashion, that their identities as game players were altered by their emerging identities as designers. Beyond the details of each study, Pelletier and Whiteman use this comparative investigation to advance larger points about the materiality of digital representation, the false dichotomy of product versus product when examining a videogame and how one learns to play it, and the artificiality of strict boundaries between physical and virtual communities of fan identity.

Concluding the volume is Chapter 8 by Deborah A. Fields and Yasmin B. Kafai. Through a detailed case study of one girl in an after-school program where students can participate in an online immersive environment, the authors pose several critical questions highlighting the complexity and challenge of identity research in online contexts. Fields and Kafai ask, When tracing the activity of an individual across physical and virtual worlds, how do we treat the identities that are enacted in different spaces? Is it fair to assume that what is enacted in the physical world is the "real" identity, and that the "play" identity inhabits only the virtual world? Does keeping these enactments distinct or separate make sense, particularly when the virtual identity engages in morally ambiguous or problematic behavior that the physical identity eschews? Finally, how does a person learn how to *be* in an immersive online environment, and what correlates exist to the social and peer influences that contribute to learning in the physical world? The authors provide provocative answers to these and more questions in this final chapter.

Constructing the Self in a Digital World

Before moving on the research studies themselves, we feel the title of this volume deserves some attention. Readers may find this odd coming at the *end* of the introduction, but the explanation builds on what has already been said.

First, the phrase "constructing the self" stems from our assertion that, whether as a developmental phenomenon with a teleological end point or as an evolving and ongoing lifelong exploration, selves are always being actively built and rebuilt. Much of the meaning we derive from life on a daily basis emerges through the process of reflecting on our experiences and converting them into narratives about ourselves (Bruner, 1992; Ochs & Capps, 1996). Further, self-construction occurs within actions both profound and mundane. Several of the chapters in this book describe contexts or curricula that are explicitly pedagogical in nature, designed to afford crystallizing opportunities for deep self-reflection and self-transformation. But these are not the only activities wherein self-construction takes place. Particularly at this point in history, when popular culture and the consumer marketplace provide endless options for self-positioning and self-expression via everyday choices, constructing the self has become a nearly constant activity (Giddens, 1991; Walkerdine, 2003). So although it is easier to see the explicit process of self-construction when engaging with a student selecting photos for a digital journal, or watching an online user creating a virtual avatar (meticulously crafting face and body parts, thoughtfully choosing personality attributes from a list, carefully preparing text for an "about me" description), as modern subjects, we are in fact constructing our selves every day, in whatever environments we inhabit.

Second, the phrase "in a digital world" encompasses any and all of the environments in which we might locate ourselves (or our selves). With this phrase we indicate not only virtual spaces, but also a physical world that has digital technology embedded within it, surrounding us and becoming increasingly normalized. Regardless of whether we are interacting via avatars or text within a virtual environment, using computer or handheld technology with our physical bodies, or reflecting on technologies across spaces, the assertion of a "digital world" still applies. Young adults in the Western world today inhabit a universe that has, from their perspective, *always* been populated by mobile phones, computers, websites, videogames, and wireless technology (Bennett, Marton, & Kervin, 2008). Because the learners in all of the studies contained in this volume are children, youth, or young adults from the United States, Britain, or Australia, this is their universe (and ours, whether we acknowledge it or not).

In sum, the world is digital, and we construct our selves in it.

References

Barab, S., Schatz, S., & Scheckler, R. (2004). Using activity theory to conceptualize online community and using online community to conceptualize activity theory. *Mind, Culture, and Activity*, 11, 25–47.

Bennett, S., Maton, K., & Kervin, L. (2008). The "digital natives" debate: A critical review of the evidence. *British Journal of Educational Technology*, 39, 775–786.

Bers, M. U. (2001). Identity construction environments: Developing personal and moral values through the design of a virtual city. *Journal of the Learning Sciences*, 10, 365–415.

Bruner, J. (1992). *Acts of meaning: Four lectures on mind and culture*. Cambridge, MA: Harvard University Press.

Buckingham, D. (2008). Introducing identity. In D. Buckingham (Ed.), *Youth, identity, and digital media*. Cambridge, MA: MIT Press.

Case, R. (1985). *Intellectual development: Birth to adulthood*. New York: Academic Press.

Chan, P. & Rabinowitz, T. (2006). A cross-sectional analysis of video games and attention deficit hyperactivity disorder symptoms in adolescents. *Annals of General Psychiatry*, 2006, 5–16.

Connelly, F. M. & Clandinin, D. J. (1990). Stories of experience and narrative inquiry. *Educational Researcher*, 19(5), 2–14.

Cope, B. & Kalantzis, M. (2004). Text-made text. *E-learning and Digital Media*, 1,182–198.

Culp, K. M., Honey, M., & Mandinach, E. (2005). A retrospective on twenty years of education technology policy. *Journal of Educational Computing Research*, 32, 279–307.

Erikson, E. H. (1968). *Identity, youth, and crisis*. New York: Norton.

Fivush, R. & Buckner, J. P. (2003). Creating gender and identity through autobiographical narratives. In R. Fivush & C. Haden (Eds.), *Autobiographical memory and the construction of a narrative self: Developmental and cultural perspectives* (pp. 149–167). Mahwah, NJ: Erlbaum.

Gajjala, R. (2004). *Cyber selves: Feminist ethnographies of South Asian women*. Lanham, MD: AltaMira Press.

Gee, J. P. (2001). Identity as an analytic lens for research in education. *Review of Research in Education*, 25, 99–125.

Giddens, A. (1991). *Modernity and self-identity: Self and society in the late modern age*. Stanford, CA: Stanford University Press.

Goffman, E. (1959). *The presentation of self in everyday life*. Garden City, NY: Doubleday.

Goldman-Segall, R. (1998). *Points of viewing children's thinking: A digital ethnographer's journey*. Mahwah, NJ: Erlbaum.

Haraway, D. (1985). A cyborg manifesto: Science, technology, and socialist-feminism in the late twentieth century. *Socialist Review*, 16(2), 65–107.

Haraway, D. (1991). *Simians, cyborgs, and nature: The reinvention of nature*. New York: Routledge.

Harel, I. (1990). Children as software designers: A constructionist approach for learning mathematics. *Journal of Mathematical Behavior*, 9, 3–93.

Harter, S. (1990).Adolescent self and identity development. In S. S. Feldman & G. R. Elliot (Eds.), *At the threshold: The developing adolescent* (pp. 352–387). Cambridge, MA: Harvard University Press.

Harter, S. (1997). The personal self in social context: Barriers to authenticity. In R. D. Ashmore & L. Jussim (Eds.), *Self and identity: Fundamental issues* (pp. 81–105). Oxford: Oxford University Press.

Harter, S. (1999). *The construction of the self*. New York: Guildford Press.

Hawkins, J. (1985). Computers and girls: Rethinking the issues. *Sex Roles*, 13(3/4), 165–180.

Hayles, N. K. (1999). *How we became post-human: Virtual bodies in cybernetics, literature, and informatics*. Chicago: University of Chicago Press.

Heidegger, M. (1982). *The question concerning technology and other essays*. Translated and with an introduction by William Lovitt. New York: Harper Perennial.

Higgins, E. T. (1996). The "self digest": Self-knowledge serving self-regulatory functions. *Journal of Personality and Social Psychology*, 71, 1062–1083.

Holland, D., Lachiotte, W., Skinner, D., & Cain, C. (2001). *Identity and agency in cultural worlds*. Cambridge, MA: Harvard University Press.

Kafai, Y. B. (1995). *Minds in play: Computer game design as a context for children's learning*. Mahwah, NJ: Erlbaum.

Kroger, J. (2007). *Identity development: Adolescence through adulthood*. London: Sage.

Lankshear, C. & Knoble, M. (2007). Sampling the "new" in new literacies. In M. Knoble & C. Lankshear (Eds.), *A new literacies sampler* (pp. 1–24). New York: Peter Lang.

Lave, J. & Wenger, E. (1991). *Situated learning: Legitimate peripheral participation*. Cambridge: Cambridge University Press.

Marcia, J. E. (2002). Identity and psychosocial development in adulthood. *Identity: An International Journal of Theory and Research*, 2, 7–28.

Margolis, J. & Fisher, A. (2002). *Unlocking the clubhouse: Women in computing*. Cambridge, MA: MIT Press.

Markus, H. & Nurius, P. (1987). The dynamic self-concept: A social psychological perspective. *Annual Review of Psychology*, 98, 224–253.

Marsh, H. W. & Hattie, J. (1996). Theoretical perspectives on the structure of self-concept. In B. A. Bracken (Ed.), *Handbook of self-concept* (pp. 38–90). New York: Wiley.

Means, B. & Olson, K. (1997). *Technology and education reform*. Washington, DC: U.S. Department of Education.

Nasir, N. & Cooks, J. (2009). Becoming a hurdler: How learning settings afford identities. *Anthropology & Education Quarterly*, 40, 41–61.

New London Group (1996). A pedagogy of multiliteracies: Designing social futures. *Harvard Educational Review*, 66, 60–92.

Ochs, E. & Capps, L. (1996). Narrating the self. *Annual Review of Anthropology*, 25, 19–43.

Papert, S. (1980). *Mindstorms: Children, computers, and powerful ideas*. New York: Basic Books.

Pinkard, N. (2005). How the perceived masculinity and/or femininity of software applications influences students' software preferences. *Journal of Educational Computing Research*, 32, 57–78.

Postman, N. (1993). *Technopoly: The surrender of culture to technology*. New York: Vintage Books.

Rheingold, H. (2000). *The virtual community: Homesteading on the electronic frontier*. Cambridge, MA: MIT Press.

Schlenker, B. R. (2003). Self-presentation. In M. R. Leary & J. P. Tangney (Eds.), *Handbook of self and identity* (pp. 492–518). New York: Guilford.

Selfe, C. & Hawisher, G. (2004). *Literate lives in the information age: Narratives of literacy from the United States.* New York: Routledge.

Steinkuehler, C. & Williams, D. (2006). Where everybody knows your (screen) name: Online games as "third places." *Journal of Computer-Mediated Communication,* 11, 885–909.

Trend, D. (2001). *Welcome to cyberschool: Education at the crossroads of the information age.* New York: Blackwell Publishing.

Turkle, S. (1995). *Life on the screen: Identity in the age of the Internet.* New York: Simon & Schuster.

Turkle, S. (2003). Interview with: Professor Sherry Turkle. *Open Door: Ideas and Voices from MIT,* July/August 2003.

Vandewater, E., Shim, M., & Caplovitz, A. (2004). Linking obesity and activity level with children's television and video game use. *Journal of Adolescence,* 27, 71–85.

Walkerdine, V. (2003). Reclassifying upward mobility: Femininity and the neo-liberal subject. *Gender and Education,* 15, 237–248.

Wenger, E. (1998). *Communities of practice: Learning, meaning, and identity.* Cambridge: Cambridge University Press.

Wortham, S. (2006). *Learning identity: The joint emergence of social identification and academic learning.* Cambridge: Cambridge University Press.

Part I

Authoring and Exploring Identity

Introduction Part I: Developmental Perspectives

Cynthia Carter Ching

Age matters. Growth is cumulative. These are two fundamental premises behind a developmental approach to studying the human experience. Developmental perspectives are founded on the idea that, whether through biological maturation or socialization and cultural expectations, the challenges and milestones an individual must master throughout the lifespan are highly contingent upon age. Likewise, as age unfolds in a linear progression from birth to death, so too unfold stages of growth in a cumulative fashion, each subsequent developmental challenge or phase building on the last. Thus, developmental research is always constructing a story about process: gaining an understanding of where a given individual is on a particular trajectory, how she came to be there, and implications for where he or she might be going next. In other words, as The King of Hearts famously advised the White Rabbit in Lewis Carroll's *Alice in Wonderland*, "Begin at the beginning, and go on until you come to the end: then stop."

Foundational Theories and Ideas

In identity research, these premises of age and growth are grounded most strongly in the pioneering work of Erik Erikson (1963), who proposed eight stages of development, each represented by fundamental identity tensions to be resolved throughout the lifespan. These phases begin in infancy and toddlerhood, when the child learns to approach relationships to others with "trust versus mistrust." Phases then progress through childhood with "autonomy versus doubt and shame" and "initiative versus guilt," as the child learns to deal with his or her growing independence. Identity tensions become critical in early through late adolescence, when the young person must begin to think about his or her relationship to others in society and create resilient ideas about the self through phases of "industry versus inferiority" and "identity versus role confusion." Early adulthood is preoccupied with finding and establishing a life-partner relationship via resolving "intimacy versus isolation." Finally, identity for middle-aged and elderly adults in Erikson's model becomes preoccupied with reflecting on one's contribution to society and leaving a lasting legacy through resolving phases of "generativity versus stagnation" and "integrity versus despair."

In comparison to other models of cognitive or psycho-social child development prevalent at the time, for example as put forward by Piaget (1968, 1972) or Freud (1989), Erikson's phases of identity development differ in three structural ways, all of which have had profound impacts on subsequent theories and research. First, Erikson's developmental challenges are not simply age-based imperatives but also draw both on biological maturation (i.e., physical capacities for self-care in early childhood, cognitive capacities for self-reflection in later childhood, and emerging sexuality in adolescence) and the shaping effects of social expectations and institutions (i.e., formal schooling in middle childhood, marriage or partnership in early adulthood). Second, unlike other stage models of development, in Erikson's theory life presents these challenges one after the other in a natural evolution; a person does not potentially become "stuck" in a particular phase at some point and unable to progress further. While resolutions to age-specific challenges can affect later development, in that, for example, an individual who learns to mistrust others in infancy and early childhood may also have difficulty forming a lasting partnership in early adulthood, opportunities for continued growth and productive resolution of challenges are found throughout the lifespan. Third, while many subsequent theories have focused almost exclusively on adolescence as the domain of identity development (e.g., Kroger, 2004, 2007; Marcia, 1983), Erikson's model is careful to articulate that while adolescence is a critical turning point for identity, constructing the self is by no means starting from scratch in adolescence, nor is it complete afterward (Erikson, 1968).

Erikson was describing what he believed to be a universal picture of human development, but as such his model has come under criticism for being largely based in the experiences of Western, middle-class individuals. Rogoff (2003), for example, has articulated that expectations for independence and autonomy in early to middle childhood vary dramatically across cultures. Other researchers have questioned the adolescent struggle to define and determine identity that has become such a naturalized part of Western understandings of youth experience. Instead, this research has found that not only is the adolescent transitional phase from childhood to adulthood configured in widely varying ways across cultural-historical contexts (Demos & Demos, 1969), but the intense struggle may also have been overgeneralized to well-adjusted youth from studies of troubled youth within Western society (Benson, Scales, Hamilton, & Semsa, 2006; Damon, 2004; Offer, Offer, & Ostrov, 2004). What this body of research on culturally and historically situated lifespan development makes clear is that while biological aging may afford cumulative phases of growth, social expectations and interpretations of that growth are highly situated and highly varied. Culture and history jointly determine how activities, norms, institutions, and social and family configurations make up the contextual side of the equation at each developmental stage.

Critical Tensions in Developmental Research

While developmental research, on identity or otherwise, is founded on theories of age-based change and cumulative growth, as situated within cultural and familial contexts, disagreement surrounds other aspects of inquiry. There exist three critical tensions within developmental perspectives that are highly relevant to the research on technology and identity contained in Part I of this volume: determinism versus constructivism, developmental timescales, and diagnostic versus participant-centered interpretation. Each of these tensions will be elaborated, accompanied by framing examples from the research studies that make up the subsequent chapters.

A theoretical continuum that has wide-ranging implications is the question of deterministic versus constructivist approaches to characterizing a developmental path or trajectory. Determinist approaches tend to look at objective phenomena in individuals' lives and examine how early indicators predict later outcomes. In these models of development, identity becomes largely a matter of self-characteristics that arise from direct experiences and social reinforcement. Specific approaches include, for example, attachment theory, which argues that relationship patterns, self-efficacy, emotional health, and a host of other factors throughout life can be traced to the security of attachment between infant and primary caregiver (Bretherton, 1985), and self-theory, in which children's beliefs about their own intelligence and ability can be attributed to social messages and their parents' patterns of praise for effort or performance (Dweck, 2000). In contrast, constructivist approaches focus not strictly on events or phenomena themselves but rather on how individuals make meaning of them. Early foundational work in this area includes Piaget's (1932) articulation of children's moral development as a function of their evolving social meanings around rules, wherein young children believe in an everlasting and unchanging set of fixed standards but older children come to an understanding of rules as socially constructed, and Erikson's (1959) assertion of the fundamental role of adult reflection and insight on past events in later identity resolution. More current work by Nelson and Fivush (2004) focuses on the critical role of self-story and scaffolded autobiographical memory (i.e., caregivers and children co-constructing stories about "what happened") for young children to develop a sense of continuous and coherent self across different contexts and experiences.

The authors in Part I of this volume come down firmly on the constructivist side of the equation, in that participants and their perspectives are at the forefront of analysis. Ching and Wang, in their chapter on photo journals in a kindergarten and first-grade classroom, and Davis and Weinshenker, in their chapter on digital video in an after-school program, take seriously the idea of storytelling as a critical component of identity development. In both these studies, the authors examine learning environments that create powerful self-story opportunities for young children or adolescents. These chapters assert that participants are actively *constructing* meanings and identities through their videos and journals, not merely representing or externalizing what they already think or believe about themselves and their experiences. When Thompson and Bouillion Diaz describe how youth learn to negotiate personal expression, usability, and aesthetics as they construct Web pages, the authors assert that these youth are not attaining an expert identity only, or even primarily, through the acquisition of marketable skills, but rather through their reflective enactments of expertise during their Web design experiences. Finally, Bers and colleagues argue that experiences themselves, in the form of technology skill-building opportunities throughout the lifespan, are worth examining only insofar as they contribute to identity and to individual and social meanings around the function of technology for improving self and society.

Another way in which the field of developmental research varies widely is the question of timescale. Traditional developmental psychological research tends to focus on lifespan or age-based development and has employed a combination of longitudinal and cross-sectional methods to capture changes over time (see review by Baltes, 1968). A sociocultural perspective, however, maintains that the lifespan of an individual, or a large subject pool of individuals, cannot be viewed in isolation. Building on Vygotsky, Cole (1990) lays out four scopes of inquiry that span a broad vision of human development: phylogenetic, which describes the evolution of the human species; cultural-historical, which accounts for shifts in meanings and practices over generations as situated within cultural contexts and historical periods; ontogenetic, which examines life-span development; and microgenetic, which is concerned with individual changes over a short period of time or even on a moment-to-moment basis. Saxe, Dawson, Fall, and Howard (1996) demonstrate how these contexts are nested, rather than independent, in that something as basic as a child's developing ability to count or solve a novel fractions problem is highly bound up with the available mathematical forms and functions in his or her cultural-historical context. Going further, Lemke (2001) argues that shorter/faster timescales, both within and beyond a human lifespan, are not only contextualized but almost always constrained by the longer/slower timescales that encapsulate them. For example, a teenage young woman learning to drive a car in a relatively short time seems normal at this point in United States history; however, a natural-adept young female motorist one hundred years ago in the same country would have been quite remarkable and unlikely. Although the relative ontological timeframe of a few months in adolescence is the same in both cases, the surrounding cultural-historical contexts of gender expectations and automotive nov-elty or ubiquity are very different.

In this volume, the authors of Part I deal with timescale in differing and complex ways. Chapters 2 and 3 are both focused on microgenetic develop-ment that occurs for adolescents over a span of a few weeks or months, as underserved youth are engaged with digital video or Web page authoring in community after-school programs. Yet while Thompson and Bouillion Diaz situate these experiences within the cultural-historical context of job prospects and professional identity for urban "at-risk" youth, Davis and Weinshenker take a more longitudinal/ontological view by following up with their participants five years later and examining the transformative potential of that microgenetic development. Bers and colleagues take a lifespan development approach to the construct of Positive Technological Development, but then they also situate this construct within a contentious cultural-historical discourse around "wired" adolescents and apply this perspective in a microgenetic analysis of how youth participating in virtual communities experience the emergence of commitment, care, and other factors. Ching and Wang's chapter is perhaps the most microgenetic on its surface, in that students create "day in the life" snapshots of their experi-ences and then reflect on them less than a week later. Yet the authors add complexity by situating the journal-making activity within ontology as con-strained by cultural-historical context, exploring developmental features of ages five through seven such as gender differences in friendship networks, as well as examining how children's journals represent cultural-historical challenges of young children adapting to the increasingly constraining institution of formal schooling.

A third and final tension in developmental research deals with diagnostic versus participant-centered meanings. Diagnostic approaches to identity development often involve instruments such as surveys, interviews, or sentence-completion tasks and attempt to place individuals on a continuum of structural stages, wherein identity relative to dispositions and values is more coherent, resolved, or clear at later stages (e.g., Hy & Loevinger, 1996; Marcia, Waterman, Mattseon, Archer, & Orlofsky, 1993). Identity development diagnosis for young children focuses more on the extent to which children have a consistent and positive sense of self across time, contexts, social configurations, and behaviors (Harter, 2003). A diagnostic focus on identity development among poor, urban adolescents often addresses the extent to which various components of identity such as beliefs or goals can serve as "protective factors" or "risk factors" in relation to behavioral outcomes like juvenile delinquency, substance abuse, or teen pregnancy (see reviews by Jessor, 1993; Rutter, 2001). Yet although these diagnostic approaches may use interviews or self-narrative as methods of assessment, ultimately, participant meanings typically take a backseat to researchers' interpretations of participants' psychological health or developmental maturity.

The authors of Part I not only take a more participant-centered approach to research and interpretation; many of them also have adapted more typically diagnostic concepts or assessment strategies toward participant-centered ends. In Chapter 1, Ching and Wang take the method of photo-elicitation often used in assessments or interventions, particularly with young children as a means of helping them elaborate on concrete stimuli rather than abstract ideas (e.g., Harper, 2002), and turn it on its head, such that children's photos and their reflections become a window into their subjective realities. In their follow-up investigation of the role of digital stories in their participants' lives five years later, Davis and Weinshenker find that intervention impact is not easily defined or assessed in objective terms. The authors pose an important question: Even if an adolescent's life does not take a more positive turn after engaging in digital storytelling, but that individual still believes creating his story was a powerful experience, what is the nature of the impact? Is increased self-awareness a valuable identity outcome in and of itself? In Chapters 3 and 4, the authors problematize a diagnostic approach to youth, particularly the construct of risk. Thompson and Bouillion Diaz challenge the notion of at-risk adolescents as passive recipients of intervention or training and instead investigate what youth bring to the table and how their perspectives affect the programs designed to help them. Finally, Bers and colleagues have developed a diagnostic developmental measure but position their work as directly challenging research and popular discourse that posits a negative or risky effect of prolonged technology use on adolescent identity and psychological health.

Conclusion

While children and youth are the focus of research represented in Part I, an age-cohort commonality is not what defines a developmental approach. In fact, that would be a poor distinction for this volume, because the learners described in Part II are all adolescents and pre-adolescents as well. Rather, across all the chapters in Part I is the common assertion that the identity-related activities participants engage in are somehow developmentally critical and have implications for future development. Identity is an ongoing project for these learners, but it is a holistic one that resembles a forward trajectory, rather than a constellation of loosely connected performances. In each case, the authors' methods are based in a model wherein identity development within a given context is an endeavor that builds on what came before and will have a significant impact on what comes after. Thus, the authors do not refer to "identity play" or "identity exploration" as much as to "identity building," "identity resolution," or "identity integration."

For all the studies in Part I, technology plays a major role in this identity development process. In the first two chapters, children and youth use digital storytelling as a medium for evolving or articulating aspects of their identities not necessarily related to technology, while the third and fourth chapters deal with youth building identities specific to technology skills and/or values. Further, while participants in these studies engage with technology within particular contexts, a major premise behind the research is that the identity work that happens as a result also has consequences for identity within and across other contexts, with or without other technologies, and over time. Collectively, the authors in Part I make the assertion that technologies can become productive tools for the age-related and continuous processes of constructing knowledge and identity, for facilitating progress in multiple timescales of development, and for helping researchers understand participant meanings.

References

Baltes, P. B. (1968). Longitudinal and cross-sectional sequences in the study of age and generation effects. *Human Development*, 11(3), 145–171.

Benson, P. L., Scales, P. C., Hamilton, S. F., & Semsa, A., Jr. (2006). Positive youth development: Theory, research, and applications. In W. Damon & R. M. Lerner (Eds.), *Handbook of Child Psychology: Vol. 1. Theoretical models of human development*. 6th Ed. (pp. 894–941). Hoboken, NJ: Wiley.

Bretherton, I. (1985). Attachment theory: Retrospect and prospect. *Monographs of the Society for Research in Child Development*, 50, 3–35.

Cole, M. (1990). Cognitive development and formal schooling: The evidence from cross-cultural research. In L. C. Moll (Ed.), *Vygotsky and education: Instructional implications and applications of sociohistorical psychology* (pp. 89–110). Cambridge: Cambridge University Press.

Damon, W. (2004). What is Positive Youth Development? *The Annals of the American Academy of Political and Social Science*, 591, 13–24.

Demos, J. & Demos, V. (1969). Adolescence in historical perspective. *Journal of Marriage and Family*, 31, 632–638.

Dweck, C. (2000). *Self-theories: Their role in motivation, personality, and development*. Philadelphia: Taylor & Francis.

Erikson, E. (1959). *Identity and the life cycle*. New York: Norton.

Erikson, E. (1963). *Childhood and society*. (2nd Ed.) New York: Norton.

Erikson, E. (1968). *Identity: Youth and crisis*. New York: Norton.

Freud, S. (1989). *Introductory lectures on psychoanalysis* (Standard edition). New York: Liveright.

Harper, D. (2002). Talking about pictures: A case for photo elicitation. *Visual Studies*, 17, 13–26.

Hy, L. X. & Loevinger, J. (1996). *Measuring ego development*. (2nd Ed.) Hillsdale, NJ: Lawrence Erlbaum.

Jessor, R. (1993). Successful adolescent development among youth in high-risk settings. *American Psychologist*, 48, 117–126.

Nelson, K. & Fivush, R. (2004). The emergence of autobiographical memory: A social cultural developmental theory. *Psychological Review*, 111, 486–511.

Kroger, J. (2004). *Identity in adolescence: The balance between self and other*. (3rd Ed.) London: Routledge.

Kroger, J. (2007). *Identity development: Adolescence through adulthood*. Thousand Oaks, CA: Sage.

Lemke, J. (2001). The long and the short of it: Comments on multiple timescale studies of human activity. *Journal of the Learning Sciences*, 10, 17–26.

Marcia, J. (1983). Some directions for the development of ego identity in early adolescence. *Journal of Early Adolescence*, 3, 215–223.

Marcia, J. E., Waterman, A. S., Mattseon, D. R., Archer, S. L., & Orlofsky, J. L. (Eds.) (1993). *Ego identity: A handbook for psychosocial research*. New York: Springer-Verlag.

Offer, D., Offer, M. K., & Ostrov, E. (2004). *Regular guys: 34 years beyond adolescence*. New York: Kluwer Academic Publishers.

Piaget, J. (1932). *The moral development of the child*. New York: Harcourt, Brace, & World.

Piaget, J. (1968). *Structuralism.* New York: Harper & Row.

Piaget, J. (1972). Intellectual evolution from adolescence to adulthood. *Human Development*, 15, 1–12.

Rogoff, B. (2003). *The cultural nature of human development.* Oxford: Oxford University Press.

Rutter, M. (2001). Psychosocial adversity: Risk, resilience, and recovery. In J. M. Richman & M. Frasier (Eds.), *The context of youth violence: Risk, resilience, and protection* (pp. 13–42). Westport, CT: Praeger Press.

Saxe, G. B., Dawson, V., Fall, R., & Howard, S. (1996). Culture and children's mathematical thinking. In R. Sternberg & T. Ben-Zeev (Eds.), *The nature of mathematical thinking* (pp. 119–144).Mahwah, NJ: Lawrence Erlbaum.

1 "This Is Me": Digital Photo Journals and Young Children's Technologies of the Self

Cynthia Carter Ching and X. Christine Wang

Childhood is populated by stories: classic stories we hear, make-believe stories we tell, and our own continuing life story that we construct as we age. To this last type of story we add and subtract pieces as we go along, changing the roles of people, settings, and events to reflect a growing understanding of the world and our place in it. Of all the developmental tasks that children must master, this challenge of the self-story is perhaps one of the most important. What will be the nature of our narrative? Will we become the protagonists in our own adventure, overcoming obstacles with confidence, gaining wisdom, and obtaining for ourselves an ultimately happy ending? Or will we find ourselves beset by tragic happenstance and the confounding actions of others, adrift in a sea of events over which we have seemingly no control?

In early childhood, almost as soon as our minds can string together two related events in time and comprehend sequence or cause and effect, this occasionally daunting project of constructing our own story begins. Fortunately, life provides an evolving arsenal of tools to help us in the task: social, cultural, familial, linguistic, and, in some cases, technological. From ancient technologies of writing to modern constellations of pixels and microchips, technological tools can serve to not only record self-narratives for posterity, but can also actually assist us in their ongoing construction.

This chapter presents a research project in which a class of five- and six-year-old children used digital photo journals to construct representations and stories of their experiences at school, and in which the authors talked with the children about their photos and journals as they were being constructed. Our analysis examines the potential of these activities to function as a type of developmental technology, through which self-representation, self-story, self-reflection, and perspective taking are all scaffolded via visual, textual, and verbal means. The chapter provides the developmental and theoretical backdrops to our study in the existing literature, our methods and findings, some insights about the affordances of the particular technologies we employed, and some challenges we encountered in terms of incorporating technology and identity practices in the early childhood classroom.

Theoretical and Empirical Background

Narrative and Development

The theoretical foundation of this study takes as its fundamental premise the idea that self-narratives, the stories we tell about ourselves, are not merely reflective of identity, but rather that they are identity. A sociocultural perspective asserts that identity development is the process of learning to be "a certain kind of person" within particular local cultures (Gee, 2001, p. 99) and involves a continuous negotiation between evolving conceptions of self and the various communities and contexts one inhabits (Lave, 1996; Lave & Wenger, 1991). Narrative, with its unique potential to organize hermeneutic conversations among events and actors in complex relation to one another, is a critical tool in constructing and molding this complicated process as it evolves (Bruner, 1991). The stories we create shape our understandings of past events and influence the construction of future stories. As Ochs and Capps (1996, p. 20) argue, "Personal narrative simultaneously is born out of experience and gives shape to experience. In this sense, narrative and self are inseparable."

But narratives do not merely relate an experienced series of events. Stories are interpretive and therefore subject to change as meanings, understandings, and audiences evolve over time. Narrative interpretations of our pasts are contingent on the perspectives of our present (Ellis & Bochner, 2003), and those narratives about the self that are the most powerful find validation in an audience and can even be constructed with or by others (Sfard & Prusak, 2005). Stories about who we are and our relation to others and to the world are critically important, because "identity talk makes us able to cope with new situations in terms of our past experiences and gives us tools to plan for the future" (Sfard & Prusak, 2005, p. 16). Whereas other scholars have described identity as a tool for understanding learning (Gee, 2001) or have described learning as a crucial shaper of identity (Tobin & Roth, 2007), Sfard and Prusak's articulation of the function of identity stories makes it clear: Learning *is* identity, and narrative is the glue that holds it all together.

In child development, self-narrative is a skill that is acquired with the help of others. Research demonstrates that autobiographical memory, the ability to consistently and spontaneously recall and relay events one has experienced in the past, shows up consistently in early childhood around age four (Nelson, 1992; Schneider, & Pressley, 1989). Self-story does not just emerge wholly formed as a developmental skill at age four, however; rather, it is scaffolded by caregivers in earlier years. Language socialization research documents the ways in which, across cultures, parents assist children younger than four years of age in remembering and telling stories about prior events, a process in which adults provide the narrative structure, tone, and stance, and children fill in key words or phrases as they are recalled (Ochs, 1993; Ochs & Taylor, 1992). Further, research by Fivush and Bruckner (2003) demonstrates that adult-assisted construction of autobiographical memory and accompanying self-narratives is critical for young children's developing sense of the self as a constant and coherent entity, with a past as well as a present existence.

Early self-narrative processes, which focus on a consistent self-as-actor over time and typically relate a bounded series of events, might thus be characterized as constructing an understanding of "who am I, and what do I do?" Self-reflection, on the other hand, might be characterized as the process of constructing an understanding of "who am I, and *why* do I do what I do?" Developmental psychology researchers typically focus on much older subjects when investigating this process, however, usually adolescents through young adults (Erickson, 1968; Marcia, 1994; Waterman, 1999). Such theories of identity development emphasize the importance of reflection toward resolving tensions surrounding ethics, beliefs, affinities, behavior, and choosing peer groups and significant others. Yet despite articulation of myriad conflicts and crises involved in the struggle for self-definition, the research literature on identity development provides precious few details regarding concrete strategies for how to resolve these tensions (see overview by Kroger, 2007), with the exception of a few researchers who focus on interventions with at-risk youth by counselors and educators (e.g., Archer, 1994). For the most part, identity, as framed in modern psychological research, seems to emerge as a psychological construct from the natural course of human development.

Technologies of the Self

Yet, this vision of identity as a spontaneous developmental phenomenon is only a somewhat recent idea. Michel Foucault, in his essay "Technologies of the Self," describes how the self was viewed in classical and early modern times: as an ongoing project requiring individual and collective effort, and as a reflective and enlightened state to be cultivated and cared for (Foucault, 1988). Practices that were viewed as being critical to the development of self included self-declaration, often accomplished through a public recounting of life stories or personal letters, and self-evaluation, a more critical practice involving confession or self-recrimination. From a historical perspective, two related stances to the development of self are identified: "know yourself," which is a more objectivist stance related to evaluation and critique; and "take care of yourself," wherein the self must be protected and given opportunities for growth. Foucault argues that throughout much of post-classical history, as primarily influenced by Christianity and the Enlightenment, an objective/evaluative "know yourself" approach to the development of self has dominated, and only in recent times, perhaps due to a post-modern concern with the fragmentation of identity (e.g., Giddens, 1991), has much consideration been given to more subjective self-declaration and self-cultivation.

The importance of audience is key in each case of self-evaluation or self-care that Foucault describes. As Foucault articulates it, self-cultivation is not a wholly individual effort, but rather takes place within and is co-constructed by a social world. In particular, Foucault argues for the importance of reconciling or reflecting on processes of self within governmentality: the restrictions on expression or presentation of self that occur via social norms, mores, and social or legal rules and regulations. Self-awareness and self-cultivation require understanding of and negotiating among these factors.

Critical also to understanding this theoretical perspective is that when Foucault uses the phrase "technologies of the self," he refers to conceptual tools and practices that aid self-cultivation or self-evaluation, such as personal letters to friends, religious confession, productive self-focused dialogue with others (i.e., responding to pointed questions about the self), and practices of listening to the self-declarations of others and subsequent contemplation. All these various practices function to communicate information and also provide, as Sfard and Prusak (2005, p. 16) articulate, "reifying, endorsable, and significant stories" about the self. Furthermore, for Foucault, technologies of the self serve not only as a means to declare or describe the self, but also as leverage for self-transformation. Thus, an additional modern example would be studies of narrative and identity in Alcoholics Anonymous (Cain, 1991; Rappaport, 1993). The formulaic addiction-and-rehabilitation story that recovering alcoholics learn to tell can be viewed as a kind of technology of the self: framing and giving meaning to experience while constructing an identity that is reified and ratified by others in a social context, and enabling the construction of an identity story that focuses on transformation through recovery.

Digital Technologies and Photo-Elicitation

What becomes obvious in Foucault's essay is that he does not have material technologies, let alone electronic or digital technologies, in mind at all. Foucault's "technologies" are social and individual practices, habits of mind, and social structures that facilitate cultivation of the self, rather than concrete objects or digital tools. Recent research, however, has examined the potential of digital technologies, as situated within social practices, for exploring cultural and religious identities via robotics (Bers & Cassell, 1998; Bers & Urrea, 2000) and personal and collective values via online avatars in a virtual city (Bers, 2001). Our current chapter not only is inspired by this work on digital technologies for identity exploration, but also incorporates the goals of visual representation via digital photography and the developmental challenge for young children of situating the self within the world of school.

In recent years, researchers have investigated the potential of photographic representation as a material technology for personal reflection, objective self-evaluation, and self-cultivation, although the purposes of such studies vary widely. The research technique of having interview subjects look at photos, either digital or print, is sometimes referred to as photo-elicitation (Epstein, Stevens, McKeever, & Baruchel, 2006) or auto-driven photographic interviewing (Clark, 1999). These methods are increasingly gaining in popularity; however, in what would seem like a critical omission from an identity perspective, reviews of photo-elicitation studies often treat as interchangeable techniques in which interviewees respond to photos taken by researchers or reflect on photos interviewees have taken themselves (Harper, 2002). Studies of these research methods find that interview subjects recall more details and converse at greater length about past events and contexts when photos are used as prompts (Epstein et al., 2006), but rarely is self-taken photography or the auto-driven interview itself framed as an intervention or explicit learning opportunity for the subject – a kind of technology of the self.

In studies where reflection on photographs is framed as a learning intervention, this experience is sometimes designed to provide an objective record of events, different from the remembered stories participants might tell. This method might thus be characterized as having a "know yourself," objective/evaluative kind of goal. An example comes from studies in diabetes education, wherein patients take pictures of the meals they eat and the insides of their refrigerators rather than completing written diet logs. Findings of these studies demonstrate that photo representation requires participating diabetics to be more objective and honest with themselves about what they actually consume (Elwood & Bird, 1983; Frost & Smith, 2002). In early childhood education in particular, photo studies often focus on increasing children's objectivity and use photographic images as tools for helping children document and remember curricular activity (e.g., Gray & Gray, 1982; Schiller & Tillett, 2004), or for helping young children understand conflict events from other people's perspectives (Forman, 1999).

Our own work takes a radically different turn from these objectivity-focused purposes for using photographic technology in learning. Instead, our research seeks to understand the *subjective* perspectives of young children in their school environments and investigate how technology can function as a medium for social negotiation and personal expression (Wang & Ching, 2003). This strategy can be characterized as more of a "take care of yourself" kind of approach. Previous reports on the study described in this chapter have examined how digital photo journals can aid technology integration in the early childhood classroom (Ching, Wang, & Kedem, 2005; Ching, Wang, Shih, & Kedem 2006), as well as the potential of digital photo journals as a developmental technology to scaffold children's raw memory and meta-memory (Ching & Wang, 2006). This chapter in particular focuses on the potential for digital photo journal activities to function as a kind of "technology of the self" for young children, helping them materially represent and psychologically reflect on their identities within the world of school.

Research Context and Data Collection Methods

In the beginning of our broader inquiry surrounding digital cameras in the early childhood classroom, our concerns were applied as well as research oriented. We were working with a diverse kindergarten/first-grade classroom of twenty-five students at a university-affiliated primary school in the Midwest. The school's educational philosophy is based on The Project Approach (Katz & Chard, 2000), wherein young children engage in long-term collective investigations of topics they choose. A key aspect of The Project Approach is that, throughout these investigation projects,

representations of student work and student thinking are created both by
the students and the teachers. Student representations typically consist of
creative installations like posters, murals, three-dimensional constructions,
and performances such as skits and songs. Typically, teachers are engaged
in more direct documentation via video and photography of student work
and student activity. In this case, the teacher at our school was a Project
Approach veteran, with decades of early childhood teaching experience.

We entered this context in the fall with three scholarly predisposi-
tions: (1) our theoretical orientation toward constructionism, the educational philosophy that posits that learning happens best when learners are
engaged in creating meaningful artifacts to share with others (Harel &
Papert, 1990; Kafai, 1995); (2) our desire to see a better integration of
technology in the early childhood classroom and its activities (Clements &
Sarama, 2003); and (3) our focus on the importance of understanding children's learning experiences from their own perspectives (Wang & Ching,
2003). After getting to know the classroom environment and the students
and teachers, we suggested a novel approach that would be constructionist, more integrated, and perspective-focused: give digital cameras to the
children and allow them to document their own ongoing activities in a way
normally reserved for teachers.

Teachers and the research team decided together that the best strategy was to use a day-in-the-life approach to digital journaling, wherein
each student was given the camera on a different day and was allowed to
take pictures of whatever interested him or her throughout the school day,
including lunch and recess. Students were told that their task was to create a digital picture book that would show parents and other visitors at
Open House "what your life is like at Prairie School." Photography was an
activity that was situated parallel to other curricular activities throughout
the year, with picture-taking and journal-making ongoing from January
through April. Members of the research team were present at the school
when students took pictures, and researchers documented students' picture-taking activity via video or fieldnotes.

Typically the day following a student's turn with the camera, but not
more than three days later, one of the authors or a research assistant sat
down with each student at a computer in the classroom to help the student
create his or her journal. Student photos from the camera were imported
into iPhoto™, and we used "book" mode, which has space for photos and
accompanying captions, to create digital journals. Researchers assisted
students with connecting the camera, downloading their photos, placing
their photos in the iPhoto™ book, and typing captions for each photo,

which the students dictated. While they were working together, researchers sometimes asked brief questions of the students about their pictures or their picture-taking experience, so that the journal-creation session also functioned as a kind of artifact-focused interview. Journal-creation sessions were videotaped and later transcribed.

Taken together, the entire data corpus for the finished project consisted of video and fieldnotes documenting children's picture taking, each child's finished digital photo journal, and each child's videotaped and transcribed journal-creation session with a researcher. For the purposes of the analysis in this chapter, we limited our analysis to the journal-creation sessions and focused on composite data units that we constructed by matching up each photo in a student's journal with its written caption and its accompanying transcribed conversation. Figure 1.1 is an example of this type of composite unit, where on the left is the student's picture and caption and on the right is the student-researcher conversation (the researcher in this case, "C," is the first author).

Research Questions and Data Analysis Methods

Whereas the previous section focused on the research context and data collection for the broader inquiry of the use of digital cameras in an early childhood classroom, this section focuses exclusively on our investigation of identity and self-narrative from the perspective of digital journaling as a technology of the self. Our research questions for this investigation were as follows:

1. How do children materially represent themselves in their digital photos and journals, and what do these representations reveal about their conceptions of self?
2. How do children represent and reflect on their relationships to the school environment, to school activities, and to other people, and what do these representations reveal about their conceptions of self?
3. What is the nature of the stories children tell about themselves in their school environment through their digital journals, and what do these stories reveal about children's conceptions of self?
4. How might the activity of creating a digital photo journal function as a kind of technology of the self for young children, and what opportunities for self-construction and self-reflection does this activity afford?

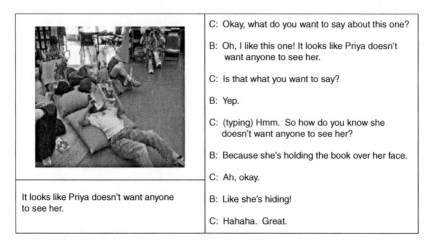

	C: Okay, what do you want to say about this one?
	B: Oh, I like this one! It looks like Priya doesn't want anyone to see her.
	C: Is that what you want to say?
	B: Yep.
	C: (typing) Hmm. So how do you know she doesn't want anyone to see her?
	B: Because she's holding the book over her face.
	C: Ah, okay.
It looks like Priya doesn't want anyone to see her.	B: Like she's hiding!
	C: Hahaha. Great.

Figure 1.1. Composite data unit with photo, caption, and transcript.

To address these questions, we focused our investigation on the composite data units described in the previous section and applied an adapted grounded theory method of analysis (Strauss & Corbin, 1998). Multiple passes were made through all of the data, first looking at each student journal picture by picture to create a comprehensive list of various kinds of representation relating to the first two research questions (material self-representation and representation of relationships to school and others). A second pass through the data, also for the first two questions, involved looking within categories and across student journals to make sure that each category was comprehensive and not unique to only a few students. Categories were adjusted, collapsed, or expanded based on this process.

The third and fourth research questions required attention to units larger than the individual pictures. For the third research question, about the nature of self-story in children's journals, we looked at each child's journal as a whole and created a list of descriptors for the types of sequencing and progression we saw displayed, as well as the tone and positioning of the photographer relative to the photographic subjects. Tone and positioning were sometimes found in the journals themselves, but more frequently were revealed in the accompanying conversations. This list was also adjusted as we compared within and across student journals. For the fourth research question, we looked at the discourse in the journal-creation sessions wherein children reflected on their own experiences as they recalled taking the pictures, and we also paid attention to the role of the researcher in scaffolding children's reflections through asking probing questions as they typed captions.

| This is me. | I wanted to take a picture of myself in the mirror, and it worked! |

Figure 1.2a-b. Literal self-representation.

Results and Discussion

Question 1: Self-Representation

Our first question was: How do children materially represent themselves in their digital journals? This is not as straightforward as it sounds, because children are behind the camera rather than in front of it, and so representation of self is more likely to be by proxy or symbolic rather than direct. We found, however, that a few children did manage to come up with clever means of putting their own bodies into their camera pictures, either by giving the camera to someone else temporarily (as in the case of Figure 1.2a) or by taking a picture of themselves in the mirror (Figure 1.2b). In other cases, children included pictures of their hands, feet, or other body parts that could be captured by the camera while they were holding it.

Far more common than bodily representation was representation by personal objects, wherein children took pictures of material things belonging to them, art construction projects they were working on or finished, and books they were reading (as in Figure 1.3a). Additionally, pictures of food the children were about to consume were also very popular, including pictures of their own lunches as well as their individual portions of various foods created in class during a science investigation about nutrition (as in Figure 1.3b).

In the cases of bodily representation and personal object representation, there are some interesting conclusions we can draw. Although fewer than half the children employed the strategy of bodily representing themselves in their journals, the fact that these kinds of representations were present shows that some children did interpret the task of making the digital photo journal as literally representing themselves within the world of school, but

| This is my book, with a really funny face! | This is pasta. We made it so we could try it. |

Figure 1.3a-b. Self-representation by personal objects.

that the constraints of the technology made this aspect somewhat difficult. (Interestingly, no children employed the strategy one often sees among teens and adults, wherein the photographer holds the camera or camera phone at arm's length from their face and snaps a blind shot without the aid of the viewfinder.) Those children who did represent themselves bodily in their journals often pointed out their strategy to the researchers during journal creation, describing their process as well as the content of the photo, as if to say, "Look what I did!" For example, in Figure 1.2b, Adrienne included a description of her process in the picture caption. Personal object photos were often taken in close-up shots, as in Figure 1.3a–b, and so they often lacked the surrounding context for the object in the photo itself. Even in these very narrowly focused shots, though, children still frequently included some kind of commentary or reflection on the context, such as their photographic intent (as in Figure 1.2b) or the purpose of the surrounding activity (as in Figure 1.3b).

Question 2: Context Representation

The second research question was how did children represent themselves in relation to their surrounding environment, including activities and routines of school, and in relation to other people. We found that a common aspect of children's journals is that they included some commentary on how pictures were situated in the schedule or rhythms of the school day, in a sense categorizing their own pictures as belonging to specific activity structures such as recess, rug meeting, choice time (Figure 1.4a), and sustained silent reading (Figure 1.4b). Our ethnographic approach to this project became helpful in analysis for this category. Due to being in the

| This the choice board with activities to do. | Dana is choosing books for sustained silent reading time. |

Figure 1.4a-b. Activities and routines of school.

classroom on a regular basis since the fall, we noticed that children focused the majority of their school-routine photos on activities that were their favorites, things we observed them enjoying and choosing for themselves over and over again when they did not have the camera. Thus, activity representation served as a type of self-representation also, and even though not many students explicitly captioned their photos with phrases like, "I like to do art at choice time," we still knew this to be the case.

When we turned our focus of analysis to how children represented themselves in a social sense, we found that children's journals were densely populated by other people: friends, peers, teachers, classroom visitors, and parent helpers. But we focused in particular on photos, captions, and student–researcher conversations that contained some elements of children situating other people in relation to themselves. A frequent strategy was using photos of other people to create a first-person plural representation, such that the subject of the photo was "we" rather than "they." Children used this strategy to represent their general ongoing actions, such as frequent recess activities ("we ride bikes outside"), as well as specific assignments and accomplishments completed with peers. Figure 1.5a is an example of this second approach, and the backstory for this photo also demonstrates the thoughtfulness with which many children created their journals. The child photographer for Figure 1.5a exerted significant effort to compose this photo before she took it, assembling her group members from the previous science unit and enlisting the help of a researcher to take their "body" down from the wall. She then finally snapped a picture after multiple tries by her group to hold up the cardboard "body" so it would not flop over.

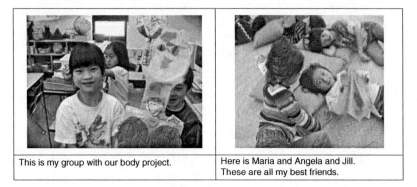

| This is my group with our body project. | Here is Maria and Angela and Jill. These are all my best friends. |

Figure 1.5a-b. Self in relation to others.

A second type of explicit self-representation in relation to others involved referencing friendship groups. Again our presence in the classroom throughout the year proved helpful in analysis, as we noted that children tended to feature close friends in their journals more than other classmates. This finding was not a surprise, as developmental research demonstrates that peers and friendships become more salient and important to children around four to six years of age (e.g., Corsaro, 1985; Rogoff, 2003). Also consistent with developmental psychology research was the degree to which girls' journals reflected not only their own friends but also an explicit awareness of friendship networks – i.e., who is friends with whom (Daniels-Bierness, 1989). Most strikingly, best friends were prominently featured in girls' journals. Unlike boys, who did include their frequent playmates in their photos but did not describe them as "friends," girls often explicitly labeled these "best friends" in their discussions and captions about their photos (as in Figure 1.5b).

Question 3: Nature of Self-Narrative

When we looked at students' journals as whole, we found that journals tended to contain self-narratives of several kinds, not only across the data corpus but also within individual journals. The first and most common type might be characterized as a "Day in the Life of Prairie School" story that reflected the progression of the day, including pictures of different kinds of activity throughout the school schedule, proceeding from morning choice time, through rug meeting, to recess, lunch, silent reading, and so on (although not all children included pictures of all activities). Because the daily routine remained relatively constant throughout the months that students took pictures, this kind of narrative was similar across student journals. The daily sequence narratives were primarily differentiated by deviations from the schedule that took place on days when particular students had the camera, such as the appearance of a guest speaker, a musical performance in the classroom, or birthday celebrations accompanied by cupcakes.

A second type of narrative, and one that was often layered over the first, reflected an approach that might be characterized as "Activities, Objects, and People I Like." This type of story was far more personal, and it varied dramatically from student to student. While students' journals typically reflected multiple activities throughout the day, the emphasis placed on those activities varied with student interest and preferences. So students who liked recess more than quiet classroom activities, for example, might include in their journals numerous pictures of outside play, accompanied by enthusiastic captions, versus only one picture of silent reading. Another feature that served to personalize journal narratives was that children tended to feature their friendship groups to the exclusion of most others, so the primary actors in a finished journal were typically unique to particular groups of friends. For example, in the friendship group of Emma, Maria, Angela, and Jill (three of whom appear in Figure 1.5b, a picture taken by Emma), the journal of each girl was largely focused on the other three girls, whereas other peers appeared in their journals only sporadically. This "I like it" strategy recalls Gee's discussion of affinity-identity, wherein one way identity can be defined is by association with self-chosen activities, peers, hobbies, and so on (Gee, 2001).

In terms of tone and positioning, we were struck by the sense of confidence that children projected through their journals and in their journal-creation sessions with researchers. Children rarely hesitated in describing their pictures and rarely revealed any sense of confusion, except insofar as they were speculating about the motivations or thoughts of other people in the pictures. Even when examining close-up pictures of blurry objects or the backs of peers' heads, with little to no background, children easily identified the subjects of their photos and placed them within the appropriate context of an activity, schedule time, or friendship group. Children's journals were also dominated by a positive attitude toward the school context, and even though they included pictures of activities and peers other than their favorites, no child explicitly captioned or discussed a photo as containing something or someone the child did *not* like.

Yet it is not accurate to say that the nature of narrative in children's journals depicted an unproblematic relationship regarding how selves are situated within school. Despite the wide variety of choices that are common in

| This is everybody raising their hands. | Sam and Jackson are sitting on chairs. They think they'll talk to their neighbor. |

Figure 1.6a-b. Representations of school constraints.

Project Approach curricula, children in our study seemed very much aware of the rules, authority figures, and disciplinary practices that also characterized their experiences in their early childhood classroom. Captions and discussions contained language that indexed rules, such as "kids aren't supposed to be in the kitchen without a teacher." Children's talk also revealed the understanding that adults determined the progression of events; for example, pictures of the teacher and teaching assistants frequently contained some oblique reference to authority, such as, "Molly is passing out math papers and giving directions for what to do."

Beyond just talking about rules and restrictions, however, a number of students chose to actively represent these aspects of their experience in their photo journals. A common type of photo appearing in many students' journals depicted children raising their hands and waiting to be called on to speak (as in Figure 1.6a). Another approach that was more rare, but still noteworthy in its revelation, were photos and captions depicting the disciplinary consequences of behavioral infractions. As an example, the photo in Figure 1.6b shows two boys sitting on chairs during rug meeting, and the caption says, "Sam and Jackson are sitting on chairs. They think they'll talk to their neighbor." Again our ethnographic approach was valuable in understanding this photo and caption, as we realized that the child photographer was indicating a practice wherein students who were too disruptive or inattentive during rug meeting were asked to leave the rug and observe quietly from chairs beyond the rug perimeter. As the year progressed, the teacher asked certain students to leave the rug almost daily, and eventually these students were expected to self-segregate and sit at the chairs automatically at the start of rug meeting. Thus, the child photographer's assertion that the two boys in her photo "think they'll talk to their neighbor" indexes not only the punishment for being disruptive at rug meeting, but also that these two boys have anticipated their own breaking of the rules and normalized the regulations and consequences thereof.

In Foucault's discussion of technologies of the self, an important aspect of self-cultivation is the acknowledgement and understanding of those social mores, taboos, and governmental/legal regulations that constrain the expression of self or even co-construct the very nature of selves that individuals display (Foucault, 1988). Although Foucault's discussion is limited to an adult world, his emphasis on awareness of constraints is equally applicable to the early childhood classroom, where a large part of the learning process at this age is adapting to behavioral expectations. As Carrere (1987) argues, early childhood is largely about learning to live in an environment where others make the rules, at a developmental time just shortly after a child figures out that he or she actually has a will of his or her own, such that the child must then immediately learn to subjugate that will to others. In our study we found that the digital journal project contained opportunities for some students to explore these issues of behavioral constraints as well.

Question 4: Creating Digital Journals as a Technology of the Self

As the findings for our first three questions demonstrate, children used the activity of creating a digital photo journal to explore and represent various aspects of themselves within their school environment, and to tell different kinds of stories about their existences at school – some reflective of their common experiences, including sequences of events and rules, and some highly personal and unique to their own preferences and friendship networks. Such representation and storytelling can be viewed as a type of developmental identity building through self-narrative as well as a type of Foucaldian self-declaration. Students also seemed proud of the journals they created and were eager to share them with others, not just with visitors at Open House but also with peers as journals were being created on-screen. In this way the journals became a compelling social artifact that had meaning for students as both a self-narrative and a personal accomplishment.

Yet there were several critical ways in which we found that we could not explore the full potential of digital journaling as a technology of the self. The first aspect was dialogue with adults. When going back over the transcribed journal-creation sessions, we found that researchers rarely asked more than one follow-up question about each picture. About a third of the time for each interview, researchers asked no follow-up questions at all, and only asked what caption a child wanted to give a given photo, typed the caption, and moved on to the next photo. We found that children typically elaborated on their photo descriptions or reflections as a result of follow-up questions, so this more in-depth questioning was useful, but they did not have opportunities to respond to questions about every photo, or to multiple questions about particularly provocative photos.

This limited amount of in-depth reflection on any given photo was largely due to three constraints. First, because the classroom goal of digital journaling was to have finished products to share with visitors at Open House, it became a high priority to ensure that each child had a completed journal that was fully populated with photos and captions by the Open House date. Second, adding to the pressure of the due date was the fact that five- and six-year-old children have limited attention spans. If journaling sessions went on longer than about thirty minutes, we found that children would get bored, fidget, and want to move on to other activities before their journals were completed. Finally, third, because students took turns, one at a time, to take photos and make their journals, journal-creation sessions required pulling students out of other activities rather than devoting class time to collective journal-making activities. Students and teachers were occasionally unwilling to give up much of their instructional time or choice time for journal creation and wanted to shorten the pull-out sessions as much as possible. A potential strategy to deal with the attention span issue might have been to spread more in-depth discussions about fewer pictures out over multiple sessions, but the deadline of Open House and the reluctance toward pull-outs made that strategy impossible. So while the sharing of digital journals at Open House provided an authentic and visible means of integrating digital journaling into the curriculum, as well as a relevant social context for sharing students' narratives, it also imposed some constraints on the inquiry process.

The second way in which digital journaling shows potential as a technology of the self, but one that was not fully realized in this project, is in the area of habitual practices and self-transformation. Developmental research on the narrative emergence of self (Fivush & Buckner, 2003) and language socialization (Ochs, 1993) demonstrates that children learn to tell self-focused oral narratives over many years of interaction with adults and peers, through having their stories shaped and focused in a social or familial context. The practices of storytelling, personal reflection, dialogue, and confession that are described by both Foucault and researchers in language socialization and child development are not one-shot opportunities, but are rather repeated practices that are integrated into the routine nature of life within social communities. The digital journal project, on the other hand, was a novelty in our kindergarten/first-grade classroom, both in terms of the technologies in use and the curricular approach. We do not know what the activity of digital journaling would look like if it were a habitual practice within this school community, or what the affordances for children's evolving personal transformation might be if we were to study such a habitual practice over time.

Future Trends and Conclusions

Technologies of the self are repeated practices, habitual ways of knowing, doing, and telling that permeate existence within social communities. As handheld and online means of documenting with photo and video, captioning, and sharing these documentations and reflections with a social audience via social media (such as Facebook, blogging, and Twitter) become more and more pervasive, we are already seeing this type of digital journaling become more of a habitual practice among older youth and adults. Further, it appears that that gaming, internet use, and cell phones are making inroads with younger and younger populations (Livingstone, 2003), so it is perhaps only a matter of time before children also develop a sense of self as "being" online and sharing multimedia personal narratives within and across their own "networked publics" (boyd, 2007). But what will be the nature of their stories with a more diffuse audience? This is clearly an area for future research.

In our digital journal project, children primarily created stories of competence, connection, affiliation, and comfort. Their stories were reflective of shared experience as well as the uniqueness of their own perspectives, social networks, and preferences. Their narratives demonstrated fundamentals of identity construction, showing that "I know how to navigate my environment, I know the people around me, I know the things I like to do, I am aware of and comfortable with the normal sequence of events (as well as deviations from it), I am a certain kind of person, and I know my own way of being in the world." Our study suggests that there is a strong potential for digital journaling as a technology of the self to help children create personal narratives that encourage reflection on the collective, governmental, personal, and social nature of their experiences and identities.

But whether schools and teachers, using Project Approach curricula or not, can support this type of activity as a habitual practice is another question entirely. Currently most K–12 schools are banning students' handheld technologies, rather than taking advantage of them (Prensky, 2006). Even in our context, where we had full support from the classroom teacher and digital journals were given an authentic and important role in preparing for

Open House, we experienced difficulties when journal-creation competed for students' time with other more established activities. Digital journaling was an addition to the learning environment, but it did not replace any other learning activities, as is often the case with incorporating new media and new literacies into classrooms and curricula (Lankshear & Knobel, 2007). If early childhood education is to realize the potential of digital technologies for exploring and representing the self within the world of school, in particular through the powerful activity of digital journaling, representation and reflection with new media must become a habitual practice, not just an infrequent novelty. Children are eager and willing to create reflective and provocative narratives; the question is, what tools will we give them to tell their stories?

References

Archer, S. (1994). *Interventions for adolescent identity development.* Thousand Oaks, CA: Sage.

Bers, M. (2001). Identity construction environments: Developing personal and moral values through the design of a virtual city. *Journal of the Learning Sciences,* 10, 365–415.

Bers, M., & Cassell, J. (1998). Interactive storytelling systems for children: Using technology to explore language and identity. *Journal of Interactive Learning Research,* 9, 603–609.

Bers, M., & Urrea, C. (2000). Technological prayers: Parents and children working with robotics and values. In A. Druin & J. Hendler (Eds.), *Robots for kids: Exploring new technologies for learning experiences* (pp. 194–217). New York: Morgan Kaufmann.

boyd, d. (2007). Why youth [heart] social network sites: The role of networked publics in teenage social life. In D. Buckingham (Ed.), *Youth, identity, and digital media* (pp. 119–142). Cambridge, MA: MIT Press.

Bruner, J. (1991). The narrative construction of reality. *Critical Inquiry,* 18, 1–21.

Cain, C. (1991). Personal stories, identity acquisition and self-understanding in Alcoholics Anonymous. *Ethos,* 19, 210–253.

Ching, C. C., & Wang, X. C. (2006). Revealing and mediating young children's memory and social cognition with digital photo journals. In S. Barab, K. Hay, & D. Hickey (Eds.), *Making a difference: Proceedings of the Seventh International Conference on the Learning Sciences(ICLS)* (pp. 85–91). Mahwah, NJ: Erlbaum.

Ching, C. C., Wang, X. C., & Kedem, Y. (2005). Digital photo journals: A novel approach to addressing early childhood standards and recommendations. In S. Tettegah & R. Hunter (Eds.), *Technology: Issues in administration, policy, and applications in K-12 schools* (pp. 253–269). Boston: Kluwer Academic Publishers.

Ching, C. C., Wang, X. C., Shih, M., & Kedem, Y. (2006). Digital photography and journals in a K-1 classroom: Toward meaningful technology integration in early childhood education. *Early Education & Development,* 17, 347–371.

Clark, C. D. (1999). The autodriven interview: A photographic viewfinder into children's experiences. *Visual Sociology*, 14, 39–50.

Clements, D., & Sarama, J. (2003). Young children and technology: What does the research say? *Young Children*, 58(6), 34–40.

Corsaro, W. A. (1985). *Friendship and peer culture in the early years*. Norwood, NJ: Ablex.

Daniels-Bierness, T. (1989). Measuring peer status in boys and girls: A problem of apples and oranges. In B. H. Schneider, G. Attili, J. Nadel, & R. P. Weissberg (Eds.), *Social competence in developmental perspective*. Boston: Kluwer Academic Publishers.

Ellis, C., & Bochner, A. P. (2003). Autoethnography, personal narrative, reflexivity. In N. Denzin & Y. Lincoln (Eds.), *The landscape of qualitative research* (pp. 199–258). Thousand Oaks, CA: Sage.

Elwood, P. C., & Bird, G. (1983). A photographic method of diet evaluation. *Human Nutrition: Applied Nutrition*, 57, 474–477.

Epstein, I., Stevens, B., McKeever, P., & Baruchel, S. (2006). Photo elicitation interview (PEI): Using photos to elicit children's perspectives. *International Journal of Qualitative Methods*, 5, 1–9.

Erickson, E. H. (1968). *Identity: Youth and crisis*. New York: Norton.

Fivush, R., & Buckner, J. (2003). Creating gender and identity through autobiographical narratives. In R. Fivush & C. Haden (Eds.), *Autobiographical memory and the construction of a narrative self* (pp. 149–167). Mahwah, NJ: Erlbaum.

Flavell, J. H., & Miller, P. H. (1998). Social cognition. In D. Kuhn & R. S. Siegler (Eds.), *Handbook of Child Psychology, Vol. 2. Cognition, perception, and language* (5th Ed., pp. 851–898). New York: Wiley.

Forman, G. (1999). Instant video revisiting: The video camera as a "tool of the mind" for young children. *Early Childhood Research & Practice*, 1(2). Online at http://ecrp.uiuc.edu/v1n2/forman.html.

Foucault, M (1988) Technologies of the self. In L. H. Martin, H. Gutman, & P. H. Hutton (Eds.) *Technologies of the self: A seminar with Michel Foucault* (pp 16–49). Amherst: University of Massachusetts Press.

Frost, J., & Smith, B. K. (2002). Visualizing health in diabetes education. In *Proceedings of CHI2002 Conference: Extended Abstracts on Human Factors in Computing Systems* (pp. 606–607). New York: ACM Press.

Gee, J. P. (2001). Identity as an analytic lens for research in education. *Review of Research in Education*, 25, 99–125.

Giddens, A. (1991). *Modernity and self-identity*. Cambridge: Polity Press.

Gilligan, C. (1986). *In a different voice: Psychological theory and women's development*. Cambridge, MA: Harvard University Press.

Gray, D. E., & Gray, R. A. (1982). Cameras and kids: Visual literacy projects for children. *Childhood Education*, September/October, 14–18.

Harel, I., & Papert, S. (1990). Software design as a learning environment. *Interactive Learning Environments*, 1, 1–32.

Harper, D. (2002). Talking about pictures: A case for photo elicitation. *Visual Studies*, 17, 13–26.

Kafai, Y. B. (1995). *Minds in play: Computer game design as a context for children's learning*. Mahwah, NJ: Erlbaum.

Katz, L., & Chard, S. (2000). *Engaging children's minds: The Project Approach*. (2nd Ed.) New York: Praeger.

Kroger, J. (2007). *Identity development: Adolescence through adulthood*. Thousand Oaks, CA: Sage.

Lankshear, C., & Knobel, M. (2007). Sampling the "new" in new literacies. In M. Knobel & C. Lankshear (Eds.), *A new literacies sampler* (pp. 1–24). New York: Peter Lang.

Lave, J. (1996). The practice of learning. In S. Chaiklin & J. Lave (Eds.), *Understanding practice: Perspectives on activity and context* (pp. 3–32). Cambridge: Cambridge University Press.

Lave, J., & Wenger, E. (1991). *Situated learning: Legitimate peripheral participation*. Cambridge: Cambridge University Press.

Livingstone, S. (2003). Children's use of the Internet: Reflections on the emerging research agenda. *New Media and Society*, 5, 147–166.

Marcia, J. E. (1994). The empirical study of ego identity. In H. A. Bosma, T. L. G. Graafsma, H. D. Grotevant, & D. J. de Levita (Eds.), *Identity and development: An interdisciplinary approach* (pp 67–79). Thousand Oaks, CA: Sage.

Nelson, K. (1992). Emergence of autobiographical memory at age 4. *Human Development*, 35, 172–177.

Ochs, E. (1993). Constructing social identity: A language socialization perspective. *Research on Language and Social Interaction*, 26, 287–306.

Ochs, E., & Capps, L. (1996). Narrating the self. *Annual Review of Anthropology*, 25, 19–43.

Ochs, E., & Taylor, C. (1992). Family narrative as political activity. *Discourse and Society*, 3, 301–340.

Piaget, J., & Inhelder, B. (1969). *The psychology of the child*. New York: Basic Books.

Prensky, M. (2006). Listen to the natives. *Educational Leadership*, 63(4), 8–13.

Rappaport, J. (1993). Narrative studies, personal stories, and identity transformation in the mutual help context. *Journal of Applied Behavioral Science*, 29, 239–256.

Rogoff, B. (2003). *The cultural nature of child development*. Oxford: Oxford University Press.

Schiller, J., & Tillett, B. (2004). Using digital images with young children: Challenges of integration. *Early Child Development and Care*, 174, 401–414.

Schneider, W., & Pressley, M. (1989). *Memory between two and twenty*. New York: Springer-Verlag.

Sfard, A., & Prusak, A. (2005). Telling identities: In search of an analytic tool for investigating learning as a culturally shaped activity. *Educational Researcher*, 34(4), 14–22.

Strauss, A., & Corbin, J. (1998). *Basics of qualitative research: Techniques and procedures for developing grounded theory*. (2nd Ed.) Thousand Oaks, CA: Sage.

Tobin, K., & Roth, W. M. (2007). Identity in science: What for? Where to? How? In W. M. Roth & K. Tobin (Eds.), *Science, learning, identity: Sociocultural and cultural-historical perspectives* (pp. 339–354). Rotterdam.

Wang, X. C., & Ching, C. C. (2003). Social construction of computer experiences in a first-grade classroom: Social processes and mediating artifacts. *Early Education & Development*, 14, 335–361.

Waterman, A. (1999). Identity, the identity statuses, and identity status development: A contemporary statement. *Developmental Review*, 19, 591–621.

2   Digital Storytelling and Authoring Identity

Alan Davis and Daniel Weinshenker

In this chapter, we explore how one form of multimedia self-expression, digital storytelling, presents new possibilities for identity formation. Today, access to complex digital authoring technologies are available to a growing number of people who are now able to present stories about themselves and their communities to a potentially huge audience through the internet. Through these stories, places once strange and impersonal take on a human face, individuals previously identified to local majorities mainly through categories such as "undocumented immigrant" or "HIV positive" emerge as individuals to new audiences, and the creators of the stories acquire greater agency in respect to their own identity at the same time that they learn about digital authoring. Our interest here is mainly in how the processes of authoring these stories and their distribution to audiences become a resource in the authoring of identity and in changing the relationship of author and audience.

The term *digital storytelling* arose from a grassroots movement that uses multi-media digital tools to help ordinary people tell their own "true stories". The term has come to be used in journalism and media studies to refer to a broad variety of emergent new forms of digital narratives (Web-based stories, interactive stories, hypertexts, and narrative computer games). In this chapter, our interest is mainly in the creation and dissemination of multi-media digital stories by groups and individuals outside of the commercial professional media.

Digital storytelling as an organized practice arose from the collaboration of Dana Atchley and Joe Lambert in Berkeley, California (Lambert, 2006). One of the stories in their initial workshop in 1993 was about Tanya, a woman struggling with AIDS, who died shortly before the story's screening. From that beginning, with its context of empowerment, the workshop approach to digital story production evolved into the Center for Digital

Storytelling (CDS), making use of intensive workshops to enable people who normally lacked technical expertise and access to digital editing equipment to make digital stories. Joe Lambert estimated that by 2008 some 12,000 digital stories had been produced in association with the Center for Digital Storytelling alone (Lambert, personal communication, 2008).

Digital storytelling facilitated in workshops usually has intentional social aspects to its development and performance. In the Center for Digital Storytelling, for example, ideas for stories arise and are shared in a "story circle" of individuals who frequently share a common experience (e.g., refugees from Somalia, teachers in urban schools, women who have experienced abuse) with strong norms of trust and mutual support (Lambert, 2006). At the end of the workshop, the individual stories are screened before the story circle. However, digital stories can range along a continuum of social involvement, from the story authored mainly alone as an act of autobiography or self-expression to a collective effort to portray community or to assert a shared perspective. Those emphasizing digital storytelling as an act of autobiography tend to view the activity as being primarily of service to the individual telling the digital story, an act linked to long traditions of theory and inquiry into the function of narrative in the construction of memory and identity. Those emphasizing the collective function understand digital storytelling as an act of group representation serving a political purpose for that group in being able to define who they are and to counter stories and impressions of them created by others, often others with greater power and resources (American Friends Service Committee, 2008). Both of these perspectives are linked by common themes of technology, learning, and identity, but there is a tension between the individual focus of the first and the collective focus of the second.

The Importance of Medium

At its core, a story is a sequence of events. But the same sequence of events, expressed as a written text, an oral telling, or a digital story combining voice narrative, visual images, and perhaps music and sound effects, can convey different messages to an audience. Each of these modal elements – voice, image, soundtrack – draws on its own implicit semiotic "grammar" (Kress, 2003; Kress & van Leeuwen, 2001). The same sentence spoken in rap cadence to a hip-hop rhythm track conveys something about the speaker that is very different from the same words spoken slowly and very quietly. The phrase "And then he left" illustrated by an image of a man in a sports car conveys a different feeling from the same phrase illustrated by close-up an image of a drop of water slowly sliding down a rusty gate or a child sitting alone. In short, the multimodal format potentially provides a much richer symbolic palette than does written text alone.

Screen media have become ingrained in the figured worlds of youth as an arena of shared experience (Alvermann & Hagood, 2000; Jenkins, 2006; Kitwana, 2002). Fashions; popular culture heroes such as athletes, musicians, and actors are known to youth primarily through screen media; and the importance of these media as new literacies are increasingly recognized by educators (Hull & Schultz, 2002; Jenkins, 2006). Messages communicated through screen media have a strong impact in shaping youth's opinions about fashion, sexuality, and status and provide a rich source of narrative motifs that young people take up in their own storytelling to address issues in their own lives (Diamondstone, 2004; Dyson, 1997). For these reasons, there is evidence that youth associate screen media with high interest and high status. Digital storytelling taps into youth's associations with screen media as preferred means of communication.

Digital stories have additional features that set them apart from other types of narratives as resources for identity. A digital story becomes "fixed" in a way that is not true of oral stories or written text. The oral story can vary each time it is told and allows the author the opportunity to reconstrue with each telling. The digital story, in contrast, involves a complex linking of narrative and imagery and is difficult to change. Once it is complete, its "telling" does not require the participation of the storyteller: It stands as a work of art, a representation apart from the teller, an "object" for reflection and critique. A digital story can also require significant planning and several days to complete, and the time spent with the story can add to its significance to the teller. These themes are explored more fully later.

Purpose and Perspective

Our own work, and the perspective of this chapter, represents a middle ground in respect to the social production and sharing of digital stories. In our collaboration, with Davis as primarily as researcher and Weinshenker primarily as digital story facilitator, we have worked in after-school multimedia clubs, neighborhood art associations, and an alternative high school with youth in the central neighborhoods of Denver in the western United States. The youth we have worked with have been between the ages of eleven and nineteen, nearly all of African American or Latino ethnicity, and nearly all from very low-income homes. A primary goal of our use of digital stories with low-income youths has been to support agency and the potential for transformative experience (Bruner, 1990; Holland, Lachicotte, Skinner, & Cain, 1998) through the reflective processes of personal-story authoring within a socially supportive community.

The objective of this chapter is to examine how the social context in which digital stories are developed and shared can mediate the ways in which the stories support the development of agency and identity for youth facing challenging transitions in their lives. We explore two cases. In the first, Marion, a twelve-year-old African American youth, creates a digital story that helps him to crystallize various activities involving airplanes into an ambition to become a pilot. In the second, Isaiah, a thirteen-year-old African American youth, creates a digital story reflecting competing pulls towards taking risks and being cool vs. becoming more serious and reflective. Follow-up interviews with these young men, now both nineteen years old, provide a retrospective interpretation of the role of digital storytelling in shaping their identities.

Background and Theory

Research on Digital Storytelling

Researchers and theorists examining digital storytelling have largely approached the phenomenon from two traditions of inquiry: sociological media study and education research informed by sociocultural theory and cultural psychology. In addition, much of the inquiry into digital storytelling embraces its potential for democratization and empowerment, drawing at times on postmodern critical theorists including Foucault (1980). Here we briefly summarize the orientation of sociological media study and then describe in greater depth the orientation of sociocultural theory in education, the primary conceptual framework we draw upon in this chapter.

Inquiry into digital storytelling from the perspective of sociological media study is well represented in the recent anthology edited by Knut Lundby (2008), *Digital Storytelling, Mediatized Stories*. A central concern is the relationship between new developments in media and social practice. Stig Hjarvard (2007) has used *mediatization* to focus attention on how communications media have come to have an impact on (*mediatize*) the social practices that they play a part in representing. Political campaigns are shaped by the constraints and affordances of television coverage. In respect to digital storytelling, how do the features of the medium itself have an impact on the practice of storytelling, including the sorts of stories people tell? Access to digital screen-based media has greatly increased interest in disseminating personal stories. Limitations of bandwidth and storage impose pressures to limit their length, and awareness of the possibility of unintended and undesired audiences, both present and future, may lead storytellers to hold back personal material (Couldry, 2008).

But the relationship between activity and tools, including communications media, is neither linear nor unidirectional. In general, the introduction of a new meditational means creates a kind of imbalance in the systemic organization of mediated action, an imbalance that sets off changes in other elements such as the agent and the mediated action in general (Wertsch, 1998). Researchers in the tradition of sociological media studies are interested in how digital storytelling's contexts and processes of production become associated with styles of interpretation and meaning, associated social linkages, and implications for power and legitimation (Couldry, 2008; Drotner, 2011).

Educational researchers addressing digital storytelling (cf. Davis, 2005; Hayes & Matusov, 2005; Hull & Katz, 2006; Kulla-Abbott & Polman, 2006; Paull, 2002) are primarily interested in how digital storytelling can serve as a developmental resource. Digital stories are examples of new literacies, and many scholars have called for schools to prepare students as informed critics of electronic communications, just as in the past they have prepared them to analyze written texts (Buckingham, 2007; Luke & Freebody, 1997). Gunther Kress and Theo van Leeuwen (Kress, 2003; Kress & van Leeuwen, 2001) have focused on the multi-modal aspects of screen media, exploring how different modes (image, movement, speech, and print) are combined in new acts of meaning. Multi-modal authoring tools previously available almost exclusively to professionals working in media organizations are now available to the general public, and have particular appeal and potential for youth (Hull & Schultz, 2002; Lambert, 2006).

Many scholars working from an educational perspective, including ourselves, have emphasized the narrative structure of digital storytelling. This inquiry tends to adopt a sociocultural perspective, attending to how the social and reflective processes of storytelling employing digital media become part of a dynamic process of changing relationships in the course of participating in social activity (Lave & Wenger, 1991, p. 53). Among these changing relationships are change in the relationship of storytellers to their stories (Davis, 2005; Hayes & Matusov, 2005), change in how storytellers think about their past and future life trajectories (Davis, 2005; Hull & Katz, 2006) and their agency in respect to advocating for themselves and pursuing their ends (Hull & Katz, 2006), change in how storytellers identify and interpret changing points in their lives (Davis, 2005; Hull & Katz, 2006), change in how they represent themselves to others and in the relationships among those exchanging stories (Lambert, 2006), and change in the relationships between the storytellers and the information they convey in their stories (Kulla-Abbott & Polman, 2006).

Narrative and Identity

Our focus here is on digital storytelling involving personal narratives: portrayals of self and self-in-community. This is the genre most frequently facilitated by the Center for Digital Storytelling because of its potential for self-definition and reflection. Here, the relationship between story and self is of particular interest and calls for a consideration of identity and the relationship between identity and narrative. We begin with narrative.

Elinor Ochs and Lisa Capps (1996, p. 19), in their comprehensive review of literature on narrating the self, argue that narrative, the telling of events in a chronological sequence, is a fundamental genre that is universal and emerges early in the communicative development of children everywhere. Jerome Bruner (Bruner & Lucariello, 1989), analyzing transcripts of the night-time soliloquies of baby Emily alone in her crib between eighteen months and thirty-six months, found that about a quarter of her soliloquies were straightforward narrative accounts: autobiographical narratives about what she had been doing during the day or what she thought she would be up to tomorrow. Bruner (1990) suggests that humans have a predisposition to organize experience into a narrative form and that the framing of experience in narrative form is fundamental to making sense of experience and retrieving it later in the form of memory. Experiments conducted in the 1980s confirmed that experience not structured in narrative is much less likely to be remembered (Mandler, 1984).

Classic studies of memory undertaken by Bartlett (1932) first demonstrated that not only does our framing of memory in narrative terms serve to recall and make sense of experience, but that the narrative framing also shapes the memory by altering our recall of events to conform to canonical representations of the social world. Shotter (1990) found that this framing served a social function, so that memories can be more readily shared with others. The process of recall and sharing involves both literal memory and interpretation (Bruner, 1990). As we narrate, we interpret what things mean, evaluate their significance, and infer why they happened. For the story to be "interesting," we emphasize discrepancies: something happened that deviated from what was expectable. Kenneth Burke (1945) formalized this into a "grammar" of dramatic narrative, arguing that a good story has five elements: an action, an actor, a goal, a scene, and an instrument – plus Trouble. Trouble consists of an imbalance or contradiction between any of the five elements. The immediate function of a story is often to make sense of a deviation from what is culturally expectable and to infer the intentions of the participants (Bruner, 1990).

Ochs and Capps (1996) offer an extensive analysis of the relationship between narrative and identity. Personal narrative is at once born out of experience and gives shape to experience. One's reflective awareness of being in the world, including one's sense of one's past and future, is shaped by one's narrative framing of experience.

> Spinning out their tellings through choice of words, degree of elaboration, attribution of causality and sequentiality, and the foregrounding and back-grounding of emotions, circumstances and behavior, narrators build novel understandings of themselves-in-the-world. In this manner, selves evolve in the time frame of a single telling as well as in the course of the many tellings that eventually compose a life. (Ochs & Capps, 1996, p. 22)

These "novel understandings" of self serve as *symbolic tools* (Vygotsky, 1934/1978) for narrators in the sense that they become available to mediate future activity. How one goes about pursuing one's ends is mediated by "who one understands oneself to be" in an unfolding chronology of experience. In this way, learning can be transformative as well as incremental: We learn from experience by internalizing symbolic representations drawn from experience, which in turn allows "qualitative transformations of one form of behavior into another" (Vygotsky, 1934/1978, p. 19). Narrative is a means by which we learn from experience by reflecting upon experience, declaring what it means, and distilling it into a symbolic form to be expressed and remembered. The process is essentially reflexive, folding back on itself: Experience is distilled into narrative, and the narrative itself becomes a tool that shapes memory and mediates future experience.

The sort of "reflecting upon experience" involved in the production of personal narrative can range from a seemingly direct rendering of memory into words, to a self-aware evaluation and interpretation of experience, often constructed in interaction with another. At its best, it involves the sort of critical reflection in which experience is recalled, considered, and evaluated in relation to a broader purpose. It is a response to a past experience that involves conscious recall and examination of the experience as a basis for evaluation and decision making and as a source for planning and action (Kegan, 1994; Schon, 1983).

The power of narrative to shape interpretations of life experience has also led to the formal use of narrative in psychological therapy. In the United States, Donald Spence (1984) and Roy Schafer (1981) explored the implications of a person re-framing his own understanding of events from his past. The Australian clinical psychologist Michael White (1990) describes narrative therapy as a process through which an individual in interaction with a trained therapist relates his or her "presenting problem" as a narrative and then works with the therapist to analyze the narrative and re-frame it in order to arrive at an affirming understanding of self. The act of telling the story aloud "externalizes" it, and this externalization allows the story to become an object of reflection:

> The underlying premise of narrative therapy is that as persons become separated from their stories, they are able to experience a sense of personal agency; as they break from their performance of their stories, they experience a capacity to intervene in their own lives and relationships. The discovery of unique outcomes, as well as the externalizing of the problem, can then be further assisted by encouraging persons to map their influence, and the influence of their relationships with others, on the "life" of the problems. (White & Epstein, 1990, p. 16)

The role of narrative in shaping identity is social, interactive, and also contentious. George Herbert Mead theorized that one's sense of who one is reflects how one is seen by others, and involves "taking the attitude of the other towards oneself" (1934/1974, p. 47). Our stories are shaped by the audiences to whom we tell them in several ways. The story we choose to tell is developed with an awareness of its hearer. The interpretations we bring to our own stories are shaped by the cultural models available to us and are reinforced by our closest associates. Hearers may dispute the telling, or may reinforce the interpretation we offer. We are positioned by others, and in important ways we experience ourselves differently in different situations, as we move from one figured world into another (Holland et al., 1998). The sincere narrative we choose to tell at a given moment reflects our perception of experience at that time and place, but may be different in the company of others at another time and place.

From a sociocultural perspective, recognizing that there is no single "identity" in an essentialist sense, to define identity in respect to personal narratives is reasonable. Dorothy Holland and her colleagues offer such a definition:

> People tell others who they are, but even more importantly, they tell themselves and they try to act as though they are who they say they are.

These self-understandings, especially those with strong emotional res-
onance for the teller, are what we refer to as identities. (Holland et al.,
1998, p. 3)

Sfard and Prusak (2005), drawing on Holland, similarly define identity in
terms of "stories about persons" that include stories one tells about oneself
and stories others tell about oneself. The most significant of these, they
argue, are the stories one tells to oneself about oneself:

There is one special identity that comprises the reifying, endorsable, significant first person stories that the storyteller addresses to herself. ... Being a
part of our ongoing conversation with ourselves, the first-person self-told
identities are likely to have the most immediate impact on our actions.
(Sfard & Prusak, 2005, p. 17).

Drawing on Holland and on Sfard, we define identity as "the enduring,
sincere, and significant first-person accounts of who we are, that we tell
ourselves and to others." We clarify that by "first-person accounts" we
do not intend to bring to mind mainly formal accounts, such as memoirs
(although we clearly include them). Rather, we refer to the brief narratives
that we use to make sense of our lives even though we normally don't
think of them as narratives ("I grew up on the South Side, and that made
me tough"; "I came to California with my parents from India when I was
only three, and when they took me to India when I was twelve to meet my
grandparents, I realized I was much more American than Indian"). This
definition privileges the perspective of the teller because, as Sfard and
Prusak claim, it is the agent's own perspective that is most likely to have
an impact on his or her actions. But even the most intimate and private of
self-assertions are social and relational. They cannot avoid employing the
interpretations made available to us through participation in culture, and
they are construed relative to a figured world of social life (Holland et al.,
1998, p. 68).

Are digital stories enactments of identity by definition? Certainly digital stories may fail to be sincere, significant, or enduring for the teller.
Produced for a grade as a class project, or to amuse an unknown audience on the internet, they often fail on both counts. Without the ongoing
support of a community, the self-realizations they report and the personal transformations they testify to are likely to fade from consciousness
without translation into action. The challenge for the educator and for
the researcher is to determine what the story and its production mean to
the person producing the story and how the potential self-knowledge and
agency are subsequently sustained in social interaction.

Research on Digital Storytelling and Identity

Empirical studies of the relationship of digital storytelling and identity development point to the importance of the social context in which digital stories are authored and disseminated. Drawing on cultural-historical activity theory, categorizing the contexts of digital storytelling in respect to the social negotiation of a shared object or purpose of the activity is useful. In the original conception of the Center for Digital Storytelling, the purpose of the workshops was to enable individuals who lacked technical expertise and equipment to tell digital stories for whatever reasons they might bring to the activity (Lambert, 2006). Authorship in this model typically takes place in an intense workshop setting rarely lasting more than three days, with expert assistance aimed at helping the author arrive at a vision for a story and to translate that vision into the digital multi-modal format. This format is most typically a two to three minute video with a narrative voice track, visual images keyed to the voice track, and sometimes additional sound effects or a music track. The CDS format emphasizes the use of still digital images, often with animation, instead of camcorder sequences, because of the time and training usually required to obtain quality production with the latter. The recent BBC projects Telling Lives (Lundby, 2008) and Capture Wales (Thurmin, 2008) are also of this type.

The expansion of this model into youth centers and after-school programs for low-income youth (e.g., ; Davis, 2005; Hayes & Matusov, 2005; Hull & Katz, 2006) generally involves an opportunity for youth to engage in digital storytelling over a period of several weeks or even years (e.g., Hull & Katz, 2006). To the extent that such programs are sustained, they are supported by a belief that they accomplish educational purposes of positive identity development and agency and that youth become skilled in the use of digital technologies that they may employ for broader purposes, including earning a living. The model remains voluntary, and the institutional goals may be implicit rather than explicit. Youth who do not come to share these goals abandon the activity or find ways to appropriate it for their own purposes (Hayes & Matusov, 2005).

A third context for digital storytelling with youth has been school and religious settings in which institutional goals are explicit. Kaare and Lundy (2008) studied a digital storytelling activity sponsored by the Church of Norway that directed youth in the authoring of "digital faith stories." Rina Benmayor (Weis, Benmayor, O'Leary, & Eynon, 2002) has employed digital storytelling as an assignment in a course on Latina Life Stories. The Australian Centre for the Moving Image (ACMI) and the Center for

Digital Storytelling have trained hundreds of teachers in Australia and the United States (respectively) to employ digital storytelling in the classroom as a means of accomplishing established educational goals (see McWilliam, 2008). All of these social contexts are distinct from informal, self-initiated efforts of groups and individuals to create digital stories as "home videos," blogs, and social networking profiles for dissemination through the internet (Brake, 2008; Lundby, 2008).

Very few empirical studies have examined the relationship between digital storytelling and identity representation and construction within the classic structure of the short workshop format. Nancy Thurmin (2008) conducted observations and interviews with participants in the Museum of London's London Voices project, and BBC Wales' digital storytelling project, Capture Wales. She found that participants perceived varying purposes for their participation: learning about multi-media tools, making a record for private use, hearing others' stories, and "having a voice" through giving the public access to their own stories (p. 95). Thurmin reported that some participants talked about the process as "therapeutic" (p. 97) and that some mentioned the value of thinking about their own and others' stories.

Kulla-Abbott and Polman (2008) and Banaszewski (2002) have studied digital storytelling in K–12 classroom settings, with some attention to self-representation. Kulla-Abbott and Polman analyzed the digital stories of 41 seventh-grade students created in a public school in the midwestern United States. Children authored personal stories, and stories about an environmental issue. The most frequent topics of the personal stories (sports, vacation travel, pets) did not seem to involve the sort of reflection that might contribute substantially to identity consolidation or change. Nonetheless, the researchers found that students were much more invested in their personal stories than in the stories about the environment. Banaszewski (2002) found a strong increase in the proportion of his fourth- and fifth-grade students who embraced an identity as "writer" after responding to an assignment to develop a digital story about a place that was special to them. Banaszewski modeled the activity first with a personal story of his own about a place special to him, and worked to create an atmosphere of trust.

Evidence that the process of digital storytelling can serve transformative purposes in respect to identity formation has come primarily out of settings in which individuals (usually youth), united by shared experience such as non-dominant status in respect to a larger social context, have spent an extended time authoring stories in a supportive and trusting community. Most of these have been in extended after-school and community settings in which the self-reflection and self-representation goals have not been confounded by grading and the need to accomplish defined educational objectives (Davis, 2005; Hull & Katz, 2006).

Context and Methods

In this chapter we draw on two ethnographic case studies* that address the general question: How does digital storytelling serve as a resource for sustained identity development for youth? Both cases are drawn from a study of seven middle school youth who completed digital stories in an after-school technology club (the Cyber Cougars) facilitated by the two authors in an urban public school over a six-week period. Five of the youth, all male, were of African American ethnicity, and two, both female, had immigrated from Nigeria. The cases reported here were selected because the youth were available for follow-up interviews five years after the completion of their digital stories.

Both cases draw on ethnographic traditions of participant observation and micro-ethnography of interaction. Weinshenker led the facilitation of the digital storytelling, and worked closely with each youth as they constructed their stories, discussing the process periodically with Davis. Davis also assisted in facilitating the activity in the role of participant observer, recording daily field notes throughout the process of creating the digital stories and afterward, when youth screened their finished products to audiences in the Cyber Cougar club and later at the University of Colorado Denver. These observations aimed at providing detailed descriptions of how the youth went about producing their stories, and at inferring the meaning and significance of the stories to their authors. Davis also recorded notes on conversations with parents of the youth regarding the meaning and significance of the stories as well as their perceptions of what the process of creating them had meant.

During the initial phase of the activity, when the youth were deciding on the script that would be turned into the voice track of their digital story, we employed methods of microethnography of interaction, especially as developed by Frederick Erickson (1986, 1992). We recorded and later transcribed each conversation with the youth as they began working on their story scripts. We then drew upon the transcripts and the various drafts of the scripts to create a chronology of changes, and analyzed these to infer

---

* Earlier versions of these cases were previously published (Davis, 2005) and are used by permission.

decision points accounting for each change from initial conversations to initial drafts and eventually to the final wording of the narrative.

Both authors participated in follow-up interviews with the youth five years after the completion of the digital stories. With the first youth ("Marion"), these involved relatively informal conversations with field notes, because we had been in periodic contact with him over the years, and the role of digital storytelling in his identity formation had settled into a consistent story, described in the next subsection. In the case of the second youth, where the significance of the digital story as a resource for identity development was much less clear, we conducted a recorded ninety-minute interview. The interview followed the form of the ethnographic interview described by Spradley (1979), beginning with "grand tour" questions first (What are you up to these days? What do you remember about working with us in the technology club?) followed by "mini-tour" questions narrowing in on more specific aspects of the activity ("What do you remember about the digital story you made?"). After eliciting his memories with minimal prompting, we then showed him the script he had written and played the digital story he had produced, and asked further questions about what he could remember about the experience and its subsequent importance to him.

We invited eighth-grade youth who had participated in our Cyber Cougars activities in previous years to participate in digital storytelling after school, and seven chose to participate on a regular basis. Second author Daniel Weinshenker explained that a digital story was a short movie, about two minutes long, that told a true story about some change in one's life. The story "tells how you changed, or how something changed for you." Daniel began by creating a "story circle" with the shared understanding that it had to be safe for everyone to tell stories without fear that anyone would make fun of them or criticize their ideas or work. Digital stories produced by youth in other settings were shown, and each of these dealt with experiences and interpretations of emotional significance to the teller. An expectation was established that digital stories dealt with matters of importance and that turning on peers who made themselves emotionally vulnerable by revealing what they cared about was not acceptable.

The first author, who had little previous experience with digital storytelling, imagined that the process of settling on a story to tell would be mainly one of selection, in that each of us has a store of significant events to relate, and the process of personal storytelling would be initially mainly a matter of selecting which one to portray. As the process unfolded, however, it became obvious that the initial processes of narration were more complex.

Youth were reluctant to share first-person accounts, and the accounts initially focused on a noteworthy event or topic, but did not associate the event with change or consequences. The rendering of these kernels into a narrative emerged in a highly interactive process, a series of conversations and story drafts and revisions before the "final" story emerged and was recorded. This process raised questions about the nature of authorship and the role of others in the formation of identity, and the description of this process became a second focus for inquiry.

When we finished, we suggested holding an informal film festival within our club. The students agreed, and we projected the finished stories onto the wall of the computer lab and broadcast the narrative soundtracks on speakers. We hadn't advertised the event, but two teachers came because one of the authors had invited them. All four youth wanted DVDs of their work to take home, and all four reported to us later that they showed them to adults in their homes. Marion, one of the youth, was surprised at his father's response. "My dad, he even got back there and watched it *again*, like you watch a movie!" he reported.

Case 1: Marion and His Airplanes

Marion, a thirteen-year old African American young man, agreed that doing well in school was important to his future, and he acted accordingly. He turned in homework and received grades of A, B, or occasionally C in academic subjects. His older brother had attended college, and Marion also spoke of attending college as well. On the other hand, he did not focus on any particular career goal or academic interest and did not have a well-organized sense of a future identity apart from the idea of going to college.

Marion was eager to author a story two days after we introduced the idea to the Cyber Cougars. "I want to tell about airplanes," he said, "and about the Ace Combat computer game that I play." Before he began to write a script, he and the first author talked about the story.

> *Marion*: I started playing Ace Combat 4, and I got real good at it. That's what I want to tell about.
> *Alan*: What is it, a computer game?
> *Marion*: Yeah, my mom got it for me because I got good grades.
> *Alan*: But you don't want to make a story just about a computer game, do you? What's important about it?
> *Marion*: I do all kinds of things about planes. I have an F16 Tomcat, and an F18 Hornet, and a P-51 Mustang, and I know all about them, how fast they fly, what armaments they have, everything.

Alan: What do you mean you *have* them? You have models of them?

Marion: Models, yeah.

Alan: Are they connected to the Ace Combat game?

Marion: Sort of, yeah. I learned about the F-18 Hornet playing Ace Combat, and then one day I saw a model of one in Walmart, and I said to my mom, "Can I buy that plane?" and she said "Yeah," and I bought it, and I made it, and then I got more.

Alan: Wow, that's interesting. And you were telling me about that Jim Meyer guy who makes models. Do you ever see him?

Marion: Jim, yeah, he's my friend. He just sent me a book about planes.

Alan: Doesn't he make models that actually fly?

Marion: Yeah. We flew RC planes together in the summer.

Alan: RC?

Marion: Yeah, RC, remote control.

Alan: So do you think that the Ace Combat game led to all that?

Marion: Sorta. And my dad's interested in planes.

Alan: He is?

Marion: Yeah, he flew in them in the war. He looks at my models and stuff.

Alan: Was your dad a pilot?

Marion: No, he just rode in them.

Alan: Wow. So, an interesting story is how just this computer game sort of led to a really big interest you have, and also a connection with your dad. You know, most people think that computer games are pretty much a waste of time. You could say that in your story.

Two days later, Marion produced a script for a story:

> My mom bought me Ace Combat 4 because I got a good report card. I started to play Ace Combat every day. The more I played it the more I gained interest in planes. One day I was in Walmart and I saw they had a model of an F-18 Hornet that I recognized from Ace Combat game. I built it and put it on a shelf above my desk.
>
> My mom asked me, "Where on earth did you learn about planes?" I said, "From my video game that you got me."
>
> At the end of school last year I overheard a guy talking about radio controlled planes. Two days ago he sent me a book about them. Now we are good friends. I could end up in the Air Force, like my Dad was, except he didn't get to fly.

All of the elements of the story were evident in the conversation from the preceding week, but before that conversation these elements did not make up a story. They lacked a chronology and the identification of a change.

The causal sequence, from the acquisition of the game, to the purchase of the first model, to the association with a remote control plane club, then the connection to his father's military experience and imagining a future as a pilot, was constructed interactively in the conversation, and then became fixed in the plot of a story. The change that was suggested was that a simple computer game had started Marion down the road to becoming a pilot. This was not an idea that was crystallized in Marion's mind before the conversation.

Alan met with Marion on October 14 to work on the script, reading one line at a time aloud and then asking questions and making suggestions. Based on those suggestions, the script expanded. All of the model planes were listed, and details that Marion had learned about them were included. The ironic twist that "most people think that video games are just for fun" was added as an introductory sentence. Then Marion recorded the script, and at that point the story line became fixed.

Marion turned next to collecting images to illustrate the story and took the digital camera home, returning with pictures of all of his models, a picture of his father, and a picture of his father's Air Force hat that was retrieved from a closet. The interaction with his father seemed significant:

> *Alan*: Marion, what about your Dad? Does he know you're doing this?
> *Marion*: Yeah, he's the first one I told.
> *Alan*: Really? What did you tell him?
> *Marion*: I told him I was doing this digital story telling, and I was doing it on the planes, and stuff like that. And he said, "Ooh!"
> *Alan*: And was he around when you took any of the pictures?
> *Marion*: Yeah.
> *Alan*: Did you ask him if he had any old pictures of himself?
> *Marion*: He's got a picture, but he's not in uniform.
> *Alan*: Does he know about Jim Meyer?
> *Marion*: Yeah! He met him.

Over the following weeks, Marion discussed the possibility of joining JROTC in high school and of joining the Marines or the Air Force. He worried about being "fragile" and told me about his injuries and allergies. The possibility of flying was becoming more real to him, and he was weighing the possibilities. The sharing of the story at home on the family DVD player was an important event for him, as already described. When our club was visited by the director of the Arts Street project of the mayor's office, Marion told her that the value of making a digital video was that he had "learned that I have an interest in planes." Clearly he knew that he had that interest before making a digital story, yet the digital story crystallized that interest into a narrative that he could use in conceiving of his future. After Marion showed his story about airplanes, it occurred to Daniel that Marion could fly in a two-seater plane through the Young Eagles program. We arranged for that to happen through Cyber Cougars, and Marion made a video about the event, and closed it with a picture of himself labeled Future Pilot. He went on to make a third video about a famous black aviator. For him, the sequence of stories made during the year seemed to be coalescing into an imagined life trajectory.

Six years have passed since Marion made his first digital story. During the intervening years, we have kept in touch with him. Marion joined Air Force ROTC in high school, maintained his interest in becoming a pilot, graduated, and enrolled in the aviation program at Metropolitan State College in Denver. In the fall of 2009 he obtained his private pilot license, and joined the Air Force. In a telephone interview he said that his participation in digital storytelling with the Cyber Cougars had had a lasting effect on his life. "It helped me figure out who I was, and what I was interested in," he said. "Before, I knew I was interested in planes. But the digital stories helped me figure out that I wanted to be a pilot".

Case 2: Isaiah Gets Serious

Isaiah was a thirteen-year-old African American youth at the time he began participating in digital storytelling. He seemed to be trying to juggle the competing expectations of his parents and teachers, on one hand, and his friends, on the other. Isaiah was popular, a successful player in the hip-hop world of his friends. He wore name-brand jerseys, expensive athletic shoes, and would occasionally "bust a move" from his hip-hop dance repertoire with athletic grace. His grades were all over the place. When he began his digital story, he was receiving a failing grade in his Language Arts class, and was almost failing in math as well – mainly, it appeared, because he didn't turn in assignments or pay much attention in class. He described himself as capable but not trying to do well in school. He said he enjoyed "clowning around."

After the introduction to digital storytelling, Isaiah said he wanted to tell a story about his birthday parties. He would show pictures of balloons, of cakes and candles, and of him "being crazy." Daniel Weinshenker reminded him that the story needed to show a change from the beginning of the story to the end. After a week, Isaiah produced this script:

> I've been bragging about my birthdays I've had since my 11th birthday. Since my 11th birthday, I don't have a lot of memories. I've been pretty

different because I have not been as straight up as before. I'm more loose, and not so boring. I make sure I'm polite to people. Like on my 12th birthday I learned how to do magic tricks, so I would be nice to people. I've been pretty informed that I make the best decisions on my birthday selections.

The main message of this initial script seems to be that Isaiah takes pride in having good birthday parties. The only changes he identifies is becoming "more loose, not so boring" and becoming "more polite to people," a phrase that sounds suspiciously gratuitous, like a morsel thrown in to appease an adult sensibility. Daniel pressed him for a deeper recognition of change.

Daniel: So Isaiah, let's talk about your script a little bit, okay?

Isaiah: Okay.

Daniel: What's the change from the beginning to the end?

Isaiah: Uh, let's see. I got older.

Daniel: So we all get older. What makes you getting older different from everyone else getting older?

Isaiah: Umm, I got longer hair, uh, I got bigger, I got taller …

Daniel: Right. So those are all physical things. What about the emotional things? What about the changes inside you? How you think? How you feel about things?

Isaiah: Uh, I think before I act now.

Daniel: Give me an example.

Isaiah: Like, um, if I was really really angry, and I wanted to fight somebody, I probably wouldn't fight them.

Daniel: What else? Are you different about school? Do you take school more seriously?

Isaiah: Yes, more seriously, and when I watched those really really drama, pulled-out movies with my mom, I get all weepy eyed.

Daniel: Really? It is kind of cool that you'll go and sit with your mom now. Did you used to do that too?

Isaiah: Oh, no. I used to be just so Isaiah …

Daniel: Tell me about the old Isaiah.

Isaiah: The old Isaiah was always running around, bumping his head, yelling, screaming, crying, all over the place. Yeah.

Daniel: I think your assignment is, under Old put one thing that you used to do, or one thing that you used to feel, the Old Isaiah, and then put how the New Isaiah feels about that. And then your job, after you do that, is to think about … give me one or two examples of those things. Because that makes a really good story. What we really need to hear from you, Isaiah, is what happened, besides just getting older, that made you change from the Old Isaiah to the New Isaiah.

Isaiah: I think I will be writing about that stuff.

Daniel: I think that would be really good. Maybe you'll show this, and some other students will see it and say, "Man. He became this new guy. And he got to be a little cooler, and stuff. I wonder how did he do that?"

In pressing Isaiah to build his story around a recognition of changes in how he acts and feels, Daniel seemed to be arguing from two assumptions. One was that the identification of a change, illustrated with specific examples, would make for "a really good story." The other was that if he thought about it, Isaiah would realize that he really had changed. Isaiah offers several possibilities of change: He thinks before he acts, he fights less, he takes school more seriously, and he cries watching "really drama pulled-out movies" with his mom. Daniel doesn't settle for any of these, and assigns Isaiah to think about changes and write them down with examples.

It is tempting to dismiss this exchange as contrived. Isaiah at this point really doesn't appear to be aware of any significant way in which he has changed over the past three years, and one might suspect that whatever he comes up with will be merely an attempt to comply with an adult's assignment, and not an authentic assertion that will be internalized. On the other hand, Isaiah is in the process of authoring his own identity, and there is no "true" version of who he is, or how he has changed. Any interpretation he arrives at will be significant to the extent that he embraces it and others accept it.

Like most of the participants in the Cyber Cougars, Isaiah participates in multiple figured worlds, in which he receives conflicting messages daily about who he is and what should matter to him. In the hip-hop world that nearly all of his peers participate in to some degree, name-brand fashion, athleticism, toughness, and street-wise savvy are key to status; crying while watching movies with one's mom and "being polite" are not. Isaiah is successful in the hip-hop world. He has friends. Other youth think he is funny. On the other hand, his father urges him to be self-disciplined and to prepare for college, and expresses concern about Isaiah's low grades. Teachers tell him that he needs to settle down and work hard. What Isaiah makes of these conflicting messages no doubt changes from place to place and from day to day. But by putting one version into a digital story and presenting it as a finished object, he takes a step toward embracing one potential identity over another, freezing it in time, and externalizing it as a possibility to contemplate.

Isaiah returned with this version of the script, which was recorded for his movie:

On my 11th birthday we had different colored balloons and when I'd get a couple of the same color I'd pop them and suck helium out. Then, on my 12th birthday I discovered that I really liked vanilla ice cream with sprinkles. And on my 13th birthday I had the biggest party ever with tons of friends and family. My mom took all of us to the movies.

Now, looking back on it all I remember how wild and crazy I was, not just on my birthday, but all the time. How I grew my hair out long and wasn't really polite to people at all. Like one time I talked back to a lady at the zoo for no reason, or I'd do crazy stunts without thinking about how hurt I could get.

Back then I didn't spend a whole lot of time with my family. I'd just go play basketball or hang out with my friends. I didn't care.

This year my friend Marcus got into a car accident and my mom drove me to go see him at the hospital. When I saw him in the hospital bed it made me think about all the dumb and stupid things I did. I didn't say anything to my mom, but I knew it inside.

I don't spend so much time away from my family anymore. Not long ago I sat at home with my mom instead of going out to play. We watched a movie together in the basement. I even got a little teary eyed.

The transformation of the story from the initial version to the final script is striking. Now the Old Isaiah is set out in detail, with persuasive examples. The contrast with the New Isaiah is well defined, certainly beyond what we would expect if the changes had been produced simply to comply with an adult's assignment. Most persuasive of all, the change is attributed to a powerful event, the visit to see his friend in the hospital who had been injured in an automobile accident.

Isaiah did not repudiate or ridicule this story when it was shown to other students in the club. He later reported taking it home and watching it with his parents, and his father subsequently came to the club on his own initiative to tell us how important this activity was for Isaiah. Three weeks later, Isaiah presented his story projected onto a large screen and spoke about it publicly in a conference on digital literacy at the University of Colorado, accompanied by his father. At that moment, he appeared to embrace the story and its making as a confirmation of his newly confirmed "maturity." He also turned in literature logs and improved his grade in Language Arts. But after that, Isaiah began to drift apart from his association with the Cyber Cougars. He made a humorous video about the club, and then started to make a murder mystery video, but this project was never finished, and by the beginning of May he and his close friend Evan had quit coming despite the fact (or perhaps because of it) that his father insisted that he attend, saying that the Cyber Cougars was the best thing happening for Isaiah.

Five and a half years after the completion of his digital story, we interviewed Isaiah at length about the experience. In contrast to Marion, what
Isaiah remembered first was not the story line of his digital story, but the
bright colors of the visual images he had used, the process of editing, and
the excitement of using the digital technology. "I definitely loved video
games, and computers," he said. "And then we started making our own videos and stuff [in the club] and that just got me hooked. And then, when I
ended up in high school, I already had a nice push." He explained that this
had led him to take a film class in high school, and then to courses in web
design and a video production class at a vocational school following graduation. He now aspired to a career in filmmaking.

Isaiah said that the attraction of the screen technology had led him to
work harder on his digital story than anything he had worked on previously.
"That was actually one of the hardest times I worked in my life," he told us.
"I was actually trying my best to make [the digital story] come out right. It
put a nice big work ethic into me. Seeing your finished product that you
put all that work into, that you thought was just for fun, or whatever, and
when you actually look at it, you're like, 'O wow! I did that piece!' ... After
editing, and playing with all the tools, you don't want to stop."

What about the transition described in the final version of the digital
story, from doing "stupid things" to getting serious? "What we couldn't
figure out," we told Isaiah, "was whether you just fixed the script for us,
or whether you actually believed it." Isaiah's response confirmed our sense
that there was no simple answer to that question. "This was mostly me
believing it," he said. It was the end of the eighth grade. Getting ready to
go to high school had been on his mind. "My dad was pushing me to buckle
down on my homework, everything like that." And Marcus's accident had
been a very big event in Isaiah's life. "It definitely like stamped a point in
my life," he said. But the impact didn't last. "Not too long after, we were
riding bikes, and I ended up getting his arm broken. We were still doing
stupid things *after* that." And during his first year of high school, Isaiah
rarely turned in homework, continued to cut classes, and ended up failing a
couple of classes. The conflicting urges to mess around and to buckle down
had not been resolved in the way suggested by the digital story.

Was the story sincere? According to Isaiah, parts of it – being rude to
the lady in the zoo, getting "teary eyed" watching movies with his mom –
had roots in actual experience, but had been "amped up" to make a stronger
point about personal change. The change he had described was something
he wanted to believe and knew was somehow best for him, but it was a
change he was not yet able to realize in behavior. It was not until his junior

year in high school, when the possibility of not graduating began to loom large – that he really began to buckle down and do what had to be done. But doing the digital story made him more aware of the choice. "I started actually thinking about it. The older I got, the less stuff I started to do. Still, I was still doing some pretty crazy stuff."

The experience of digital storytelling had been a resource for identity development for Isaiah in different ways than we had thought. By connecting with his interest in other screen technologies such as video games, it had led him to what he looked back on as the most sustained and concentrated effort of his life (apart from sports) up to that time, a blend of "fun" and effort that resulted in a product that gave him a sense of accomplishment and an inkling that this was something rewarding to continue to do. His newly found "work ethic" was connected with his claim in the story that he had become more mature, but in the short run, that new maturity was mainly a realization that he had found an interest that he could connect, on occasion, with school. He discovered that he wanted to be a film-maker, a professional creator of digital stories.

Conclusion

These two cases are illustrative of fundamental and interconnected ways in which digital storytelling can serve as a resource for identity construction for youth and low-income youth in particular: as an introduction to multi-media authoring, opening up new possibilities for self-presentation and storytelling in general, and as a means of identity developing through the process of constructing, presenting, and reflecting upon a particular first-person story.

For nearly all of the several dozens of youth from low-income homes Weinshenker has worked with through the Center for Digital Storytelling, digital storytelling has served as an introduction to multi-modal digital authoring, and the appeal of the medium has drawn youth to the activity. The youth who participated in our middle school after-school club came initially because they wanted to use multi-modal digital technology. If we had proposed a project of telling personal stories only through text, we believe most would not have persevered. Before these students engaged in digital storytelling, screen media had been a major source of messages that shaped their values and their view of the world. To author their own multi-modal messages opened new possibilities of personal agency. For Isaiah, ongoing participation in digital storytelling has become an element of identity, as he expressed in his interview: "We started making our own videos and stuff [in the club] and that just got me hooked." We know that many of the youth who first encountered digital storytelling through CDS have continued to gain skill in digital authoring.

The transformative potential of digital storytelling also lies in the reflective process of discovering and objectifying the story itself. Digital stories that have transformative potential for the author begin with the willingness of the storytellers to identify significant experiences, reflect on them, and share the reflections with others. These actions involve risk and call for safety, especially when the process is carried out in a group. For Marion and Isaiah, that process began with the facilitator creating a norm of safe disclosure, including the presentation of stories by other youth dealing with experiences with personal emotional significance. The establishment of norms of safety and self-disclosure through the development of a "story circle" (and the understanding that violators would no longer participate) allowed exchanges that would have been risky in the ordinary environment of an inner-city middle school.

Stories that are significant for young authors are rarely initially well formed in their authors' minds. As in the cases described here, they may begin as an event or person or topic that is salient for the teller, but with little sense of either a narrative structure or an awareness of potential meaning. Self-reflection is a developmental accomplishment. Robert Kegan (1994, p. 27) pointed out that for adolescents to be able to identify inner motivations, hold onto emotional conflict internally, or be psychologically self-reflective, they must step outside of their immediate categorical reality. Their experience must be transformed into an *object* of contemplation (Kegan, 1994, p. 32). Many adolescents cannot readily do this without the scaffolding of an adult. Marion began with his interest in airplanes, Isaiah with his pride in his birthday parties. These initial images and themes gradually were shaped by the storytellers into narratives. They developed in the course of telling mini-stories to the adult facilitators, who elicited interpretations, repeated them back for confirmation, suggested links between one mini-story and another, pressed for authenticity, and probed for elaboration and detail until the overarching story emerged for the teller working in anticipation of an audience.

These stories emerged over a period of more than six weeks from beginning to end. In the course of producing them, the storytellers returned to their stories perhaps a hundred times, first reviewing what they had written and considering changes to the script, then recording themselves reading the script, and later adding mages and a second soundtrack to the narrative track. This process encourages the dual processes of accepting or appropriating the story as an interpretation of life experience (Wertsch, 1998) and at the same time externalizing the story as an object of reflection (Kegan, 1994; White & Epstein, 1990).

The combining of multiple modalities, particularly spoken narrative and visual images in digital stories distinguish them from written text in important ways. After completing their scripts, Marion and Isaiah rehearsed reading their scripts aloud many times and then recorded them in sections, listening to the recordings as they emerged. For both youth, this was the first time they had heard a recording of their own voice, and it sounded to them almost as though someone else was telling their story. Isaiah depicted his former "crazy" self by using Photoshop to make his hair blond and by using animation to cause the image to spin. He used a contrastingly serious photograph to emphasize the change he had undergone. Marion ended his story with the image of his father's Air Force hat. These elements of image and voice serve both to externalize and objectify the story and to link its themes to visual images with strong emotional associations.

The role of digital storytelling as a tool in the authoring of identity is clearer in the case of Marion than in the case of Isaiah, but there is evidence that each story served as a tool in the process of self-authoring in different ways. In both cases, the youth reflected on events of his or her life and organized them into a coherent narrative that had not existed beforehand as an object of contemplation. Each of these narratives held the potential to contribute to a more developed "imagined life trajectory" for the teller. For the time being, Marion saw himself as a future pilot, and Noah tried to embrace the idea that he had moved on from his former "wild and crazy" self. Each of the storytellers had also developed proficiency with a variety of technical tools, from scanning and digital photo editing to video editing, and these newly acquired tools also became incorporated into a more competent sense of self. From that point on, however, the significance of these realizations depended on how they were reinforced and reshaped in the ongoing process of positioning and answering (all within the constraints of larger, slower-moving systems) through which lives are authored.

Future Trends

The model of workshop-assisted digital storytelling expanded enormously between 2004 and 2009. Growth took place within the United States in a variety of institutional contexts, including schools and universities, museums, and the expansion of field offices of the Center for Digital Storytelling. But more significantly, large projects were undertaken with institutional sponsorship in Scandinavia, the United Kingdom, Australia, New Zealand, and the Netherlands. Despite a worldwide economic downturn at the time of this writing, it seems likely that such projects will continue and expand in the long run, especially as a means of exploring the relationship between individual and group identity (e.g., Capture Wales) and the linking of historical experience to personal story (e.g., Somali-Bantu Project Voice).

There is also evidence that digital storytelling is expanding in K–12 education, in response to a recognition of the importance of digital tools in the world economy (*technology*) and, to a lesser extent, in recognition of a need to expand the concept of literacy to include both authoring and critique involving screen media. Ironically, the latter initiative is still referred to as "alternative literacies" in an age in which people under the age of thirty-five receive most of their long-distance communications digitally (Hull & Schultz, 2002). The attention to identity development and life trajectories that has characterized digital storytelling outside of schools is less evident in K–12 initiatives, and seems likely to remain so, given the current focus of schools in most countries on mastery of standards that have little to do with art or the interpretation of life experience.

The most important trend in respect to digital storytelling is the de-institutionalization of the form and its place with other forms of Web 2.0 expression. Technological developments in the past five years have made digital storytelling available to millions of individuals in the first world without the need for schools, workshops, or multi-media centers. Digital cameras and voice recorders are now incorporated into most cell phones, and easy-to-learn video-editing software now comes as standard applications with Apple computers (in the form of iMovie) and Windows-based computers (in the form of Movie Maker). In short, nearly anyone with a cell phone, a computer, and an internet connection can potentially create a voice-narrated digital story and upload it to the internet. The production of such stories remains "mediatized" by the technological tools required for their production and dissemination. How will the format of such stories evolve, and how will the reciprocal relationship of messages and technology continue to shape one another? What is the nature of the social networks in which they are exchanged? How do these digital stories shape outsiders' perceptions of groups who previously had no direct access to their stories? How do they contribute to the enactment of agency by individuals who previously were voiceless outside of their immediate social circles?

References

Alvermann, D. & Hagood, M. (2000). Fandom and critical media literacy. *Journal of Adolescent and Adult Literacy*, 43, 436–446.

American Friends Service Committee (2008). Project Voice and digital storytelling. http://www.afsc.org/midatlantic/ht/display/ContentDetails/i/71778.

Banaszewski, T. (2002). Digital storytelling finds its place in the schools. *Multimedia Schools*, 9(1), 32–40.

Bartlett, F. (1932). *Remembering: A study in experimental and social psychology.* Cambridge: Cambridge University Press.

Brake, D. (2008). Shaping the "me" in MySpace: The framing of profiles on a social networking site. In K. Lundby (Ed.), *Digital storytelling, mediatized stories: Self-presentations in new media* (pp. 285–300). New York: Peter Lang.

Bruner, J. (1990). *Acts of meaning.* Cambridge: Harvard University Press.

Bruner, J. & Lucariello, J. (1989). Monologue as narrative recreation of the world. In K. Nelson (Ed.), *Narratives from the crib* (pp. 73–97). Cambridge, MA: Harvard University Press.

Buckingham, D. (2007). *Beyond technology: Children's learning in the age of digital culture.* Cambridge: Polity.

Burke, K. (1945). *A grammar of motives.* New York: Prentice Hall.

Couldry, N. (2008). Media and the problem of voice. In N. Carpentier & B. de Cleen (Eds.), *Participation and media production. Critical reflections on content creation* (pp. 15–26). Bristol: Intellect Press.

Davis, A. (2005). Co-authoring identity: Digital storytelling in an urban middle school. *Technology, Humanities, Education and Narrative (THEN Journal)*, 1, 1–12. Retrieved Dec. 16, 2008 from http://thenjournal.org/feature/61/.

Diamondstone, J. (2004, March). *Jasmine makes a scary movie: A multi-modal analysis of an adolescent's popular culture literacy.* Paper presented at the annual meeting of the National Council of Teachers of English Assembly for Research (NCTEAR), Berkeley, CA.

Drotner, K. (2011). Children and digital media: Online, on site, on the go. In J. Qvortrup, W. Corsaro, M.-S. Honig & G. Valentine (Eds.), *Palgrave handbook of childhood studies* (pp. 360–374). London: Palgrave Macmillan.

Dyson, A. (1997). *Writing superheroes: Contemporary childhood, popular culture, and classroom literacy.* New York: Teachers College Press.

Erickson, F. (1986). Qualitative methods in research on teaching. In M. C. Wittrock (Ed.), *Handbook of research on teaching* (pp. 119–158). New York: Macmillan.

Erickson, F. (1992). Ethnographic microanalysis of interaction. In M. D. LeCompte, W. Millroy, & J. Preissle (Eds.), *The handbook of qualitative research in education* (pp. 201–225). New York: Academic Press.

Foucault, M. (1980). Truth and power. In C. Gordon (Ed.), *Power/knowledge: Selected interview and other writings 1972–1977* (pp. 109–133). New York: Pantheon Books.

Hayes, R. & Matusov, E. (2005). From "ownership" to dialogic addressivity: Defining successful digital storytelling projects. *Technology, Humanities, Education and Narrative (THEN Journal)*, 1, 22–34. Retrieved Dec. 16, 2008 from http://thenjournal.org/feature/75/.

Hjarvard, S. (2007). Changing media, changing language. The mediatization of society and the spread of English and medialects. Paper presented at the International Media Association 57th Annual Conference, San Francisco, May 24–28.

Holland, D., Lachicotte Jr., W., Skinner, D., & Cain, C. (1998). *Identity and agency in cultural worlds.* Cambridge, MA: Harvard University Press.

Hull, G. & Katz, M.-L. (2006). Crafting an agentive self: Case studies of digital storytelling. *Research in the Teaching of English*, 41(1), 43–81.

Hull, G. & Schultz, K. (2002). Connecting school with out-of-school worlds. In G. Hull & K Schultz (Eds.), *School's out! Bridging out of school literacies with classroom practice* (pp. 32–60). New York: Teachers College Press.

Jenkins, H., with Puroshotma, R., Clinton, K., Weigel, M., & Robison, A. (2006). *Confronting the challenges of participatory culture: Media education for the 21st century* (Occasional paper). Cambridge, MA: MIT Comparative Media Studies Program. Retrieved October 21, 2009 from http://www.newmedialiteracies. org/files/working/NMLWhitePaper.pdf.

Kaare, B. H. & Lundby, K. (2008). Mediatized lives: Autobiography and assumed authenticity in digital storytelling. In K. Lundby (Ed.), *Digital storytelling, mediatized stories* (pp. 105–122). New York, NY: Peter Lang.

Kegan, R. (1994). *In over our heads: The mental demands of modern life.* Cambridge, MA: Harvard University Press.

Kitwana, B. (2002). *The Hip Hop Generation.* New York: Basic Books.

Kress, G. (2003). *Literacy in the new media age.* London: Routledge.

Kress, G. & van Leeuwen, T. (2001). *Multimodal discourse: The modes and media of contemporary communication.* Oxford: Oxford University Press.

Kulla-Abbott, T. & Polman, J. (2008). Engaging student voice and fulfilling curriculum goals with digital stories. *Technology, Humanities, Education and Narrative (THEN Journal)*, 5. Retrieved Dec. 16, 2008 from http://thenjournal.org/feature/160/.

Lambert, J. (2006). *Digital storytelling: Capturing lives, creating community.* (2nd Edition). Berkeley, CA: Digital Diner Press.

Lave, J. & Wenger, E. (1991). *Situated learning. Legitimate peripheral participation.* Cambridge: Cambridge University Press.

Luke, A. & Freebody, P. (1997). Critical literacy and the question of normativity: An introduction. In S. Muspratt, A. Luke, & P. Freebody (Eds.), *Constructing critical literacies: Teaching and learning textual practice* (pp. 1–18). Creskill, NJ: Hampton.

Lundby, K. (2008). Introduction. In K. Lundby (Ed.), *Digital storytelling, mediatized stories: Self-representations in new media* (pp. 1–20). New York: Peter Lang.

Mandler, J. (1984). *Stories, scripts and scenes: Aspects of schema theory.* Hillsdale, NJ: Lawrence Erlbaum Associates.

McWilliam, K. (2008). Digital storytelling as a "discoursively ordered domain". In K. Lundby (Ed.), *Digital storytelling, mediatized stories* (pp. 145–160). New York: Peter Lang.

Mead, G. (1934/1974). *Mind, self, and society.* Chicago: University of Chicago Press.

Meadows, D. (2003). Digital storytelling: Research-based practice in new media. *Visual Communication*, 2, 189–193.

Miles, M. & Huberman, M. (1994). *Qualitative data analysis: An expanded sourcebook.* 2nd Edition. Thousand Oaks, CA: Sage.

Nelson, M. E. & Hull, G. A. (2008). Self-presentation through multimedia: A Bakhtinian perspective on digital storytelling. In K. Lundby (Ed.), *Digital storytelling, mediatized stories* (pp. 123–144). New York: Peter Lang.

Ochs, E. & Capps, L. (1996). Narrating the Self. *Annual Review of Anthropology*, 25, 19–43.

Paull, C. (2002). *Self-perceptions and social connections: Empowerment through digital storytelling in adult education.* Unpublished doctoral dissertation, University of California at Berkeley.

Schafer, R. (1981). Narration in the psychoanalytic dialogue. In W. J. T. Mitchell (Ed.), *On Narrative* (pp. 25–49). Chicago: University of Chicago Press.

Schon, D. (1983). *The reflective practitioner.* New York: Basic Books.

Sfard, A. & Prusak, A. (2005). Telling identities: In search of an analytic tool for investigating learning as culturally shaped activity. *Educational Researcher*, 34(4), 14–22.

Shotter, J. (1990). The social construction of forgetting and remembering. In D. Middleton & D. Edwards (Eds.), *Collective memory* (pp. 120–138). London: Sage.

Spence, D. (1984). *Narrative truth and historical truth: Meaning and interpretation in psychoanalysis.* New York: Norton.

Spradley, J. (1979). *The ethnographic interview.* Belmont, CA: Wadsworth.

Thurmin, N. (2008). "It's good for them to know my story": Cultural mediation as tension. In K. Lundy (Ed.), *Digital storytelling, mediatized stories: Self-representations in new media* (pp. 85–104). New York: Peter Lang.

Vygotsky, L. (1934/1978). *Mind in society.* Cambridge, MA: Harvard University Press.

Weis, T., Benmayor, R., O'Leary, C., & Eynon, B. (2002). Digital technologies and pedagogies. *Social Justice*, 29(4), 153–167.

Wertsch, J. (1998). *Mind as action.* Oxford: Oxford University Press.

White, M. & Epstein, D. (1990). *Narrative as therapeutic tool.* New York: W. W. Norton.

3   Building Identities as Experts: Youth Learning in an Urban After-School Space

Carol Cuthbertson Thompson and Lisa Bouillion Diaz

Over the past two decades we have become accustomed to think-ing of youth as experts with technology, although this perception does not often apply to urban youth. Youth whose schools are understood to be poor and whose economic prospects are dim seem unlikely candidates for con-sideration as experts in much that matters to the middle-class world that surrounds them. Policy makers and others ascribe a variety of ethnic and social identities to urban youth, frequently in terms of problems that need solutions; as McLaughlin (1993) noted, however, the local construction of identity is often at odds with these ascribed identities.

Urban youth organizations that have embraced use of emerging tech-nologies have created avenues through which youth can form and assert their own identities. The Social And Public Art Resource Center (SPARC), for instance, supports youth expression and activism through digital mural projects. The possibilities of multidimensional meanings within digital media become a vehicle through which youth can "amplify and widely disseminate their social consciousness" (Sandoval & Latorre, 2008, p. 99). In the case of SPARC and similar urban youth programs, digital tech-nology positions youth in the role of expert, conveying counternarra-tives (Gutiérrez, Baquedano-López, Alvarez, & Chiu, 1999; Soep, 2006) that disrupt and challenge images constructed by others to represent who they are.

In this chapter we focus on the case of Hopeworks, an urban youth development program in Camden, New Jersey, that brings youth and adults into intentional conversation and collaboration around a similar technology project. More specifically, we seek to shed light on how youth identities as "expert" are constructed across different roles within collabo-rative youth–adult activities. We argue that these negotiations of expertise are an essential dimension of youth identity formation and preparation to participate in adult worlds. Technological learning environments that mediate these negotiations and bridge youth–adult worlds are especially important in contexts where race, language, and socioeconomic status contribute to youth marginalization.

At Hopeworks, youth join the program as "trainees" in Web page development or mapping and, upon successful completion of the initial curriculum, are employed to work collaboratively with Hopeworks staff on commissioned Web page design projects. We focus on one such project in which several youth were asked to construct Web sites for the author of a widely used book series for middle and high school–age readers. The two media in play in this project – the very old one of books and the new one of Web design – exemplify the way in which technologies currently "coexist" (Buckingham, 2007, p. 14). The project further brought together author, reader, and Web designer roles in which the youth and adults contributed diverse expertise. For example, the author, a Caucasian, wrote about African American urban youth, with whom the Hopeworks youth had much in common. In designing Web sites for the author, the urban youth who read and loved his books would be called on to enact identities not only as experts of their own lives as students and readers but also as technology designers. The adult staff with whom they worked were more technologically expert in Web design but less expert in the lives of urban youth or in the exigencies of book publishing (see Figure 3.1). The project was thus constructed with considerable fluidity in who was an "expert" at any given time (Jacoby & Gonzales, 1991). In this chapter we examine how this fluidity made possible the eventual identification of the youth as professionals and experts. And, more to the point, we look at the ways in which youth identities as experts were connected and manifested in a technological task, and in fact could not have happened without it.

Background and Theory

The transformative potential of community-based organizations as sites for youth development has been well documented (Cole, 1996; Heath & McLaughlin, 1993; Hull & Greeno, 2006; Hull & Katz, 2006; Larson, Walker, & Pearce, 2005; McLaughlin, 1999; McLaughlin & Heath, 1994; Mahoney, Eccles, & Larson, 2005; Sefton-Green, 2006). CBOs are noted for their freedom from constraints such as high-stakes testing and pressures to cover standardized content, and we are interested here in their potential as sites for youth to encounter and prepare for participation in new adult worlds (e.g., Larson et al., 2005). More specifically, we examine

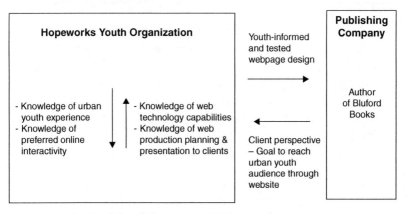

Figure 3.1. Youth-adult collaboration on Web page design.

how youth negotiate different identities and roles in their work within collaborative design projects with peers and adults.

Adult program leaders play an important role in helping youth to develop the social capital needed for entry into adult worlds by providing youth with access to adult resources, information, support and encouragement (e.g., Chavez & Soep, 2005; Jarrett, Sullivan, & Watkins, 2005). At the same time, youth come to these programs with their own toolkits of experience, knowledge, and expectations. Programs that prioritize outcomes of youth empowerment and ownership may lean toward more youth-centered activities, while programs that seek to facilitate specific skill development may lean toward more adult-centered activities. The research of Larson and colleagues (2005) identifies distinct development benefits to both program structures.

Whichever model a program chooses, preparation for youth participation in adult worlds requires a concomitant focus on acquiring expertise. Although, as Lajoie (2003) argues, there is a paucity of research on exactly how novices become experts, there is agreement that novices progress through three predictable stages of expertise: acclimation, competence, and proficiency (Alexander, 2003; Hatano & Oura, 2003; Sternberg, 2003). In the acclimation stage, as Alexander (2003, p. 11) notes, "learners have limited and fragmented knowledge," and they attend to "surface-level" features of a domain. Learners in the stage of competence have basic working knowledge and are able to begin to think more deeply about their tasks. Alexander argues that the increase in learner interest corresponds to this deepening knowledge. Proficiency is marked, as Bransford, Brown, and Cocking (1999) and Alexander (2003) note, by an ability to see patterns,

high engagement, and a desire to ask searching questions. These characteristics bespeak some control of the domain. However, as Hatano and
Oura (2003) argue, real proficiency is gained when learners participate in
professional worlds with real audiences. In distinguishing between performance of a task for a teacher and one for a real world audience, Hatano
and Oura contend that the former, which has to do with getting things
right, will actually leave learners stuck at the novice level, whereas the latter will promote expertise. As Thompson (2011) argues, expertise further
requires opportunities to take on the imagined point of view of a prospec-
tive audience. Learners at this stage are usually necessarily highly engaged,
and the move into expertise is evidenced by changes in values and identity
(Hatano & Oura, 2003).

A key design challenge in creating these conditions for expertise development is finding ways to break down the often-static roles of
"teacher" and "learner" (or "expert" and "novice") within educational learning environments. As illustrated in this chapter, opportunities for youth to
authentically apply and exercise their growing expertise require more than
a simple transfer of power or decision making from adults to youth. Rather,
these opportunities must involve active collaboration and dialogue through
which participants negotiate and construct shared meaning across diverse
experiences. This reciprocal exchange and mutuality in participation create
the possibility for a "third space" (Bhaba, 1994) between otherwise distinct
youth and adult worlds. Expertise in this overlapping space is defined by
valued roles within each community of practice (see Figure 3.2). The contribution of diverse bodies of knowledge, role types, and practices creates
a space of asymmetrical relationships (Gutiérrez, Baquedano-López, &
Turner, 1997) in which young people are given opportunities to construct
identities as experts that integrate their individual experiences and values.

In studies of classroom learning, a framework of "third space" (Bhaba,
1994) has been used to conceptualize opportunities for creating bridges
between youth and adult knowledge and practices, as well as to create a
space for learners to intentionally challenge and renegotiate the practices
that are valued in school (Gutiérrez et al., 1997, 1999; Gutiérez, Rymes
& Larson, 1995; Moje et al., 2004; Soja, 1996). Bhabha and others (e.g.,
Moje et al., 2004) have focused on the potential for third-space encounters to destabilize dominant norms and assumptions by bringing together
different interpretations and experiences with those signs and symbols.
"Building bridges is a necessary part of what makes third space because it
helps learners see connections, as well as contradictions, between the ways
they know the world and the ways others know the world" (Moje et al.,

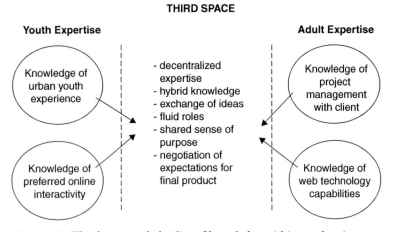

Figure 3.2. Third-space as hybridity of knowledge within overlapping contexts of practice.

2004, p. 44.) Youth programs with technological projects are particularly well suited for this kind of bridge building. Cole's Fifth Dimension (1996), Vásquez's La Clase Magica (2003), Goodman's Documentary Workshop (2003), Hull's D.U.S.T.Y. project (Hull & Nelson, 2005) and Youth Radio (Chavez & Soep, 2005) are among the well-known examples. Many smaller projects also exemplify this trend (e.g., Vasudevan, 2006).

In the Hopeworks project, there are numerous instances in this case study in which youth take up the practices and even language of adult partners in their efforts to understand the author's intentions for the Web site. Of particular interest in this project is the inherent tension in youth representing youth, while the Web design process also required that they represent the author's intents and expectations to their peer group. Rather than simply developing the insights needed to "cross over" into and successfully participate in a new context, youth in this case were called upon to nimbly navigate and mediate between two communities. This study thus represents a shift in questions of *identity* to questions of *identity in practice*. That is, we assume identity formation to be dynamic (Bucholtz & Hall, 2004), emergent (Duranti, 1997; Wenger, 1999), and a process that forms and reforms over time through improvisation and self-authoring (Holland, Lachicotte, Skinner, & Cain, 1998). Identity in practice is inseparable from participation in the context of a community (Lave & Wenger, 1991; McLaughlin, 1993; Rogoff, 1995; Wenger, 1999). The focus from this perspective is on the activities in which youth have learned and are learning to participate, rather than only on the knowledge that they have acquired. This shift reflects an emphasis on one's ability to interact with and orient oneself within different physical and social environments (Sfard, 1998).

The Hopeworks project creates bridging between youth and adults by leveraging the affordances of Web 2.0 technologies. With the rapid expansion of information communication technologies (ICTs) we have witnessed a shift in focus from information delivery and access to collaborative knowledge sharing and construction. The increasing ubiquity of these social software tools has renewed discussions of pedagogical possibilities for learners of all ages (see, for example, Cope & Kalantzis, 2009). Microcontent, collaboratively developed content by different users, is among the frequently noted aspects of Web 2.0 technologies (e.g., Alexander, 2006; McLoughlin & Lee, 2007). Early studies suggest that this knowledge-building activity with Web 2.0 technologies can be linked to evidence of increased idea generation, collective problem solving, and knowledge refinement. In one such study, Lee, McLoughlin, and Chan (2007) examine the role of learner-generated podcasts as catalysts for knowledge creation. Through the involvement of undergraduates in the role of "student-producers," this study found that the collaborative creation of podcasts facilitated knowledge building activities including progressive problem solving (cf. van Aalst & Chan, 2001), democratization of knowledge, and epistemic agency, "whereby students expressed their ideas, listened to divergent opinions and maintained a focus on improving the outcome" (Lee et al., 2007, p. 513). The Hopeworks study presented in this chapter further illuminates the ways in which identity construction is linked to these knowledge building activities, and the ways in which those opportunities are mediated by both the technologies at the center of the design task and the social structures of the learning environment designed to support this collaborative work.

Methods and Results

Settings and Participants

At the time of this study Hopeworks had been established for seven years. It is located in an old Camden, New Jersey, church parsonage in an area of extreme poverty. From the front porch, the youth can see the major bridge to Center City Philadelphia across the river, but the Camden neighborhood that surrounds Hopeworks exemplifies the consequences of industrial decline. Many of the surrounding row houses a block away have been boarded up or have porches that are essentially cages, and the county incinerator produces a fine dust that blankets many nearby neighborhoods. Camden's unemployment figures are more than twice the state average (Brubaker, 2009). Although there has been some gentrification on the riverbank that faces Philadelphia, the city of Camden remains the repository for the sewage, a population of incarcerated people, and the trash from the rest of the much wealthier Camden County that surrounds it. During the year in which most of this study was conducted, Camden's crime rate, ranked twice as the nation's highest (Gettleman, 2004; Wood, 2005), continued to rise (Katz, 2008).

About half of Camden's residents are African American, and about 34 percent are Hispanic with Mexicans as the newest immigrants. Fifty-seven percent of Camden's children live in poverty (Camden Poverty Trends, 2012). One-third of the population lived in households with yearly incomes under $15,000; another 23 percent have household incomes under $30,000 (Poverty Benchmarks Project, 2007). The socioeconomic characteristics of the population of Hopeworks mirror those of Camden. The youth who attend the after-school program (Hope Through School, or HTS) are ages fourteen through eighteen; during the day they attend a variety of schools, including charters, parochial schools, and the local public schools. But academic achievement for Camden youth is problematic. Forty-two percent of residents do not have high school diplomas, and only 11 percent hold bachelors (or higher) degrees. The Camden City schools are classified under No Child Left Behind criteria as needing improvement; at Camden High School and Woodrow Wilson High, fewer than 40 percent of students meet state standards. Six months prior to the Bluford project, graduation rates for the class of 2006, though rising, were 42 percent at Camden High and 67 percent at Wilson (Poverty Benchmarks Project, 2007). However, students at the competitive magnet school (Medical Arts) score at the level of all students in New Jersey.

Hopeworks was established by one Jesuit and two Lutheran parishes to help local youth find pathways to college or to jobs with good pay. From the beginning its youth development mission has been expressed through technology, and the youth train in the areas of either Mapping or Web Design. Youth who have dropped out of high school attend the Day Program; youth fourteen and up who are still in school attend the HTS program, which meets three afternoons a week. The population of the Day Program is between ten and fifteen; HTS usually numbers fifteen to twenty. The youth are paid stipends while they complete their training, and if they qualify for production work they earn slightly above New Jersey minimum wage. The Literacy Program provides academic support for all of the youth including help with SAT prep and college application. Poor school performance requires youth to temporarily stop work and spend their time in "homework help," unpaid, until they are caught up. The Formation Program helps youth explore their goals for the future. Though Hopeworks is a nonprofit, the Web Design and Mapping businesses help fund the youth development program, which is designed as an apprenticeship in which youth take on increasing responsibility. The organization has ties to the surrounding community in multiple ways, often offering training and services. Hopeworks is thus a relatively unusual hybrid of business, youth development, community engagement, and connection to various levels of school.

Youth who enter the program usually do so in Web Design, where they follow an online curriculum. They sit elbow to elbow in one of two training rooms, each of which seats eight youth. The seating arrangement and the apprenticeship structure encourage the youth to use more expert others as resources when they are stuck. Once the youth have completed work in Internet Basics, HTML1 and HTML2, Photoshop, and Dreamweaver they construct their personal Web sites, which they must present to the assembled community of youth and staff.

The construction of a site is the first major occasion for identity work since the project requires trainees to address questions intimately involved in self-examination and self-presentation: Who am I here? How do I explain the decisions I made about my site? The presentations are also displays of competence since youth who complete their sites to the satisfaction of trainers can move out of their roles as trainees and assume new roles as designers involved in production work with clients. The presentations mimic those that they will make to clients. As the youth begin to learn their new roles as designers, they become more expert at seeing Web pages the way designers do and also at thinking and talking like designers as they work and make presentations to clients. Their move into central participation (Lave & Wenger, 1991; Rogoff, 1995) is thereby linked both to shifts in identity – from youth to professional, from novice to expert advisor of adult clients – and to the technology that defines the roles they play.

The Bluford Web design project in which the youth were engaged during this study was in many ways similar to other Web design projects in which youth had been involved since their training. Like those training projects it required the youth to develop a site from scratch and present it – though at a much more sophisticated level. It thus represented the kind of project that forms the basis for nearly all of the work at Hopeworks. However, unlike others, the Bluford project was a collaborative effort of all parts of the organization. The Literacy, Formation, Mapping, HTS Training, and Web directors worked together to establish a clear pathway for participation by all of the HTS youth. They also established a series of deadlines for each stage of the project, which culminated in a presentation to the Bluford author and the publisher. Another, larger difference was the expanded role that the youth were asked to play. Typically youth in production have completed training and passed their tests; they do the "grunt work" of adding content to sites and carrying out the designs of adult staff. This time, however, the youth designers had full reign to imagine and invent Web sites that both represented the author's intentions in and interests of youth readers

Data Collection and Analysis

This empirical research is part of a larger six-year participant observation study at Hopeworks during which the lead author sat in on work sessions, meetings, and conferences. The lead author initially examined the apprenticeship structure of the HTS program, in particular the ways in which the more experienced youth used their increasing facility with new technologies and their attached social languages to advance their understanding of practices and to help newcomers get started (Thompson, Putthoff, & Figueroa, 2006). The second author had conducted research at the organization for three years and had sat on the board for two years.

Over the six-year study, Hopeworks continued to explore new projects through which it could involve youth in apprenticeship and presentation, with a growing focus on the latter. One of the questions that emerged for the researcher was whether these presentations were opportunities for the kinds of learning that encouraged shifts in identity. What roles were the youth taking on or being assigned by staff as they presented their work?

The data considered in this chapter were collected and analyzed by the lead author throughout the Bluford Web site project, which began in October 2007 and extended through January 2008. The lead author attended Hopeworks one or two times a week throughout the four-month period and read two Bluford books along with the youth. The data include extensive field notes, audio and video recordings of community practices including the presentations to the community and the book series author, video- and audio-taped interviews of both youth and staff, images of the Web sites the youth designed, the books themselves, and the PowerPoint presentations made to the author by the youth. The four youth designers and the staff were interviewed twice.

The transcripts discussed here are excerpted from the over one hundred pages collected. Although the lead author was not present during the presentation to the author, she did have the video recording of the presentation in its entirety. Moerman's (1988) transcription conventions were used with the audio tracks, and the thematic coding techniques outlined by Miles and Huberman (1994) were used with all data. Based on the lead author's earlier work (Thompson, Puttholf & Figueroa, 2006, Thompson, 2009) initial coding organized data into the categories of role, community practice, professional language, and technology use. As coding progressed, a series of sub-codes helped develop understanding of subtler features in the data. Role sub-codes include Camden resident, student, trainee, designer, presenter, reader, novice, expert, self-representer, and identity. Community practice sub-codes included physical use of technology, project (further divided into adult initiated and youth initiated), preparing for presentation, community presentation, scaffolding questions, collaboration, reflection, curriculum, and group assessment. Professional language included being able to articulate questions and statements using professional language and audience awareness. Technology use included tool use, problem solving, asking questions, improvisation, and assessment.

As the analysis was conducted, several features became clear. First was the identification of all participants including staff and client as "expert" or "novice" depending on the part of the project in which they were engaged. The youth, we already knew, struggled with the expectations of outsiders in accordance with ascribed socioeconomic identities. Another even more interesting theme began to emerge. We had seen Hopeworks as multifaceted, but the second author's assessment of the organization as an example of a "third space" helped us examine the data for places in which identify formation was linked to events of reciprocal exchange and mutuality (Bouillion Diaz, 2009) rather than to more linear or discrete movements from novice to expert or adult to youth decision making. The lead author performed member checks at various stages of the data collection in order to ensure accuracy and conducted interviews with youth and staff to understand their perspectives on what had been learned during the project. Duranti (1997), Goodwin (1994), and Levinson (1992) provided helpful models for analyzing discourse in professional practice and the socialization of new community members into participation through the talk engaged in by participants as they worked. The talk provided a window into the multiple kinds of expert-novice identification and mutual exchange across different experience, knowledge, and expectations occurring within the activities of the Web site design and presentation. Particularly noteworthy were the ways in which youth, staff, author, and youth used these activities as opportunities for reflection.

Data and Results

To understand the ways in which the Bluford book project contributed to the trainees' construction of their identities as experts and professionals, this section looks first at the project phases and then at the stages of expertise through which the youth move.

The Project Phases

This project was typical of work in which the Hopeworks Web Design Program engaged: a client, in this case the book author, approached Hopeworks for help with Web design knowing that the production team consisted of youth trainees under the mentorship of Hopeworks staff. It was atypical, however, in that instead of a finished live site, the author wanted the trainees' help in understanding the kind of Web site to which his readers would respond. The author also wanted to see what the youth would invent as possibilities for the Web site if there were no limits. By paying Hopeworks to provide him with an array of possibilities, he was commissioning the youth to think visibly (Collins, Brown, & Holum, 1991) rather than to make products. Even the more experienced youth had been design assistants whose jobs were to implement the designs of the adult staff rather than to conceptualize their own sites, so this project would stretch their skills. To ensure that the project was delivered on time, the adults at Hopeworks, including the Web Design directors (Jon and Gavin), the Literacy director, the Formation director, and the Operations director, established project phases, each with its own deadline.

In the initial phase everyone in the HTS program, including adult staff, read most of the books in the Bluford series. All of the youth then identified the central themes in the series by acting the narratives out in puppet shows, creating raps, and writing poetry from the points of view of different characters. In community-wide discussions, the youth then identified the themes in the books that most interested them: family, friendship, and death. Finally all the youth worked together to establish the characteristics that they thought would be most important in a site: simplicity; the capability for users to customize, to rate content, and to contribute their own writing, raps, and personal experience; and finally the availability of music and videos.

In the second phase, four youth (Raquel, Rick, Maria, and Amir) volunteered to work as designers on the project (the remaining youth were informed that they would later play the role of critical audience). For about a month the youth designers worked with Gavin and Jon's help to construct prototype sites that would respond to the themes of the books and incorporate the functions that all of the HTS youth had requested.

In the third phase, the designers would present their work to three in-house audiences. This use of a critical audience was a frequent pedagogical strategy that adult staff felt helped model the design process for newcomers who did not have enough technical expertise to code and compose finished Web sites. The youth designers were to present their work to the other youth twice for feedback on Web site usability and interest, and then use that feedback to revise their sites as needed. The last in-house presentation would be to the adult staff who would make sure that the Web site designs were functional and that the youth's presentations were articulate. In the fourth and final phase, the youth designers would present their work to the author and the publisher. To demonstrate how the youth began to acquire and use their knowledge, the next sections first look briefly at their experience with design tools and then move to an examination of their acquisition of proficiency and their identification as experts.

The Youth and Their Experience with Technology

All of the youth in the after-school program were learning to use the technologies of the Map Design or Web Design programs, but those who became designers were, in general, more technologically advanced than were the youth who took on the role of audience. Even within the group of the four youth designers, however, there was considerable variability in Web experience. The youth discussed at length in the following section, Rick and Raquel, had less experience than most of the other youth designers then working in production. Rick had been in the Web Design Training Program before moving into Map Design; Raquel had little Web training and had moved directly into the Map Design. Maria, who plays a minor role in the discussion, was quite experienced in design implementation; she had also been the Youth Web Design trainer. Two other youth played important supporting roles: Alejandro, who occasionally offered help to Rick, was the Lead Youth Web Designer and a veteran of the training program. Ajua, who made some useful critical comments about Raquel's site, was in training but had not yet constructed her own personal Web sites or passed her production test.

The youth were thus in quite different stages when they began the project. However, since the designers for the first time had the freedom to create their own sites from scratch, even the quite-experienced Maria would need to learn new skills, new ways of thinking about design, and the professionalism attached to the role. All of the designers would be in charge of their own presentations, and they had to think about their audience and their own habits of work. In examining their construction of design expertise and identification as experts and professionals, using the commonly accepted stages of expertise as markers is helpful. As Alexander (2003), Hatano and Oura (2003), and Bransford (1999) suggest, novices must first become acclimated before they can establish competence and then expertise. In the data presented across these stages, we are particularly interested in uncovering how the trajectories of youth identity formation are mediated by different aspects of the activity context. Supported by these data and elaborated in the findings section, we discuss how the participation structures in the Hopeworks program combined with the affordances of Web 2.0 technologies to create a "third space" connecting youth and adult worlds. Further, we argue that this space – characterized by overlapping goals, diverse expertise, mutual exchange, and reciprocity – created unique opportunities for the youth participants (one in particular) to construct identities as experts in ways that integrated their individual experiences and values. For urban youth and other marginalized populations, we argue, these opportunities are critical in protecting the agency needed for successful transition into professional workplace communities.

The First Stage of Constructing Expertise: Becoming Acclimated.

In the initial brainstorming process for the project the staff had frequently reminded all of the youth that this was not school and that they should not feel constrained by ideas of "right" and "wrong." So, as the designers began to think about their sites, Gavin reminded them to be both inventive and to understand what worked and what didn't and why. This injunction, however, presupposed some understanding of the function of Web sites as examples of real-world professional interactivity, an understanding that Rick did not yet have. He appeared not to take the process seriously: he frequently avoided the keyboard, instead trying to engage in banter with Maria and Raquel or leaning back in his chair just staring at the screen. When he began an early version of his site, he added his name prominently as a title: "Copyright Rick 5, since 1991" (the year of Rick's birth), an addition that drew a rejoinder from Gavin:

GAV: You got your "Copyright Rick. Rick 5 since 1991," you might want
to think about that. if you have a serious site and you put a wacky title it
loses something, y'know? The font you had before was just fine.
RICK: I don't remember what it was. Oh yeah.

In a subsequent version, Rick changed the position of his name from "title"
to "author" but retained its large type. Gavin looked at it and said gently
that he "might not want to make that the second biggest item on page."
This urge to sign one's name occasionally manifested itself in the work of
the youth least confident about their problem-solving abilities; it may indicate a retreat to the more comfortable role of student, where signatures on
art objects and other papers are not unexpected but sometimes substitute
for deeper thinking. With the deadline for the first community presentation
looming, Gavin asked Rick to think about what he would want as a visitor
to a Web site, noting that "sometimes you just have to take best idea and
follow through." These interactions between Rick and Gavin helped Rick
begin to see a Web site as a professional artifact. As Goodwin (1993) has
demonstrated, this kind of talk between participants around the "theories,
artifacts, and bodies of expertise" (p. 606) that are characteristic of a profes-
sion allows novices to understand what they are seeing and doing.

How to consider the two-dimensional composition of the Web site was
something that all of the youth struggled with as they designed their sites.
They had to keep in mind not only the themes of the books and the desires
of the rest of the Hopeworks youth but also how to structure a site that
would have visual appeal. With the size and position of his name Rick had
learned about the importance of proportion, and as he developed his site he
had to address the concept of representation. His search for a background
pattern led him to a fleur-de-lis pattern, and when Gavin asked him about
his choice, Rick mentioned that he simply liked the design. Since Gavin
had asked the designers to look at sites with visual appeal, Rick's find was
a somewhat useful stepping-stone into thinking about pattern, and it also
provided the opportunity for exploring the idea of symbolic representation. Once Gavin explained what the fleur-de-lis represented, Rick quickly
understood that it was not a good choice for his site. He and Gavin used
the opportunity to talk about the relation of color and shape and to think
about other patterns that might be useful. Rick found a Web site with the
covers of the Bluford books and found an image of a brick wall that became
the foundation for his site.

The following week Rick worked to construct the sizes of the titles and
the function buttons of the site against the pattern of the wall, and Gavin
helped him learn to see the site as an example of the category "Web site,"

with attributes that internet visitors would expect. This partly involved understanding the hierarchy of a site. Gavin rolled his chair over to Rick's computer and the two of them sat looking at the screen. Gavin showed him how to emphasize the titles with a series of keyboard moves:

> *Gav*: this will make your titles stand out a little bit. usually the titles are bigger and bolder than the subtitles
> *Rick*: another font?
> *Gav*: no but if they're bold they stand out better. [turns to another youth]
> *Rick*: I need BULLets?

Rick's mistaking of "bullets" for "bold" was both a mark of his inexperience and of the noise level in the small design room where Gavin and the four youth worked elbow to elbow. Rick added the bullets to the page. When Gavin turned back to Rick, he returned to the issue of hierarchy:

> *Gav*: [looks at design, which now has bullets] no, you gotta manipulate the bricks. could the text be manipulated a little more, bring it out.
> *Rick*: what do you mean.
> *Gav*: make it more prominent
> *Rick*: make it bigger?
> *Gav*: you are the designer. you can put bullets next to the items, change the color. it's about how you have your text organized.

In this apparently simple interchange both design issues and role are under discussion. Rick was just learning what to emphasize and how to do it. His uncertainty about Gavin's direction about the text led to his desire for specificity about how to make things "prominent." Although Gavin's answer does not appear to recognize that Rick's use of bullets was probably because of his misunderstanding, his answer does take the bullets into account as a possible solution. It also places Rick firmly in charge, since Gavin's last statement opens with the declarative comment, "you are the designer."

A week later, Rick was still working on his site before the first presentation to all of the HTS youth. Alejandro, one of the older production youth who was also a trainer, stopped by to take a look. Sitting next to Rick, he began to point at the screen:

> *Alej*: if you do this with the text it will blend in. so what you want to do is give it some kind of accent to it. I experimented with all this stuff, but this part right here, it's got too many colors and doesn't flow. you want the text to be readable.
> *Rick*: how 'bout the words in this color text.
> *Alej*: remember I told you earlier about this style of text. [shows with keyboard clicks] I'm not sure if you have it in here. maybe something like

that, and also what you want to keep in mind is this is about a BOOK. [clicks on font.] that type of font, but if it's not available go back to colors [(5.0)[1]; chooses a font]. oops that's too crazy you don't want that. if I came to a website like this I'd say oh it's too plain, so you want to work with this. remember what you do most is attract them to the site, make it appealing to the eye. pick some of your favorite colors and see how you can transfer them into here. experiment. that's what Photoshop is all about.

Alejandro's advice ties the technological tools of Photoshop and Dreamweaver tightly to his articulation of Rick's purpose: attracting viewers. When Rick wondered whether to change the color of the text, Alejandro suggested looking for a font appropriate to the subject – a book. He modeled for Rick a way to consider an inappropriate choice ("oops that's too crazy"). Finally Alejandro advised Rick to experiment as a way of getting to a workable solution: attracting viewers. At this acclimation stage Rick still exhibits the characteristics of a learner whose knowledge is both "fragmented" and concerned with the "surface features" (Alexander, 2003, p. 11) of Web sites. Both Gavin and Alejandro helped Rick construct his knowledge by identifying the visual phenomena on the screen and then tying them to the project purpose; this new knowledge lays the ground-work for the next stage of expertise, competence.

The Second Stage of Expertise: Competence

As Alexander (2003) has noted, the move into competence is demonstrated when learners have gained a "foundational body of domain knowledge" (p. 12) and are engaged in the process because of their own interest. Although they no longer need to depend completely on their environment to develop their work, they still use a mix of "surface level and deep processing strategies" (p. 12). Several weeks into the project, Amir, Rick, and Raquel could handle the tools of the technology with some confidence. Both they and their youth audience began to see how the sites could be connected to professional prac-tice. The move into this stage was marked by an increase in critical assess-ment of the sites in presentations to the community; the designers learned to use the evaluation of others to revise their work. First, though, Gavin encouraged them to use other sites that they found interesting and could use as models in some way. Maria and Raquel found a site that had animations they found particularly engaging, and Maria showed it to Gavin. Though the

---

[1] Numbers in parentheses indicate length of pause in conversation.

site was about cakes and not books, she was interested in its functions rather than its subject matter. Gavin asked what she thought about the site:

> *Gav*: so what makes this site successful?
> *Mar:* the FOOD
> *Gav*: let's see the images. [Maria clicks on link]. The images are really good. What if you went to the cakes section and the images were really bad, blurry.
> *Mar*: well what's the point of having them if they are? (5.0)
> *Mar*: Is this Flash?
> *Gav*: Yes. [Pause while they click on image] I like how this disappears.

In this brief interchange, Maria not only indicated that she could use part of the site as an analog for her own, but also that she also understood its limitations. Her answer to Gavin's question about why the site was successful indicated that she was clearly interested in the power of a good image to entice a visitor. The conversation about the animated images also was an opportunity for her to identify that particular animation as Flash, and Gavin focused briefly on one of its attributes. Amir, whose own work often lagged but who had also developed a good critical eye, remarked, "I often go to websites and think what I could do better." These remarks indicate an increasing depth in Amir's thinking about the design process as he began to link it to professional models.

Gavin also asked the designers to enlarge their sphere of competence by seeing their roles as part of a business structure. Although the staff had downplayed it for much of the design process, Gavin reminded Maria that the organization of the site and the appeal to the visitor were also linked to the work plan for which the designer would be paid:

> You have to think, how can I organize that? It's like having something laid out on a desk – it helps you know how to build the website. Information gets plugged into something called "the scope of work" – information for clients – an outline step by step. That way they know exactly what they are getting. Proof that we did exactly what we said we were going to do.

Gavin then sent the designers back to the list of attributes that the other HTS youth had initially requested as part of their preparation for the first community presentation. In making their presentations, Gavin said, the designers would need to think about how to present their work understandably to their audience so that they would get the "feedback that will help you hone your designs."

All of the youth had taken part in sessions in which adult staff presented their own design work to all of the youth in the organization for feedback; such critiques modeled ways for the youth to think and talk about what they were seeing. The staff took youth comments seriously, and in so doing, indicated that the critiques weren't only for the benefit of the youth. The designers thus had an organizational model for publicly talking about their work and getting useful feedback. Hopeworks planned three in-house presentations before the final presentation to the author. The first was to a small group of youth, the second to all of the HTS youth, and the third to the Director of Operations and Jon, the other Web director, and Gavin. All the presentations took place in the conference room on the second floor, which seated everyone if some youth sat on the floor. A projection screen was set up at one end of the room, and the presenting youth stood next to it as one of the other designers clicked on the different features of the site.

As the first presentation got underway, Raquel stood next to the screen at the front of the room, pointed to the home page of her site, and discussed its functions, one of which would allow viewers to click on different characters to get more information. When she finished, Jon opened up the discussion. Several of the youth noted that Raquel's slogan – "Bluford inspires" – seemed to index the kinds of language used by adults in school settings and was unlikely to appeal to the youth audience they were hoping to attract. They then began to critique the site's reliance on bright colors as appealing once again to the wrong audience. Amir provided a blunt opinion:

> *Amir*: I think they'd [the colors] be all right if you're aiming for a younger audience, but the Bluford books are meant for students in HIGH school, this would be aimed more at a middle school to high school grade level, it's kind of kiddie –
>
> *Youth2*: – yeah, it's still not that bad because but people like colorful stuff like this and without something, ooh what's this? then people not going to pay attention to it
>
> *Youth3*: What about colors, make it colorful
>
> *Amir*: not to be insulting, Raquel, but if I went to a site like this I'd think these colors are boring – make me think this site is for Winnie the Pooh or something,
>
> *All*: hahahahahaha
>
> *Ajua*: he's right but she –
>
> *Amir*: – I'm sorry, I'm sorry. but they're primary colors, elementary
>
> *Youth2*: they're basic colors
>
> *Raq*: all RIGHT, all RIGHT. hahaha. using colors in the crayon box.
>
> *Jon*: so these are basic colors, so Raquel you're talking about the crayon box,

Youth1: such fun!

Youth2: bring it on!

Jon: ok, ok

All: hahahahaha.

Jon: so bring it back to the colors, so if if these colors are looking pretty K-through-6 what kind of colors can we use? Maria, what do you think.

Maria: I [like the colors

Youth3: [red is good

Jon: let's just try one at a time

Maria: I like the colors but I think that they're, if you change them up, like where they're at and stuff, it'll be good, and I think that the red is –

Raq: – I have to fix it –

Maria: – and there's too much space.

Raq: I gotta move the books over. I was axing Jon if I should [unintelligible] and he said maybe you should, maybe you should, and that's not an answer

Jon: ooohhhh –

All: hahahaha

Ajua: he says you have to think on your own

Raq : ok I'll fix 'em

Amir: I think you should darken some of the colors if not change them because dark colors will be –

Maria: – it reminds me of –

Raq: – I'll do darker colors.

Ajua: but not TOO dark color or it's something Goth and they'll say I don't want to see this I'm not into that.

Jon: cool.

In this section of transcript, the youth audience immediately homed in on the issue of audience awareness, and Jon used their comments ("the colors … are Winnie the Pooh") as organizing features for assessment. One of the salient features of this section of transcript is the role the younger youth played in discussing Raquel's site. Although Jon acted as facilitator, the assessments were articulated chiefly by the youth. Most saw Raquel's primary colors as appealing to a much younger audience. Raquel, who had worked hard on her site, initially resisted changing her colors, but Maria and Ajua's suggestions of somewhat darker colors (that wouldn't be so "Goth" as to scare the audience away) helped their colleague find a compromise. Jon later framed the discussion of neutralizing Raquel's colors in terms of their "urban" quality, one that would index the locales in the books. Just how neutral or "urban" the colors should be was debated well into the presentation of the sites to the author. (Raquel later damped the colors down, and the author called them "a bit drab.")

Raquel's comment toward the end that Jon hadn't answered her question may have indicated that she was experiencing the difficulties all the designers were having with merging the interests of multiple audiences. Amir was struggling with his own site, which remained incomplete, but he was an articulate, if blunt, critic. Rick had his own moment on the "hot seat," when Jon remarked that his "aggressive background" would work only with one or two books but not the entire series. Maria's design received mostly positive comments.

The discussion turned next to the functions of the sites, and here there was unanimity between designers and the HTS youth. Because the HTS youth had prioritized interactivity as a primary characteristic they wanted in the site, the designers had incorporated surveys, quizzes, bulletin boards, spaces to post poetry, drawing contests, drop boxes about each book, and a MySpace-like space for each character as ways to inform readers about each character, and, as one youth said, "get them interested in several books or the series." Ajua, one of the youth audience members, also was hopeful that the final site could include "people being creative with writing their own endings and changing chapters" in the books for which the site visitors would vote. She also suggested incorporating a bulletin board on the site and changing the featured book weekly; Rick suggested showcasing rap and video. This discussion about interactivity was evidence of the growing engagement of all the youth as the site construction began to reflect their growing interest in using the technology; Alexander (2003) has noted this connection between knowledge and growing interest in a domain as learners achieve competence. The youth left that presentation immediately after Thanksgiving with a good bit of feedback, which they began to incorporate in their sites to varying extents. They had an immediate deadline for the second presentation to all the HTS youth a week later. That presentation did not go well. Maria reported, "I am trying to show them [the other HTS youth] the design; they are in corner talking, not paying attention. There was not much feedback and it was really forced" (interview, December, 12, 2008). She placed some of the blame on the newer youth in the larger group and noted in frustration that the designers had already incorporated the themes they had suggested. Jon's assessment of the presentation was harsher; he called it "a borderline disaster." Raquel had her back to the audience as she looked at the screen, and Amir forgot his glasses and could not see what he was doing. "We got to see where the weaknesses were," Jon said, and there was only one week more of prep time before the presentation to the staff and a final week before the presentation to the author (interview, January, 16, 2008).

By the time of the third in-house presentation, to the staff, Rick said he couldn't "wait to show everyone my design – I've got it all ready." This was a huge step for the usually laconic Rick. When he saw that only the staff were present, he was visibly disappointed, saying that he had thought the youth would be there too and complaining later that he hadn't had enough feedback in the second presentation. By the time he presented his site, he did so with confidence.

> *Rick:* this is the internal page for when you want to CREATE a book, title, author, don't know how that is going to work out, how many chapters. [here's the] character reference, cover art, and "about the author," and the back of each book where it gives the picture of all of the other books.
>
> *Gav:* is this part of your proposal because it should be, because it is a really cool idea.

The youth were aware that Gavin was quite sparing in his praise, so this assessment of Rick's work was unusual. Raquel earned similar praise from Jon when he saw how she had integrated a personality quiz into her site, noting that it was "the first time I've heard how this could be used in a class – you go on the site and you take the trivia challenge … and you're almost more about the class part, so when … the author comes in he might be interested – this isn't just about free time." The staff restricted the remainder of their comments to understanding how each site worked and what still needed to be done to achieve the goals each youth had set. Almost all of their comments in the 67 minutes of presentation and feedback focus on the interactivity of the sites – the games, the polls, the surveys, and the opportunities for writing raps and stories. As the final presentation to the community ended, it was clear that the designers and audience alike had mastered much of the design process, had a clearer understanding of the requirements of the role of designer, and were able to articulate to their proxy clients (the other youth) the reasoning behind their choices.

The Third Stage of Expertise: Proficiency

Although the staff had acknowledged Rick's and Raquel's work, they paid more attention to Maria's. Maria had been working in Web Design production for a year, and she had been the youth trainer in the 2007 Summer Program; her job there had been to help the younger youth learn the design curriculum. She was thus clearly identified by the staff as one of

Image 3.1. Maria's site.

the most proficient of the HTS youth and had already played the role of expert as a professional trainer within the organization. She needed to spend only a little time mastering Flash, and she had continually demonstrated her competence in implementing Gavin's and Jon's designs and at working independently. She made quick progress with her own site, which was an elegant set of colored rectilinear shapes with tabs for the different functions (see Image 3.1). Because of the file folder motif, it was eye-catching, organized, and business-like, and the staff frequently referred to her site as a model for the other youth. Maria had also presented at conferences, and as she prepared for the presentation to the author, she was confident.

Rick's work (see Image 3.2), in contrast, was viewed by the staff as much less proficient than Maria's. And when it was time for the presentation to the author, Rick's newly developed confidence temporarily left him. He repeated to Gavin and Jon that he couldn't do the presentation. Jon reported that he and Gavin insisted that Rick go through with his presentation, arguing that the author was "going to be here in five minutes – you can't pull this" (interview, January 16, 2008). The other youth, Jon reported,

Image 3.2. Rick's site.

"pulled each other up," and Rick was able to deliver a well-thought-out presentation of his site.

Rick's site used a brick wall as a backdrop. The bolded title about which he and Gavin had talked several weeks earlier was clear and prominent, and his copyright remained discreetly visible at the bottom of the site. The faces of four characters, about 50 percent transparent, were positioned on the brick wall at the sides and bottom. One of the site functions was a creation gallery, where, Rick said, "you'd create your own book or MySpace page." The author responded first to the function, which, since Bluford had sold a million books in the previous year, might mean that there could be a daunting number of postings to the site. He explained to the youth that his publishing company was actually smaller than Hopeworks, remarking, "I so see the power of what you're doing that I fear the response!" In this comment the issues of the youth's choices, backed and encouraged by the staff, were contextualized in the realities of the marketplace. The author went on to discuss how Rick's site worked visually, noting his use of color and the kind of "graphic intensive look" that the book covers represent.

AUTHOR: I like the brick wall, where'd you get that.

RICK: I thought it related to *Search for Safety*. [one of the books in the series]

AUTHOR: And it goes to the edginess I mentioned earlier, you don't want to get slammed against brick and it speaks to city. It also speaks to 2 books and their setting without saying a word.

In his written response to the youth sent a few weeks later, the author assessed the strengths of Maria's and Raquel's sites but noted that they tended to appeal to a readership younger than his. Rick's site, however, he saw as "building on the cover images and connecting visually with what readers see. ... This is innovative and engaging" (e-mail communication to Hopeworks, January 7, 2008). He referred to Rick's site in two of his four suggestions for the home page. Like the feedback from the HTS youth and the staff that identified Maria as an expert, this feedback from the author identified Rick as expert. Although the staff had viewed Rick's site as less proficient than Maria's, the author clearly identified Rick's site, more than the others, as having made the link between author and reader a visible one. Rick's site was a mark of his growing expertise as a thoughtful designer who made good use of the author's intentions and built on them. He mentioned later that one of the hardest things had been "figuring out what kind of site [the author] would like," that he'd made one and hoped for the best (interview, January 16, 2008). Rick's quiet pride in having constructed a Web site that was useful in an adult world – thereby indexing the world of professionals – along with his newly gained ability to talk to his client about his work signaled his identification of himself as a perceptive and capable designer.

Findings Summary

The data indicate a high level of engagement on the part of the four youth designers as they played their multiple roles. The youth were already adept users and makers of internet artifacts when they began the project, and they quickly became interested readers of the series who found it easy to identify with the characters whose age, ethnicity, and urban and class status mirrored their own. As students, they also could see themselves as representatives of other readers their age. Their relation to these readers changed, however, as they moved into designing the Web sites and mentally positioned these readers as their own potential audience. In designing their sites, they also became representatives or agents of the author in the new technological format. Their relation to the author was thus a dual one

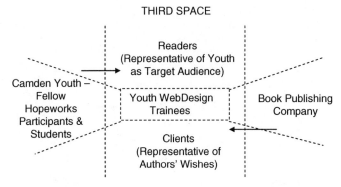

Figure 3.3. Fluidity of roles within overlapping contexts of practice.

since he had asked them to represent youth readers, but the design process required that they also represent him. Additionally, the youth were designers-in-training in a business set up for the express purpose of training them. The Web sites themselves thus became the locus of overlapping business interests and representations.

This complexity enabled a great deal of occasional frustration as well as fluidity in roles and expert/novice identifications (see Figure 3.3). The collaborative youth-adult design activities brought together a wide array of linguistic, social, and cognitive resources situated in a real world context. The adult staff at Hopeworks made their thought processes available to the youth (Brown, Collins, & Duguid, 1989), who then learned how to "think visibly" (Collins et al., 1991) in solving design problems and anticipating needs of an internet audience. Also, in order to consider the needs of the author's audience both for the books and the Web sites, the youth needed to articulate their thinking, a hallmark of expertise (Radziszewska & Rogoff, 1991). Through discourse and the sharing of tasks, skill, and meaning were co-constructed across this web of expertise, opening paths of transformed participation for both youth and adults. Youth acquired knowledge, competence, and proficiency as they assumed increasingly complex roles in activities with others, representing a change in participation over time (Lave & Wenger, 1991; Rogoff, 1990).

Of particular interest is the way in which the growing identification of the youth as expert was encouraged by the practices within the project phases (see Table 3.1). In Phase 1 all the youth became immersed in the subject matter of the books, but the focus was not yet on the technology. Phase 2 generally corresponds to the acclimation that the designers underwent as they worked on the mechanics of their sites, linking their

Table 3.1. *Project Phases and Stages of Expertise*

Project Phase	Phase 1: Read, understand author's work	Phase 2: Construction of "draft" Web sites	Phase 3: Presentation of "draft" sites to community	Phase 4: Presentation of final sites to client
Expertise stage (youth who reached stage in parentheses)		Acclimation (Rick, Raquel, Maria, Amir)	Competence (Rick, Raquel, Maria, Amir)	Proficiency (Rick, Raquel, Maria)
Participants	All HTS youth	Youth designers, Web Design adult staff, Alejandro	All youth, designers, and HW staff	Youth designers, HW staff, author, publisher

Note: HTS = Hope Through School; HW = Hopeworks.

composition to both the technological requirements of the internet and to the experiences and interests of potential users. The youth were aware of using themselves as reference points in deciding on Web site functions; it was an awareness they articulated repeatedly as they worked and one reinforced by the staff, who continually asked what they would like to see in the sites if they were visitors. As Maria noted, "I didn't want it to be boring ... I had to think of what we would want to see" (interview, January 16, 2008). At this stage the designers' knowledge was a mix of surface and deep understanding.

Within Phase 3, with its requirements for articulation to a critical audience, all four designers acquired competence, if somewhat unevenly. Raquel, Rick, and Maria all had functional sites. Amir's was promising, and his growing competence could be seen in his clear critiques. At this stage, however, the youth were still presenting to audiences who would understand much of what the designers were doing, since these audience members had provided some of the requirements for the site functions. Rick, who frequently had few words to say, became a good presenter who cared deeply about demonstrating his hard work. This phase also enabled Raquel to demonstrate her growing competence. Neither staff nor youth initially identified her as expert, and she chafed under Jon's refusal to provide pat solutions. With more work, however, she effectively connected the classroom to the author's audience, clearly articulating how the site could be used for more than just entertainment and earning praise from both Jon and, later, the author.

Phase 4, with its focus on a presentation to the clients (publisher and author), required that the youth think of themselves as assuming professional roles. To perform well, they needed finished Web sites, an ability to anticipate new questions, and to respond to client needs rather than to those of their peers. Maria, Raquel, and Rick presented their workable sites articulately, though Rick's stage fright indicated his awareness that this presentation held new demands. Maria, already positioned as expert, enjoyed being able to claim sole credit for her work: "They [staff and author] told us to do what you want. Here I usually have to do what *they* want; I think it came out pretty good" (interview, October 23, 2008). That Amir's site was unfinished indicated that he had not yet reached this stage.

It is difficult to overemphasize the importance for the youth of the professional interactions with the author. They particularly liked working with him as a client because, as Raquel later remarked (personal interview, January 15, 2008): "He was easy to work with because he thinks like a teenager; he knows what we would want ... so it wasn't a bit difficult." When the researcher remarked that she guessed that an author of a book for teenagers would probably have to be able to think like one, Raquel responded, "He's like a big kid; he's all interested in what people would want but he could still think about his business. How much time it's going to actually take to build [the site]."

In this last comment, Raquel acknowledged the business constraints with which the author was dealing – which seemed to interest rather than disappoint her. Her assessment of the author as able to imagine himself into their world was a complement of youth's own imaginings of themselves and other readers into his – not only into the stories, but also into his larger intentions for the series and the readers. It was rare for the youth to have the opportunity to work with a client interested in thinking his way into their world – a world frequently dismissed by powerful adults. The adult staff at Hopeworks also took on an unusual role as encouragers of the designers' perspectives as youth, while simultaneously helping them learn to think more like professionals.

The youth identity work was, of course, uneven. While Maria engaged her identity as an already competent designer and trainer of others, Rick struggled with his. It was only when he took down his own name as title for the site – a sort of faux identity – and began to work seriously that he began to construct an identity much deeper and more urgent than would have been possible without the books, the needs of an audience, and the

help of the adult staff. Like the other designers, Rick began to use his multiple identities (student, reader, Camden resident) as space that made the
construction of his identity as an expert possible. The multiple avenues
and audiences helped the youth draw connections across multiple sites
of thinking and acting. This multiplicity offered another benefit as well.
Rick, for example, was frequently positioned as "less expert" compared
with the others by the staff, partly because of his distractible, and somewhat inarticulate, manner. His design, while acknowledged to be worthy,
was less interesting to the staff than Maria's. The author, however, saw
the design as a more expert understanding of his books, his intent, and
the needs of the audience. These identifications of youth as more or less
expert demonstrate the complexities of assessing expertise in fluid situations – with potential consequences for the roles youth choose to play.
The mutual exchange of perspectives and identities around a common
but emerging technology has, as we argue in the next section, profound
implications.

Future Trends

This project had a high value for the youth designers for a number of
reasons. One key element that emerged in the data was the connected-
ness to valued communities of practice: to an author the youth valued, to a
new worldwide community of peers, and to the worlds of professional Web
designers and book publishers. As Brown, Collins, and Duguid (1989);
Greeno and his colleagues (1996); Lave and Wenger (1991); Cole (1996);
Cole and Wertsch (n.d.); and Rogoff (2003) all have noted, learning that
occurs in real-world projects is better remembered and transferred to new
situations. Engagement is further heightened when youth are able to take
on increasingly complex tasks, responsibilities, and roles that have meaning to them (Cole, 1996; McLaughlin & Heath, 1994). Youth involvement
and identity are also profoundly affected when youth are publicly acknowledged for their growing expertise (Heath, 1998, 1999).

     As reflected in the example of the Bluford Web Project, technology
is often an area in which youth prize and enact expertise. As Luke and
Carrington (2002) observe, the link between technology and community
is a powerful one for adolescents struggling to define the ways in which
they will participate in the multiple worlds in which they live. This study
further reveals the role that internet and communication technologies
can play in bringing diverse communities of practice into conversation –
thereby creating third-space learning opportunities. These technologies

are socially constructed across a web of interactions through which they are put to use for different purposes within different communities. As "boundary objects" (Harvey & Chrisman, 1998), they serve to distinguish differences while also providing common points of reference among collaborators. Drawing from a review of literature on participatory design of new technologies, Muller (2003) emphasizes mutuality and reciprocity as defining qualities in third space interactions between technology "designers" and "users." Bouillion Diaz (2009) examines the affordances of emerging technologies in creating these conditions within youth-adult collaborations and the related possibilities for youth development in out-of-school programs. New technologies, and related projects such as the Bluford Web site, will have value and meaning for all participants only when the knowledge and experience of all collaborators are leveraged in the design process. These activities require "mutual education, negotiation, creation of understanding, and development of shared commitments" (Muller, 2003, p. 10). In the Bluford case, peer-group presentations played an important role as "dress rehearsals" for the final presentation to the author who had commissioned the Web site. These peer presentations provided a vehicle for articulation of understanding that would otherwise remain tacit and largely subconscious. The Web site models as artifacts served as an important reference point as well, making visible the understanding, intent, and expectation of the individual youth designers, while also facilitating concrete checks as to whether alignment with the author's intents for the site had been achieved.

While communication technologies will undoubtedly continue to evolve and change, few would question their ubiquity in our future lives. The implications of this ubiquity have led to cross-disciplinary examinations of changing paradigms for learning (Cope & Kalantzis, 2000) and constructions of race and identity (Everett, 2008). However, as Vadeboncoeur (2006) has noted, it is the kinds of participation that hold keys to development, rather than the organizational or technological "subject." Organizations that are not involved with technology can also combine learning with opportunities for youth to take on increasingly complex tasks, responsibilities, and roles. A growing body of research argues that participation structures are a focal mediating force through which youth interpret and act upon the perceived opportunities, expectations, and constraints for interaction within a given context. At the same time, this chapter and the other work in this volume illuminate participation structures with technology that use youths own experiences as a foundation for their development and learning.

Conclusion

The Web design project discussed in this chapter is an example of how programs for youth can link technology, expertise, and identity. The use of new technologies often requires novices to continually assess their control of their technological tools (Lin, 2001) their understanding of the subject matter with which they are working, and the functionality of their projects. To assess these, novices must begin to engage in some degree of self-reflection. More sophisticated learners then begin to assess the success of their work by using professional criteria. Projects that use technological tools and artifacts can result in new systems of authority as youth progress from knowledge acquisition to competence to proficiency. It is clear, for example, that practices of preparation to real-world audiences of other professionals require the kinds of reflective thinking that go beyond "getting it right" into a deeper set of questions about meaning, audience, and point of view. Poor urban high school youth who reach the stage in which they are acknowledged to be playing the role of professional have certainly formed new identities because they have acquired new expertise that integrates and builds upon their previous lived experiences.

This chapter lays out the ways in which certain kinds of structures encourage this dual formation of expertise and identity, arguing that the youth's identities as expert designers were forged in part because of these other identities as experts on the experience of students, employees, urban youth, and users of technologies. Forming an identity as an expert can be difficult for youth who may have expertise but not see themselves as experts. This is especially difficult if adults do not recognize the value in a youth's work. As Lin (2001) argues, we draw both the roles available for playing and our perception of ourselves as learners from our social context. How that context is structured, then, will affect youth identity.

How best to incorporate this kind of learning experience for youth is an ongoing question. As Sefton-Green (2006) and others have argued, we no longer need to make the case for out-of-school contexts as the site of informal learning; we need instead to focus on the kinds of pedagogical strategies and learning opportunities in which youth can thrive. This need is especially acute for urban youth whose access to learning opportunities outside of school may be quite limited. When a project also connects them to adult worlds, it has an even greater valence; the connection to a valued author encouraged the youth to toggle mentally between their own reactions, purposes, and interests as well as those of imagined peers. These kinds of reflection are an important locus of development.

Although Hopeworks is somewhat unusual in its mix of youth development, business, and technology, it is not alone (Radio Arte and Youth Radio, among others in the United States, have nonprofit apprenticeship programs in online radio production for urban youth). We hope that the practices described in this chapter add to the discussion of pedagogical strategies that have application to other youth development programs, and perhaps, to schools as well.

References

Alexander, P. A. (2003). The development of expertise: The journey from Acclimation to Proficiency. *Educational Researcher*, 32(8), 10–14.

Bhabha, H. K. (1994). *The location of Culture*. London and New York: Routledge Press.

Bouillion Diaz, L. (2009). Creating opportunities for ubiquitous learning with geospatial technologies: Negotiating roles at the borders of youth and adult practice. In B. Cope & M. Kalantzis (Eds.), *Ubiquitous learning* (pp. 100–108). Champaign: University of Illinois Press.

Bransford, J., Brown, A., & Cocking, R. (1999). *How people learn: Brain, mind, experience, and school*. Washington, DC: National Academy Press.

Brown, J. S., Collins, A., & Duguid, P. (1989). Situated cognition and the culture of learning. *Educational Researcher*, 18, 32–42.

Brubaker, H. (2009). South Jersey faring worse on jobs than Philadelphia area. *The Philadelphia Inquirer*, November 29.

Bucholtz, M. & Hall, K. (2004). Language and identity. In A. Duranti (Ed.), *A companion to linguistic anthropology* (pp. 369–394). Malden, MA: Blackwell.

Buckingham, D. (2008). Introducing identity. In D. Buckingham (Ed.), *Youth, identity, and digital media* (The John D. and Catherine T. MacArthur Foundation Series on Digital Media and Learning; pp. 1–24). Cambridge, MA: MIT Press.

Camden poverty trends (2012). Camconnect.org, http://www.camconnect.org/dat alogue/2010CamdenPovertyRates.pdf

Chavez, V. & Soep, E. (2005). Youth radio and the pedagogy of collegiality. *Harvard Educational Review*, 75(4), 409–434.

Cole, M. (1996). *Cultural psychology: The once and future discipline*. Cambridge, MA: Belknap Press of Harvard University Press.

Cole, M. & Wertsch, J. V. (n.d.). Beyond the individual-social antimony in discussions of Piaget and Vygotsky. Online at http://www.massey.ac.nz/~alock/virtual/colevyg.htm

Cope, B., & Kalantzis, M. (2000). *Multiliteracies: Literacy learning and the design of social future*. New York: Routledge.

Collins, A., Brown, J. S., & Holum, A. (1991). Cognitive apprenticeship: Making thinking visible. *American Educator*, 15(3), 6–11, 38–46.

Duranti, A. (1997). *Linguistic anthropology*. Cambridge: Cambridge University Press.

Everett, A. (2008). Introduction. In A. Everett (Ed.). *Learning race and ethnicity: Youth and digital media*. The John D. and Catherine T. MacArthur Foundation Series on Digital Media and Learning. Cambridge, MA: MIT Press.

Gettleman, J. (2004). Camden's Streets go from mean to meanest: Life and death in a city called America's most dangerous. *New York Times*, pp. B1, B5.

Goodman, S. (2003). *Teaching youth media*. New York: Teachers College Press.

Goodwin, C. (1994). Professional vision. *American Anthropologist*, 96(3), 606–633.

Greeno, J. G., Collins, A. M., & Resnick, L. B. (1996). Cognition and learning. In D. C. Berliner & R. C. Calfee (Eds.), *Handbook of educational psychology* (pp. 15–45). New York: Macmillan.

Gutiérrez, K., Rymes, B., & Larson, J. (1995). Script, counterscript, and underlife in the classroom: James Brown versus Brown v. Board of Education. *Harvard Educational Review*, 65, 445–471.

Gutiérrez, K., Baquedano-López, P., & Turner, M. G. (1997). Putting language back into language arts: When the radical middle meets the third space. *Language Arts*, 74(5), 368–378.

Gutiérrez, K., Baquedano-López, P., Alvarez, H., & Chiu, M. (1999). A cultural-historical approach to collaboration: Building a culture of collaboration through hybrid language practices. *Theory into Practice*, 38(2), 87–93.

Harvey F. & Chrisman N. (1998) Boundary objects and the social construction of GIS technology. *Environment and Planning*, 30(9), 1683–1694.

Hatano, G. & Oura, Y. (2003). Commentary: Reconceptualizing school learning using insight from expertise research. *Educational Researcher*, 32(8), 26–29.

Heath, S. B. (1998). Working through language. Kids talk: Strategic language use in later childhood. In S. Hoyle & C.T. Adger (Eds.), *Kids talk: Strategic language use in later childhood* (pp. 217–240). New York: Oxford University Press.

Heath, S. B. (1999). Dimensions of language development: Lessons from older children. In A. S. Masten (Ed.), *Cultural processes in child development: The Minnesota symposium on child psychology: Vol. 29* (pp. 59–75). Mahwah, NJ: Erlbaum.

Heath, S. B., & McLaughlin, M. (Eds.) (1993). *Identity and inner city youth: Beyond ethnicity and gender*. New York: Teachers College Press.

Holland, D., Lachicotte, W., Skinner, D., & Cain, C. (1998). *Identity and agency in cultural worlds*. Cambridge, MA: Harvard University Press.

Hull, G. & Greeno, J. (2006). Identity and agency in nonschool and school worlds. In Z. Bekerman, N. Burbules, & D. Keller (Eds.). *Learning in places: The informal education reader* (pp. 77–97). New York: Peter Lang.

Hull, G. & Katz, M. L. (2006). Crafting an agentive self: Case studies of digital storytelling. *Research in the Teaching of English*, 41(1), 43–81.

Hull, G., & Nelson, M. (2005). Locating the semiotic power of multimodality. *Written Communication* 22(2), 224–261.

Jacoby, S. & Gonzales, P. (1991). The constitution of expert-novice in scientific discourse. *Issues in Applied Linguistics*, 2(2), 149–181.

Jarrett, R. L., Sullivan, P. J., & Watkins, N. D. (2005). Developing social capital through participation in organized youth programs: Qualitative insights from three programs. *Journal of Community Psychology*, 33, 41–55.

Katz, M. (2008, September 23). N.J . murder rate falls, but rises in Camden. 9/23/2008. *Philadelphia Inquirer*. Retrieved November 13, 2008, from http://www.philly.com/inquirer/local/20080923_N_J__murder_rate_falls__but_rises_in_Camden.html.

Kendon, A. (1990). Spatial organization in social encounters: The F-formation system. In A. Kendon (Ed.), *Conducting interaction: Patterns of behavior in focused encounters* (pp. 209–238). Cambridge: Cambridge University Press.

Lajoie, S. P. (2003). Transitions and trajectories for studies of expertise. *Educational Researcher*, 32(8), 21–25.

Larson, R., Walker, K., & Pearce, N. (2005). A comparison of youth-driven and adult-driven youth programs: Balancing inputs from youth and adults. *Journal of Community Psychology*, 33, 57–74.

Lave, J., & Wenger, E. (1991). *Situated learning: Legitimate peripheral participation*. Cambridge: Cambridge University Press.

Lee, M. J. W., McLoughlin, C., & Chan, A. (2007). Talk the talk: Learner-generated podcasts as catalysts for knowledge creation. *British Journal of Educational Technology*, 39(3), 501–521.

Levinson, S.C. (1992). Activity types and language. In P. Drew & J. Hertiage (Eds.), *Talk at work: Interaction in institutional settings* (pp. 66–100). Cambridge: Cambridge University Press.

Lin, X. (2001). Designing metacognitive activities. *Educational Technology Research & Development*, 49(2), 23–40.

Luke, A. & Carrington, V. (2002). Globalisation, literacy, and curriculum practice. In R. Fisher, M. Lewis & G. Brooks (Eds.), *Language and literacy in action*. London: Routledge/Falmer.

Mahoney, J., Eccles, J. & Larson, R. (Eds.) (2005). *Organized activities as contexts of development: Extracurricular activities, after-school and community programs*. Mahwah, NJ: Erlbaum.

McLaughlin, M. W. (1993). Embedded identities: Enabling balance in urban contexts. In S. B. Heath & M. W. McLaughlin (Eds.), *Identity and inner city youth: Beyond ethnicity and gender* (pp. 36–67). New York: Teachers College Press.

McLaughlin, M. W. & Heath, S. B. (1994). Learning for anything everyday. *Journal of Curriculum Studies*, 26(5), 471–489.

McLaughlin, M. (1999). *Community counts: How community organizations matter for youth development*. Washington, DC: Public Education Network.

McLoughlin, C. & Lee, M. J. W. (2007). Social software and participatory learning: Pedagogical choices with technology affordances in the Web 2.0 era. In *ICT: Providing choices for learners and learning. Proceedings ascilite Singapore 2007*. 664–673. Online at http://www.ascilite.org.au/conferences/singapore07/procs/mcloughlin.pdf

Miles, M. B. & Huberman, A. M. (1994). *Qualitative data analysis: An expanded source book*. (2nd Ed.) Thousand Oaks, CA: Sage.

Moerman, M. (1988). *Talking culture: Ethnography and conversation analysis*. Philadelphia: University of Pennsylvania Press.

Moje, E. B., Ciechanowski, K., Kramer, K., Ellis, L., Carrilo, R., & Collazo, T. (2004). Working toward third space in content area literacy: An examination of everyday funds of knowledge and discourse. *Reading Research Quarterly*, 39(1), 38–70.

Muller, M. (2003). Participatory design: The third space in HCI. In J. Jacko & A. Sears (Eds.), *The human-computer interaction handbook* (pp. 464–481). Mahwah, NJ: Lawrence Erlbaum Associates.

Poverty Benchmarks Project. (2007). *Poverty in the city of Camden*. Retrieved November 13, 2008 from www.lsnj.org/PDFs/budget/PovertyCityOfCamden041107. pdf

Radziszewska, B. & Rogoff, B. (1991). Children's guided participation in planning imaginary errands with skilled peer or adult partners. *Developmental Psychology*, 27(3), 381–389.

Rogoff, B. (1990). *Apprenticeship in thinking: Cognitive development in social context.* New York: Oxford.

Rogoff, B. (1995). Observing sociocultural activity on three planes: Participatory appropriation, guided participation, and apprenticeship. In J. Wertsch (Ed.), *Sociocultural studies of mind* (pp. 139–164). New York: Cambridge University Press.

Rogoff, B. (2003). *The cultural nature of human development.* New York: Oxford University Press.

Sandoval, C. & Latorre, G. (2008). Chicana/o artivism: Judy Baca's digital work with youth of color. In A. Everett (Ed.) Learning race and ethnicity: Youth and digital media (The John D. and Catherine T. MacArthur Foundation Series on Digital Media and Learning; pp. 81–108). Cambridge, MA: MIT Press.

Sefton-Green, J. (2006). *New spaces for learning: Developing the ecology of out-of-school education* (Hawke Research Institute Working Paper Series No. 35). Magill, South Australia: University of South Australia, Hawke Research Institute for Sustainable Societies.

Sfard, A. (1998). On two metaphors for learning and the danger of choosing just one. *Educational Researcher*, 27(2), 4–13.

Soep, E. (2006). Youth mediate democracy. *National Civic Review*, 95(1), 34–40.

Soja, E. W. (1996). *Thirdspace: Journeys to Los Angeles and other real-and-imagined places.* Malden, MA: Blackwell Publishers.

Sternberg, R. (2003). What is an "expert student"? *Educational Researcher*, 32(8), 5–9.

Thompson, C. (2009). Rehearsals and roles: Youth participation frameworks in one youth organization. *Linguistics and Education* 20(4): 328–349.

Thompson, C. (2011). Absent audiences: Youth identity formation in preparations for performance. *Journal of Language, Identity, and Education*, 10(1), 22–40.

Thompson, C., Putthoff, J., & Figueroa, E. (2006). Hopeworks: Youth identity and technology. In D. Buckingham & R. Willett (Eds.), *Digital generations: Children, young people, and the new media* (pp. 313–329). Mahwah, NJ: Lawrence Erlbaum.

Vadeboncoeur, J. (2006). Engaging young people: Learning in informal contexts. *Review of Research in Education*, 30, 239–278.

Vásquez, O. A. (2003). *La Clase Mágica: Imagining optimal possibilities in a bilingual community of learners.* Mahwah, NJ: Lawrence Erlbaum.

Vasudevan, L. (2006). Looking for Angels: Knowing adolescents by engaging with their multimodal literacy practices. *Journal of Adolescent and Adult Literacy*, 50(4), 252–256.

van Aalst, J. & Chan, C. K. K. (2001). Beyond 'sitting next to each other': A design experiment on knowledge building in teacher education. In P. Dillenbourg, A. Eurelings, & K. Hakkarainen (Eds), *Proceedings of the First European Conference on Computer-Supported Collaborative Learning* (pp. 20–28). Maastricht, the Netherlands: Universiteit Maastricht.

Wenger, E. (1999). *Communities of practice*. New York: Cambridge University Press

Wood, S. (2005, November 21). "Most dangerous" label strikes Camden again. *Philadelphia Inquirer*. Accessed online November 28, 2005, from http://www.philly.com/mld/inquirer/news/local/13221055.html

Wortham, S. (1994). Mapping participant deictics: A technique for discovering speakers' footing. *Journal of Pragmatics*, 25, 331–348.

4 Positive Technological Development: The Multifaceted Nature of Youth Technology Use toward Improving Self and Society

Marina Bers, Alicia Doyle-Lynch, and Clement Chau

Too often youth experiences with technology are framed in negative terms (e.g., cyber-bullying, sexual predation, invasion of privacy, addiction to videogames or massively multiplayer online games [MMOGs]). For example, works such as those by Li (2007) on cyber-bullying especially among schoolmates; Grusser, Thalemann, and Griffiths (2007) on videogame addiction and aggression; and Palfrey and Gasser (2008) on new challenges faced by digital natives, especially regarding online safety and privacy, all highlight the dangers and perils of new technologies. The literature has pointed to many risk factors including poor home environment, lack of parental oversight, depression, history of abuse, and substance use as correlates to poor choices and negative uses of new technologies (see Schrock & boyd, 2008, for an extensive overview).

The work presented here on Positive Technological Development (PTD) is an attempt to both identify and foster an alternative to this deficit discourse about youth's experiences with technology. Researchers such as Jenkins, Purushotma, Clinton, Weigel, and Robison (2009), from a media studies perspective, and Resnick (2008), from an educational technologies focus, have also taken a positive approach to understand how children use technology. PTD complements this work by adding the psychological and developmental science perspective. PTD builds on previous work on Positive Youth Development (Benson, Scales, Hamilton, & Semsa, 2006; Damon, 2004) that looks at pathways of thriving individuals in the first two decades of their lives and parallels its origins as a reaction to a prevalence of discussion about "at-risk" youth that ignores positive development. The focus on positive process informs the work presented in this chapter; the underlying assumption is that youth are already using technologies, and can use them even in better ways, if presented with educational opportunities, to construct their sense of identity as having agency toward promoting changes in their own selves and society. This chapter presents a measurement tool that establishes and operationalizes the PTD construct, and in turn provides a way to evaluate outcomes of technologically rich educational experiences for youth.

Since the early 1960s, the growing field of educational technology has developed assessment instruments to examine how learning with and about computers happens based on the constructs of computer literacy and technological fluency. From an outsider's perspective, both constructs are similar and both address the questions of what it means to successfully use technology for teaching and learning (National Research Council Committee on Information Technology Literacy, 1999). However, there is a difference between these constructs. Computer literacy, defined by researchers such as Luehrmann (1981, 2002), Hoffman and Blake (2003), and Livingstone (2004), is about developing instrumental skills to improve learning, productivity, and performance by mastering specific software applications for well-defined tasks, such as word processing and e-mail, and knowing the basic principles of how a computer works. By contrast, technological fluency includes instrumental skills but focuses on enabling individuals to express themselves creatively with technology (Papert, 1980). Seymour Papert (1980) described fluency as the ability to use and apply technology as effortlessly and smoothly as people use language.

Recent research has also suggested that in addition to computer literacy and technological fluency, students' attitudes toward computer technologies may also influence their use and experience of computer and technology-mediated learning (Coffin & MacIntyre, 1999; Tsai, Lin, & Tsai, 2001). Because of the changing digital media and technology-rich environment that surrounds today's youth, the use of technology is multifaceted (Jenkins et al., 2009). The ability to use technology meaningfully in the context of learning no longer rests only on skills but also on a variety of psychosocial and emotional factors. Teasing apart these various dimensions is an important task in understanding the sources of variations among youth's attitudes toward technology use and self-efficacy.

For instance, gender differences in students' technology use have been a topic in the literature in the past decade (Kafai, 1996, 1998).When taken as a whole, many researchers have found that male students tended to score more positively in attitude toward technology or higher in technology self-efficacy tests than do female students. However, recent studies have taken a closer examination of this gender issue and found that gender differences may be rooted in terms of approach and goals (Ching, Kafai, &

Marshall, 2000). Gunn, McSporran, MacLeod, and French (2003) argue that male students tend to take a more exploratory and developmental approach and are less swayed by technical problems, whereas female students are more practical and instrumental in their technology use. Because there is evidence to suggest differences in various aspects of technology use, research must take steps to pull apart these various dimensions of the use of technology.

Given the multitude of contexts and purposes for which youth utilize computers for learning (both in and out of school), our comprehension of their technology-related behavior must now expand beyond computational literacy and fluency. While cognitive factors are important, the social, cultural, emotional, civic, and moral dimensions of technology use should also be acknowledged. The construct of PTD was developed to provide the theoretical basis to design and evaluate technology-related experiences that take into consideration the individual attitudes and the psychosocial processes influencing the positive uses of computers by youth in the context of their developmental trajectories (Bers, 2008b).

PTD attempts to describe youth development in technology-rich settings while acknowledging that computers use is no longer limited to teaching and learning in school settings. Young people use computers at home, at work, in the library, and in after-school settings. They use them to communicate with friends, to listen to and exchange music, to meet new people, to share stories with relatives, to organize civic protests, to shop for clothing, to engage in e-mail therapy, and to find romantic partners (Subrahmanyam, Greenfield, Kraut, & Gross, 2001). While all these activities involve both computer literacy and technological fluency, the skill set needed goes beyond them. PTD describes the process of youth development in technological settings and provides a model for how development can be enhanced by promoting certain individual and social assets. For example, positive technological development involves developing competence and confidence regarding computer use. However, it is also important for youth to develop character traits that will help them use technology safely to communicate and connect with other people, and to envision the possibility of making a better world through the use of computers (Bers, 2008b; Ribble, Bailey, & Ross, 2004). PTD is in alignment with current Informational and Communications Technology (ICT) standards, such as the Framework for 21st Century Learning, that emphasize the integration of both the technical skills of digital technologies and an understanding of the ethical and social issues surrounding the use of such tools (Partnership for 21st Century Skills, 2011).

Theoretical Framework

PTD draws on two bodies of work: Papert's (1980) constructionism, which looks at the role of computers in education, and the positive youth development approach proposed by applied developmental science (e.g., Lerner et al., 2005). Following Piaget, constructionism might best be defined as a constructivist philosophy for educational technologies. However, while Piaget's (1953) theory was developed to explain how knowledge is constructed in our heads, Papert (1980, 1993) pays particular attention to the ways that such internal constructions are supported by constructions in the world, for example, through the use of computers. By creating an external object to reflect on, people are more likely to construct internal knowledge and develop technological fluency in a playful way (Resnick, Martin, Sargent, & Silverman, 1996). Thus, constructionism is both a theory of learning and a strategy for education. Constructionism informs PTD by focusing on the design of computational tools for learning (Barab & Squire, 2004; Collins, Joseph, & Bielaczyc, 2004) and by providing guidelines for the development of technologies for exploring issues of self and identity (Bers, 2001; Bruckman, 1998; Bryant, Forte, & Bruckman, 2005).

While historically the computer literacy movement has taken an ethically neutral approach, PTD as a framework for design, implementation, and evaluation takes a stance regarding positive ways for youth to engage with technology. PTD is guided by current research on positive growth in developmental science and developmental psychology. Applied developmental scientists look at cognitive, personal, social, emotional, moral, and civic characteristics of young people to study positive youth development (Lerner, Wertlieb, & Jacobs, 2003). The use of the term "positive" connotes the promotion of valued characteristics and activities (i.e., developmental assets) that would lead a young person toward a good developmental trajectory (i.e., development toward improvement of one's self and society). Researchers in developmental science (e.g., Damon, 2004; King & Furrow, 2004; Larson, 2000; Scales, Benson, & Mannes, 2007; Theokas & Lerner, 2006) contrasts the positive youth development movement as fostering and engendering healthy behaviors with the prevention model that targets at-risk youth before these behaviors even appear. Recent research by Lerner et al. (2005) frames the various developmental assets into the six C's of positive youth development: competence, confidence, character, connection, caring, and contribution. Researchers see pathways to promote thriving individuals as the basis for developing personhood and a civil society. Taken together, these characteristics reflect a growing consensus about what is involved in healthy and positive development among people in the first two decades of their lives and the promotion of healthy communities (Scales, Benson, Leffert, & Blyth, 2000). This multidimensional framework for thinking about young people's experience is particularly important in today's technology use. As new technologies are developed, young people appropriate them in different ways, even subverting the original intent of the designer, to satisfy their own developmental and contextual needs. Thus, understanding the multiple ways in which technology can have a positive impact is an important task for researchers interested in the role of technology in identity construction. While the six C's were first theorized to describe the different aspects of young people's day-to-day experiences, the PTD framework extends them to those specific experiences that are mediated by computer technologies.

Drawing upon an interdisciplinary and integrative look at constructionism and applied developmental science, the positive technological development (PTD) framework offers a way to understand positive youth development in a technology-rich context. PTD is both a theoretical construct and a proposed pathway in which opportunities for promoting the six C's are encountered through participation in technologically rich intervention programs that support positive behaviors through engagement with computers and other innovative technologies (Bers, 2006). The six constructs that compose PTD are defined in Table 4.1. These constructs form the basis of the Positive Technology Development Questionnaire (PTDQ) for measuring change after an intervention. The PTDQ provides a window into identity in two ways: (1) at the intrapersonal level, by including information regarding an individual's feeling of comfort and skill with the use of technology and his or her sense of moral compass, and (2) at the interpersonal level in terms of increased agency that technology can provide toward caring, connecting, and contributing to others.

Measuring Factors and Correlates

The Positive Technological Development Questionnaire (PTDQ) was constructed based on the PTD framework to provide a way to measure the multifaceted use of technology in learning contexts in a way that is relevant to the twenty-first century. To this end, the PTDQ uses an applied developmental science approach while drawing on existing theories regarding technological fluency and literacy. Understanding that youth development is contextualized and multifaceted, the PTDQ is framed by the six C's as proposed by the applied developmental sciences framework and brings

Table 4.1. *Definitions of the 6 C's of Positive Technology Development*

Competence	An ability to use technology, to create or design projects using the computer in order to accomplish a goal, and to debug projects and problem solve
Confidence	A sense of oneself as someone who can act and learn to act successfully in a technology-rich environment and find help when necessary and have perseverance over technical difficulty
Caring	A sense of compassion and willingness to respond to needs and concerns of other individuals, to assist others with technical difficulties, and to use technology as means to help others
Connection	Positive bonds and relationships established and maintained by the use of technology
Character	Awareness and respect of personal integrity and moral and social values while using technologies in responsible ways and an ability to express oneself using technology.
Contribution	An orientation to contribute to society by using and proposing technologies to solve community/social problems

together existing technological literacy and fluency constructs in a way that appreciates the inter-relatedness among the different constructs in the context of technology use.

Currently a number of measurements are proposed to assess individuals' "technological abilities" in a variety of ways depending on the particular theoretical framework from which the measurement is created. Some measurements are designed to assess an individual's ability to operate the computer and the internet. For example, Turner, Sweany, and Husman's (2000) Computer Interface Literacy Measure evaluates students' ability to navigate the graphical user interfaces of basic operating systems, standard applications, and the internet. However, as computer technologies develop and new tools and paradigms emerge, knowledge in basic operation may not be enough. Bunz (2004) extends on mere interface literacy to include network-based technologies as part of what is deemed important "technology skills." His Computer-Email-Web (CEW) fluency scale was developed with the understanding of the importance and pertinence of internet technologies in young people's lives. The PTDQ draws and adapts these measurements and, using the vocabulary of the applied developmental science approach, frames these constructs as *technological competence*. For example, the PTDQ proposes statements such as "I am able to create or design projects on the computer from an idea to a finished work" on a 5-point Likert scale.

Cassidy and Eachus (2002) go beyond basic operation to include self-efficacy (or self-efficacy beliefs) to be a necessary component for successfully using computer technologies to complete tasks. Their Computer User Self-Efficacy (CUSE) scale has been widely used to help educators identify students who may have difficulty engaging with technologies in their learning environments. The PTDQ adapts the constructs and items from this work and frames them as technological confidence defined as the assurance or consciousness of one's powers of reliance on oneself to learn and accomplish certain tasks using technologies, rather than the ability to know how to do them now. An example confidence scale item is "I feel confident that I can learn how to use a new computer program."

The increase of both technological competence and technological confidence are evaluated in most educational programs that focus on promoting technological fluency and computer literacy. However, most recently, with the surge of Web 2.0 technologies and the emphasis on collaborative and cooperative learning paradigms, researchers started to focus on social aspects in learning with and about technology.

Scholars in the field of computer-mediated communication (CMC) began to develop constructs and measurements that focus primarily on the internet as a unique social phenomenon. Rather than evaluating uses of standard computer usage such as word processing or computer programming, CMC scholars focus on networked-based uses of computers to mediate communication and peer relationships (Herring, 2002) and have developed constructs such as Internet Social Capital (Williams, 2006). By evaluating technologies as tools to bridge relationships and bond with others, Williams and others (e.g., Kraut et al., 2002) found that contrary to common criticism of internet communication (e.g., Putnam, 2000), online bonding or online in-group activities do not predict insularity. Furthermore, there is a strong and significant positive relationship between bonding with similar in-group online peers (such as peers through video games, interests and hobbies, etc.) and bridging to make contact with people unlike oneself and meeting new people. Spitzberg (2006) developed the Computer-Mediated Communication (CMC) questionnaire to measure knowledge about uses of networked computers for CMC purposes as well as levels of motivation. CMC scholars argue that in today's technology-rich environment, not only are computer technologies used for computation and processing tasks, but they are also tools for connecting and bonding with others. Using the applied development science vocabulary, we frame these constructs in our PTDQ as *technological connection* and *technological caring*. While the connection items focused on one's use of technologies to affiliate with others and participate in affinity groups, the caring items focused on building emotional ties with other individuals and using technologies to show signs of care and assistance. For example, items such as "I use the computer to be part of different groups and communities" are used to measure the connection construct, whereas items such as "I use the computer to learn more about the people who I care about" and "I am part of a virtual community on the internet where I give and receive advice" are used to measure caring.

Finally, Jenkins, Purushotma, Clinton, Weigel, and Robison's (2009) work on New Media Literacies (NML) illuminates a new set of skills to the healthy social and educational development of today's young people. Competencies such as collective intelligence and appropriation are argued to foster "good" uses of technologies to promote community involvement, and competencies such as judgment and negotiation promote "good" decision-making. In a related study, Gardner and colleagues' (James et al., 2008) GoodPlay project also taps into the various ethical dimensions in the digital media experiences of today's youth, and primarily focuses on aspects such as authorship, participation, identity, credibility, and privacy. While there is no existing scale that specifically measures these constructs, our PTDQ frames these ideas as *technological contribution* and *technological character*, respectively. The contribution dimension includes items such as "I can give back to my community using my computer and/or my computer skills," and the character dimension includes statements such as "I do not engage in behaviors that I think are bad when using computers."

We have previously piloted the PTDQ for evaluating robotics-based educational interventions with young children and their parents (Bers, 2007a; Chau & Bers, 2006) and for measuring developmental trajectories in young adults' attitudes and use of technology for engaging in community activities (Chau, 2006; Chau & Bers, 2010). This chapter presents a study assessing the validity of the hypothesized six Cs structure behind the PTDQ and supports the findings with qualitative data.

We first present a confirmatory factor analysis (CFA) to examine the hypothesized structure of the PTDQ. CFA is factor analysis method that allows researchers to test whether a proposed theoretical factor structure is supported empirically. Here, the proposed structure is a six-factor structure (i.e., the six C's). By applying CFA to the PTDQ, we are able to examine whether the six C's "exist" within the PTDQ as well as the strength of the factors as individual, but interrelated constructs.

Following the CFA, we examine gender differences in the relationship between the six C's and youth's attitudes toward technology. Given the evidence in the literature that points to potential gender differences in students' attitude toward technology use, we were interested in providing a working example of how the PTDQ could supplement previous work and help understand how males and females differentially experience enjoyment regarding their use of technology. The goals of this second analysis are two-fold. First, to further the process of validating the PTDQ by examining its relationship with other constructs related to technological development. Second, to demonstrate the utility of the PTDQ in applied settings as a tool that can be used to evaluate differential positive uses of technology by youth.

Methods

Participants

The Positive Technological Development Questionnaire (PTDQ) was administered to 188 undergraduate students enrolled at a liberal arts university in Northeast United States. The researchers recruited freshman students during orientation as they registered for orientation activities to participate in a questionnaire survey as part of a study to examine the extent to which computer and related technologies can facilitate social and civic engagement on campus (Bers, 2007, 2008b). All participants volunteered to complete the survey questionnaire without incentives.

In the current analysis, only questionnaires with 90 percent completion (i.e., 24 out of 27 questions answered) were included to optimize the validity of the results. These criteria left us with a total of 186 participants. The final participant group was comprised of 103 (55.40%) females and 83 males (54.60%) and ranged in age from 17 to 24 with a mean age of 19 ($M =$ 19.01, $SD = 1.74$). The sample was 62.9 percent Caucasian, 8.4 percent Asian American, 5.4 percent Latino American, 5.4 percent African American, and 17.8 percent biracial or other. Among the participants, 15 percent were engineering students, 81 percent students of arts and sciences, and 4 percent undecided. To minimize selection bias, recruitment specifically targeted students enrolled in a variety of orientation programs including a technology-based civic engagement program (19.35%), a fitness program (38.71%), an outdoor exploration program (9.68%), and others (32.25%).

Measure

The PTDQ is composed of twenty-seven items that tap into the six C's (caring, character, competence, confidence, connection, and contribution) of positive technological development. Participants were given the following instructions: "Below are some statements about your attitudes towards technology. Please let us know how much you agree with each statement." Participants respond to each item statement using a 5-point Likert scale where a response of 1 indicated strong disagreement with the statement and a response of 5 indicated strong agreement with the statement. As a scale, sum scores of the 27 items may range from 27 to 135. For this current sample, sum scores on the PTDQ ranged from 49 to 134, with an average total score of 89.72 (*SD* = 20.54). This reflected an item average of 3.25 for the sample, indicating that this sample does not represent the floor of the scale. Potential limitation to the generalizability of this study is addressed in the Discussion. The full PTDQ is presented in Appendix A.

In addition to this questionnaire, participants also completed a standard demographic questionnaire including age and gender, as well as a nine-item scale that addressed various aspects of math, science, technology, and engineering activities. Of this nine-item scale, because the current study primarily focuses on students' use of and attitudes toward technology, only the item, *enjoyment in technology use* ("I enjoy using technologies and computers") is included in this analysis.

Results

Statistical Validation of the PTDQ

A series of confirmatory factor analyses (CFA) were conducted using the software package, Mplus4.1 (Muthén & Muthén, 2007) to examine the validity of the theorized six-C's model of positive technological development thought to underlie the PTDQ. Model fit was assessed using four fit statistics: chi-square (χ^2), Comparative Fit Index (CFI), the Tucker-Lewis Index (TLI), and the root mean square error of approximation (RMSEA). A nonsignificant χ^2 value suggests a good model fit. However, because χ^2 is highly sensitive to sample size, the ratio of χ^2 to degrees of freedom (*df*) was used to evaluate the model. A χ^2/df value between 2 to 3 indicates good model fit (Carmines & McIver, 1981). RMSEA scores <.05 suggest "good" fit, scores between .05 and .08 suggest "moderate fit," and scores between .08 and .1 suggest "adequate" fit (Brown & Cudeck, 1993). On both the TLI and the CFI, values >.09 indicate good model fit (Hu & Bentler, 1999).

Factor analysis typically involves testing a series of models, using the findings from each model to inform modifications of subsequent models. Examples of modifications that may be made in this process include deleting questionnaire items all together, or moving individual question-naire items to be associated with a different factor. All model modifications should be based both on data and on theory. For example, a questionnaire item that read, "I know how to make computer projects (e.g., images, animations, songs, videos, robotic constructions) to express things that I value" was associated with "character" in our original model. Results from the CFA, however, suggested that this item was a stronger predictor of "competence." As a team, we determined that such a modification to the questionnaire would make sense theoretically and moved this item to be connected with competence.

In our CFA procedure, five items from the PTDQ were demonstrated to be significantly associated with several factors, rather than with a sin-gle factor. As such, these items were removed from the model and the questionnaire. The final model of the PTDQ presented in this article (see Figure 4.1) includes twenty-two items. The CFI and TLI fit indices of the final model suggested good model fit (χ^2/df =2.134, CFI =.901, TLI =.882, RMSEA =.078). A thorough review of the results did not suggest additional changes that would both improve model fit and hold up theoretically. The CFA procedure is based on the tenants of regression analysis and its output can be similarly interpreted (Kline, 2004). For example, item 4 is associated with "caring" and has an R^2 value equal to .336. Following the same proce-dure one would use to interpret a regression analysis, it can be deduced that item 4 accounts for 33.6 percent of the variance in the construct "caring." A complete report of individual item means, standard deviations, standard-ized beta coefficients and R^2 values can be found in Table 4.2.

To further test the reliability of the model structure suggested in the final CFA model, Cronbach's alpha coefficients, which measure the internal consis-tency of a scale, were calculated for each of the six C's (Cronbach, 1951). The alphas for character (α =.735), competence (α =.904), confidence (α =.892), connection (α =.813), and contribution (α =.814) all exceeded .70, suggest-ing "good" internal consistency. The alpha for the caring scale (α =.608) sug-gested a "fair" internal consistency. Please see Appendix A for a complete list of questionnaire items and their corresponding and final factor association.

Gender Differences in Technology Use

After the confirmatory factor analysis procedures established a measure-ment model, participants' data were aggregated to provide six sub-scores of PTD. Ordinary least squares (OLS) regression analyses were conducted to examine the moderating effect of gender differences on the relationship

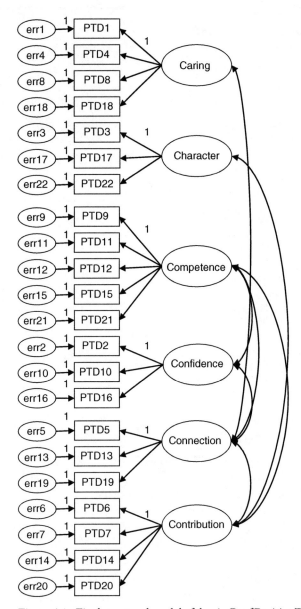

Figure 4.1. Final structural model of the six Cs of Positive Technology Development (model 4).

Table 4.2. *Descriptive Statistics, Standardized Structure Coefficients, and R^2 values for the Final Confirmatory Factor Analysis Model*

Initial Item #	Factor	M	SD	Standardized Beta Coefficient	Z-Score	R^2
1	Caring	3.31	1.02	0.311	0.00	0.097
4	Caring	2.50	1.41	0.579	4.56	0.336
8	Caring	2.92	1.12	0.588	5.30	0.346
18	Caring	3.10	1.21	0.581	4.95	0.338
3	Character	3.65	1.12	0.695	0.00	0.484
17	Character	3.38	1.13	0.793	12.79	0.629
22	Character	3.46	0.97	0.572	8.54	0.328
9	Competence	3.34	1.25	0.781	0.00	0.610
11	Competence	2.76	1.29	0.752	12.05	0.566
12	Competence	3.04	1.35	0.871	15.80	0.759
15	Competence	2.97	1.41	0.853	16.55	0.727
21	Competence	2.96	1.26	0.787	12.94	0.619
2	Confidence	3.76	1.05	0.804	0.00	0.646
10	Confidence	3.87	1.12	0.869	14.65	0.756
16	Confidence	3.68	1.10	0.906	16.22	0.821
5	Connection	3.08	1.44	0.679	0.00	0.461
13	Connection	2.09	1.25	0.631	7.85	0.398
19	Connection	2.88	1.21	0.700	9.26	0.489
6	Contribution	3.67	1.18	0.714	0.00	0.509
7	Contribution	3.97	0.91	0.579	8.75	0.336
14	Contribution	3.02	1.25	0.862	11.66	0.744
20	Contribution	3.82	1.05	0.622	8.41	0.387

between the six positive technology development constructs and participants' enjoyment of technology use.

Among female participants, the overall regression model was statistically significant, $F(6, 87) = 7.89, p < .001, R^2 = .40$. Among the six C's, only the confidence scale significantly predicted female participants' enjoyment of technology use (see Table 4.3). This significant positive association between female participants' technological confidence and their enjoyment using technology, when controlling for all other Cs, suggested that despite variations in female participants' level of competence in technology, their confidence made the largest contribution to their reported enjoyment. This finding is consistent with literature cited earlier in the introduction regarding the importance of the confidence factor when understanding women and technology, and it echoes works by researchers such as Bannert and Arbinger (1996), Cassell and Jenkins (1998), and Cooper and Weaver

Table 4.3. *Regression Analysis for Predicting Enjoyment of Technology Use with the 6Cs of Positive Technology Development by Gender*

Variables	B	SEB	βʃ
Male Participants			
Caring	.23	.18	.22
Character	.71	.22	.52**
Competence	−.35	.17	−.39*
Confidence	.27	.20	.21
Connection	−.38	.16	−.34*
Contribution	.38	.19	.34*
Female Participants			
Caring	.21	.18	.17
Character	.20	.19	.15
Competence	.001	.13	.001
Confidence	.32	.19	.35**
Connection	−.06	.13	−.05
Contribution	.13	.13	.12

Notes: R^2 = .46 for male participants; R^2 = .40 for female participants. B = standardized coefficient; SE = standard error; β = unstandardized coefficient.
*$p < .05$; ** $p < .01$.

(2003) that suggest female students' attitudes and relations toward technology could be largely attributed to the extent to which they could realize and recognize their technological abilities and skills.

The regression model for male participants was also statistically significant, $F(6, 54) = 8.54, p <.001, R^2 = .46$. Whereas only the confidence factor was a significant predictor of enjoyment of technology use among female participants, results showed that character, competence, connection, and contribution factors were all highly predictive of male participants' enjoyment of technology use (see Table 4.3). These results indicated that there is a significant moderating effect in the relationship between the six Cs and enjoyment of technology use. Caring was not found to be a predictor for either males or females. These results might be due to several reasons that are discussed in the Future Work section.

Guiding Program Development

This section presents a case study to illustrate how the PTD framework can be used to implement a particular technology-based youth program to reflect the various factors associated with positive youth development. The Active Citizenship through Technology (ACT) was a pre-orientation program designed for incoming freshman to a northeastern university (Bers, 2008b) to explore issues of civic engagement and community. Students came together for three days and used the Zora virtual environment (Bers, 2001) to create a campus of the future, engage in exploration of the role of the university in promoting civic engagement with the community, and build a peer-social network before the stress and demands of the academic year begin. The ACT program is designed so students, in the process of developing their campus of the future, can first learn about the real campus by interviewing faculty, students, and administrators and then discuss how they could improve its facilities and its policies and curricular offerings and explore the relationship between their campus and the local neighborhoods and communities. The goal is to immerse youth in a high-tech playground where they can acquire civic knowledge and skills, as well as experiment with civic behaviors and democratic participation.

The design of the intervention was informed by the PTD framework and activities were implemented to address each of the C's of the theoretical model. In terms of competence and confidence, students used the Zora tools to create a virtual campus similar to the ones they know, with spaces such as the Mike Jonas Student Center, the Math and Science Building, the Orwell Language Hall, the Winifred Mandela Library, and the Jumbo Appetite, a dining hall where "themed meals are served and a suggestion box [is provided] where requests for particular food can be made." But the students have also developed virtual exhibits to educate students, faculty, and community members about issues of concern to all. In terms of connection, students used Zora to find peers who were interested in similar issues and together they created their Zora projects – virtual exhibit halls to display information, research, and ideas about an area of interest. For example, a student was interested in the arts and invited other participants to collaborate with her to create the Art and Community House. The following log excerpt shows the Zora-supported collaborative process they engaged in to build the house:

> *Mary*: Arts are slowly disappearing in schools
> *Tom*: Because it's mostly money oriented, the arts don't bring as much as football games
> *Brittany*: I know that certain school districts on long island have had to cut out arts programs
> *David*: It is the same here
> *Mary*: Why did they cut the budgets?

> *Brittany*: There just wasn't enough money coming in from the state I guess for funding
> *Mary*: but why couldn't they just cut the other stuff as well?
> *David*: spending too much on other things ... they figure its easier to get rid of the public art education
> *Mary*: it's really sad that politics has infiltrated the school system
> *David*: there are plenty of private places but people have to pay more and obviously they don't like that
> *Alex*: so what are we doing?
> *Danny*: earth to jenny: politics and public schools are obviously linked
> *Tom*: Now that some of us have a topic that fire us up, what should we do? Go off and build and make our case house?
> *Mary*: who wants to work with me on the arts?
> *Brittany*: let's put pictures of art and theater and music up.

The resulting Art and Community House contained fifty-eight objects, including nineteen message boards, each with a piece of information regarding funding, school, and the arts (e.g., results from Gallup polls, statistics about slashing of funding in various states, and various venues in which the university could take action in bringing arts and music to the community and its citizens); seventeen photographs and images of various types of arts and related subjects (e.g., a child playing the piano, a ballerina, the logo for Americans for the Arts, a local community performance space) each accompanied with a description; and various three-dimensional objects such as music notes and dancing characters to populate the room. Figure 4.2 illustrates a screen capture of the Arts and Community House in the Zora virtual environment. As shown by this example, students were able to connect with each other based on shared interests and engage in a collaborative project.

In terms of caring, students were active in online chat. For example, the Zora Activity Log recorded 3,612 lines of chat over the three days. They discussed issues such as student life, policies/rules for graduation, internet, administration, and student services. Following is an excerpt of a conversation in which students discussed funding for students' clubs, showing their caring about the well-being of the community.

> *Peter*: Are we going to have fun student clubs? Do clubs have to give back to the community?
> *Melanie*: If you are giving back to the community, should you get more money?
> *Alan*: Should we fund the clubs?
> *Peter*: Every year, they give their proposal ... then they decide ... and get their permission.

Figure 4.2. A virtual house in the Zora environment about bringing drama into the community.

> *David*: If you are giving back to the community, you should get money. Why put money into clubs?
>
> *Peter*: If it lasts then that is good; but if you are new, you start-off with the minimum amount.

In terms of character, students used Zora's values dictionary feature to think about personal and moral values that their virtual campuses of the future should cherish. For example, they logged thirty-six values entries and eighty definitions in the values dictionary. Some of the values were academic curiosity, defined as "keeping your mind open to diversity in learning"; integrity, defined as "keeping to ones morals"; tolerance, defined as "the ability to not allow differences to get between you and others"; and trust, defined as "knowing that others will not take advantage of your vulnerabilities."

   In terms of contribution, students proposed recommendations of how their future virtual campus could make an impact in the socioeconomic situations in the neighborhood communities. For example, some students chose to focus on the relationship between the local town police and the university police by interviewing police officials to understand better if and how the surrounding communities benefit from the campus police.

Based on this information, participants created a virtual exhibit hall called the Police case study. This house contained twenty-three objects, of which there were four message boards at each of the corners to represent four discussion topics. At each corner were related images and photographs as well as three-dimensional objects to provide visual support for the discussions. The topics included a comparison of salaries between the university and public police forces. This discussion topic was accompanied by statistics and graphs about salaries as well as graphics and text images displaying the types of jobs and roles at each of the police forces. In another corner was a discussion about jurisdiction for on campus violations such as "dealing with alcohol [abuse] on campus." To illustrate an example, participants included photographs of beer cans and the game beerpong to accompany this topic, as well as a three-dimensional structure illustrating the game in action. There was also a topic about how the two forces can work together to address university students' violations in the community such as noise and complaints by community citizens. Images of recent news photographs were displayed along with the message board to provide some relevance of the topic and the pertinence to these particular students. Finally, a display about the types of crimes that students have committed on campus and in the neighborhood communities accompanied by charts and web links was created in the last corner.

Other students chose to focus on the role of the universities, in particular the education, child development, and psychology departments, to provide childcare and educational opportunities for members of the surrounding communities. The resulting virtual public house (Figure 4.3) was called No Preschooler Left Behind and had a welcoming description: "We believe that kids should be allowed to keep their arms and legs to get quality childhood education."

Besides police and early education, some students chose to do research about public interest issues such as the impact of comprehensive exams in the learning environment and state-mandated curriculum and the positive impact that athletics programs and art education programs can have on a local community. Instead of writing ideas and results of their research in a paper or action plan, they used Zora to develop a virtual exhibit to teach others about their findings. For example, the high-stakes testing Massachusetts Comprehensive Assessment System (MCAS) house was populated by a series of five images of bar graphs and accompanying message boards to discuss about differences in standardized test score results in the five communities neighboring the university. There was also a Test Your Knowledge corner where questions from recent standardized tests

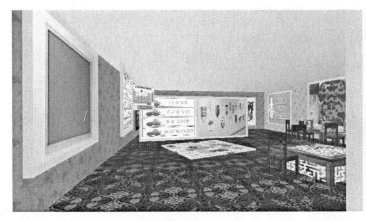

Figure 4.3. A virtual house in the Zora environment about educational issues in the community.

were posted, and visitors were encouraged to try out some of these test questions and to comment their thoughts about the test. In another corner of the house, a participant linked from an external website a video presentation about the standardized testing practice as well as web links to official Web pages of the state.

The ACT pre-orientation program provides an example of how the PTD theoretical construct can guide the design and evaluation of an intervention program aimed at engaging youth in using technologies in positive ways. While ACT focuses on providing opportunities to use the Zora virtual environment for civic engagement with college students, other programs developed within the PTD framework can utilize the PTD constructs to put their own values-in-practice while utilizing a wide range of technologies.

Discussion

This chapter reports an effort to theorize and validate a new instrument that measures positive technological development. The PTDQ aims to bring the multifaceted approach of applied developmental science to our understanding of the role that technology may play in the lives of individuals, in particular regarding their own self-improvement and contributions to society. Both dimensions, the intrapersonal and the interpersonal, are important to consider in an integrated way when thinking about identity. While it is indeed needed that young people become technologically fluent, especially in today's technology-rich and technology-dependent society, our goal is to extend beyond an ability to use technology to also focus on using technology to make positive contributions to the development of self and of society. The six Cs of positive technological development, as we have conceptualized here, provide a framework for supporting this work and the PTDQ provides a way to measure change after an intervention. As the fields of education and as new areas such as cyberpsychology start to tap into the potential of new technologies to provide or augment programs aimed at helping young people construct their sense of identity, the PTD framework and its derived instrument present new opportunities for conceptualizing programs to support differential positive uses of technology by youth and differential ways to evaluate success and failure of the interventions regarding each of the desired domains of impact, represented by the six C's.

Results from the confirmatory factor analysis support the validity of the hypothesized six C's structure of the PTDQ. In addition, the Cronbach's alpha scores calculated in alignment with the final model structure ranged from .608 to .904 and support the reliability of each of the six individual scales that makeup the PTDQ. Furthermore, the second set of regression analyses illustrated the utility of the PTDQ for examining the multidimensionality of technology use when measuring participants' enjoyment or attitudes about technology. Results showed that among females, confidence is a highly significant predictor of enjoyment of technology use. On the other hand, when considering the male sample, character, competence, connection, and contribution were all strong predictors for enjoyment. By examining the individual facets or factors the overarching construct of positive technological development, this analysis was able to identify sources of gender difference in students' attitudes toward and engagement with technology. Results for these analyses further add to the current discussion about the sources and bases for gender differences, digital divide, and participation gap. By identifying relevant social and personal factors (connection, caring, character, and contribution) in addition to the traditional cognitive factors (competence and confidence) that are typically accounted for by the literacy and fluency frameworks, this study illustrates and further supports the multifaceted nature of the relationship between technology and youth development. Further research and in-depth analyses are needed to examine how these developmental factors may influence actual usage of technology and, in turn, how variations in youth technology use contribute to different developmental outcomes.

One limitation to the present study is the relatively small sample size (*N* =186 after discarding incomplete questionnaires). While the current findings suggest preliminary support for the proposed six-factor structure of the PTDQ, it is thought that future examinations of the PTDQ using larger and more diverse samples will further substantiate the six Cs model of positive technological development. This particular sample also reported relatively high average total score of 89.72(SD = 20.54), indicating a mean of 3.23 at the item level. Not only might social desirability effects have contributed to students reporting higher scores; the use of a college student sample also limited the generalizability of this study to the other populations. In addition, because the goals of this study were mainly to assess the PTDQ, participants were not asked to report in detail their actual technology use such as time spent using technology, types of activities engaged with technology other background variables such as classes taken that might have influenced their attitudes, and so on. These are important variables to consider when measuring attitudes and enjoyment.

By integrating constructs from the applied development science literature with the educational technologies and the computer medicated communication literatures, the PTDQ can be used by educational technologists and experts in youth development and communication media researchers to understand the various ways in which technologies can promote positive youth development. The PTDQ can be used to measure change from before to after a technology-rich educational intervention and can guide the development of a technology-rich curriculum to explore the six dimensions of positive technological development. While the present confirmatory analysis demonstrates the validity and reliability of the PTDQ for the college-age youth described earlier, in order to understand how young people are using technologies for their psychosocial development, it is best to integrate the use of the PTDQ with qualitative methods for data collection that provide ethnographic insights into young people's ways of thinking about technology in their lives.

Future Directions

The work presented in this chapter introduces the research construct of positive technological development and the validation of an instrument to evaluate it. PTD is an attempt to develop a theoretical framework that integrates both psychological and sociocultural dimension of identity. Thus, the emphasis is on investigating both intrapersonal characteristics that might have an impact on the use of technology (such as competence, confidence, and character) and interpersonal ones (such as caring, connection, and contribution) that situate the individual within a larger social context. The PTD framework acknowledges the cognitive aspects of technology use such as skills, fluency, and decision making, as well as contextualizes the use of technology within a social and civic ecology, promoting relationships and civic actions. In addition to shifting the discussion of youth development and youth technology use from the deficit paradigm to a positive and asset promotion discourse, this study also highlights the necessity for researchers to look at technology use through a multidimensional lens. Not only did the analysis reveal the utility of a measurement that could help partial out factors contributing to variances and gender differences in technology use and attitudes, it also identified places for education, intervention, and promotion. For example, results from this study called attention to the relationship between female enjoyment of technology use and their technological confidence, despite varying levels of competence. It is our hope that future work in the area of technology and identity will help shift away the public discourse from deficit models that depict youth's use of technology as associated with negative personal and social outcomes.

Appendix A

The Positive Technological Development Questionnaire

-You and technology-

Below are some statements about your attitudes toward technology, please let us know how much do you agree with them on a rating scale from 1 (strongly disagree) to 5 (strongly agree).

	Please circle One
When working with someone on the computer, I make sure that they understand everything I am doing.	1　2　3　4　5
Learning about technology is easy for me.	1　2　3　4　5
I can express my ideas, my values, and myself by using the computer.	1　2　3　4　5
I am part of a virtual community on the internet where I give and receive advice.	1　2　3　4　5
I have met new people through the use of computers.	1　2　3　4　5
I can imagine ways of using technology to make the world a better place.	1　2　3　4　5

(continued)

Appendix A (*continued*)

	Please circle One
I believe that by using new technologies people can find new ways to contribute to their communities.	1 2 3 4 5
It is important for me to teach others the things that I already know about computers.	1 2 3 4 5
I am able to create or design projects on the computer from an idea to a finished work.	1 2 3 4 5
I feel confident that I can learn how to use a new computer program.	1 2 3 4 5
I can debug or fix computer projects or programs when something goes wrong.	1 2 3 4 5
I know how to make computer projects (e.g., images, animations, songs, videos, robotic constructions) to express things that I value.	1 2 3 4 5
I have found support groups on the internet.	1 2 3 4 5
I can contribute to my community using my computer and/or my technical skills.	1 2 3 4 5
I know how to make or design my own projects with computers (images, animations, songs, robotic constructions).	1 2 3 4 5
I feel confident that I can figure out how to use new features of a program on my own.	1 2 3 4 5
I am able to learn computer applications that help me express myself in different ways.	1 2 3 4 5
I use the computer to learn about the people who I care about.	1 2 3 4 5
I actively use the computer to be part of different communities.	1 2 3 4 5
I can imagine positive ways to use computers for our society.	1 2 3 4 5
I have an advanced understanding of how a computer works.	1 2 3 4 5
I feel good about myself when using the computer	1 2 3 4 5

Removed Items

##. Because of my technical skills, I can connect with people in many different ways.

##. I use computers to connect with other people who think and feel the same way as I do.

##. I know that I can figure out how to create or design projects on the computer from an idea to a finished piece of work.

##. I know how to use the computer as well as, or better than my peers.

##. I know what is good and bad behaviors regarding the use of internet.

References

Bannert, M. & Arbinger, P. R. (1996). Gender-related differences in exposure to and use of computers: Results of a survey of secondary school students. *European Journal of Psychology of Education*, 11(3), 269–282.

Barab, S. & Squire, K. (2004). Design-based research: Putting a stake in the ground. *Journal of the Learning Sciences*, 13(1), 1–14.

Benson, P. L., Scales, P. C., Hamilton, S. F., & Semsa, A., Jr. (2006). Positive youth development: Theory, research, and applications. In R. M. Lerner (Ed.), *Theoretical models of human development. Volume 1 of Handbook of Child Psychology* (6th ed.). Hoboken, NJ: Wiley.

Bers, M. (2001). Identity construction environments: Developing personal and moral values through the design of a virtual city. *Journal of the Learning Sciences*, 10(4), 365–415.

Bers, M. (2006). The role of new technologies to foster positive youth development. *Applied Developmental Science*, 10(4), 200–219.

Bers, M. (2007a). Project Interactions: A multigenerational robotic learning environment. *Journal of Science and Technology Education*, 16(6), 537–552.

Bers, M. (2007b). Positive Technological Development: Working with computers, children, and the Internet. *MassPsych*, 51(1), 5–7, 18–19.

Bers, M. (2008a). *Blocks to robots: Learning with technology in the early childhood classroom*. New York: Teachers College Press, Columbia University.

Bers, M. (2008b). Civic engagement and the Internet: Developing technologically-rich educational programs to promote civic participation online and offline. In L. Bennett (Ed.), *Digital media and civic engagement* (MacArthur Foundation Series on Youth and Digital Learning; pp. 139–160). Cambridge, MA: MIT Press.

Bers, M. & Chau, C. (2010). The virtual campus of the future: Stimulating and simulating civic actions in a virtual world. *Journal of Computing in Higher Education*, 22(1), 1–23.

Brown, M. W. & Cudeck, R. (1993). Alternative ways of assessing model fit. In K. A. Bollen & J. S. Long, *Testing structural equation models* (pp. 136–162). Newbury Park, CA: Sage.

Bruckman, A. (1998). Community support for constructionist learning. *Computer Supported Cooperative Work (CSCW)*, 7(1–2), 47–86.

Bryant, S., Forte, A., & Bruckman, A. (2005). Becoming Wikipedian: Transforming of participation in a collaborative online encyclopedia. In *Conference proceedings of the 2005 International ACM SIGGROUP Conference on Supporting Group Work* (pp. 1–10). New York: ACM Press.

Bunz, U. (2004). The Computer-Email-Web (CEW) fluency scale: Development and validation. *International Journal of Human-Computer Interaction*, 17(4), 479–506.

Carmines, E. G. & McIver, J. P. (1981). Analyzing models with unobserved variables. In G. W. Bohrnstedt & E. F. Borgatta (Eds.), *Social measurement: Current issues* (pp. 65–115). Beverly Hills, CA: Sage.

Cassell, J. & Jenkins, H. (Eds.) (1998). *From Barbie to Mortal Kombat: Gender and computer games*. Cambridge, MA: MIT Press.

Cassidy, S. & Eachus, P. (2002). Developing the computer user self-efficacy (CUSE) scale: Investigating the relationships between computer self-efficacy, gender, and experience with computers. *Journal of Educational Computing Research*, 26(2), 133–153.

Chau, C. & Bers, M. (2006). Positive technological development: A systems approach to understanding youth development when suing educational technologies. In S. Barab, K. Hay, & D. Hickey (Eds.), *Proceedings of the International Conference of the Learning Sciences* (pp. 902–903). Mahwah, NJ: Lawrence Erlbaum.

Chau, C. (2006). Associations between online civic engagement and personal characteristics among late adolescents (Master's thesis). *Masters Abstracts International*, 44(6), 3006.

Ching, C. C., Kafai, Y. B., & Marshall, S. (2000). Spaces for change: Gender and technology access in collaborative software design. *Journal for Science Education and Technology*, 9(1), 67–78.

Coffin, R. J. & MacIntyre, P. D. (1999). Motivational influences on computer-related affective states. *Computers in Human Behavior*, 15, 549–569.

Collins, A., Joseph, D., & Bielaczyc, K. (2004). Design research: Theoretical and methodological issues. *Journal of the Learning Sciences*, 13(1), 15–42.

Cooper, J. & Weaver, K. D. (2003). *Gender and computers: Understanding the digital divide*. Mahwah, NJ: Lawrence Erlbaum.

Cronbach, L. J. (1951). Coefficient alpha and the internal structure of tests. *Psychometrika*, 16(3), 297–334.

Damon, W. (2004). What is Positive Youth Development? *The Annals of the American Academy of Political and Social Science*, 591, 13–24.

Grusser, S. M., Thalemann, R., & Griffiths, M. D. (2007). Excessive computer game playing: Evidence for addiction and aggression? *CyberPsychology & Behavior*, 10(2), 290–292.

Gunn, C., McSporran, M., MacLeod, H., & French, S. (2003). Dominant or different? Gender issues in computer supported learning. *Journal of Asynchronous Learning Networks*, 7(1), 14–30.

Herring, S. (2002). Computer-mediated communication on the Internet. *Annual Review of Information Science and Technology*, 36(1), 109–168.

Hoffman, M. & Blake, J. (2003). Computer literacy: Today and tomorrow. *Journal of Computing Sciences in Colleges*, 18(5), 221–233.

Hu, L.-T. & Bentler, P. M. (1999). Cutoff criteria for fit indices in covariance structure analysis: Conventional criteria versus new alternatives. *Structural Equation Modeling*, 6, 1–55.

James, C., Davis, K., Flores, A., Francis, J., Pettingill, L., Rundle, M., & Gardner, H. (2008). *Young people, ethics, and the new digital media: A synthesis from the GoodPlay Project*. Chicago: MacArthur Foundation.

Jenkins, H., Purushotma, R., Clinton, K., Weigel, M., & Robison, A. (2009).*Confronting the challenges of participatory culture: Media education for the 21st century*. Chicago: MacArthur Foundation.

Kafai, Y. B. (1996). Gender differences in children's constructions of video games. In Patricia M. Greenfield & Rodney R. Cocking (Eds.), *Interacting with video* (pp. 39–66). Norwood, NJ: Ablex.

Kafai, Y. B. (1998). Video game designs by girls and boys: variability and consistency of gender differences. In J. Cassell & H. Jenkins (Eds.), *From Barbie to Mortal Kombat: Gender and computer games* (pp. 90–114). Cambridge, MA: MIT Press.

King, P. E. & Furrow, J. L. (2004). Religion as a resource for positive youth development: Religion, social capital, and moral outcomes. *Developmental Psychology*, 40, 703–714.

Kline, R. (2004). *Principles and practice of structural equation modeling* (2nd Edition). New York: Guildford Press.

Kraut, R., Kiesler, S., Boneva, B., Cummings, J., Helgeson, V., & Crawford, A. (2002). Internet paradox revisited. *Journal of Social Issues*, 58, 49–74.

Larson, R. W. (2000). Toward a psychology of positive youth development. *American Psychologist*, 55, 170–183.

Lerner, R., Lerner, J., Almerigi, J., Theokas, C., Phelps, E., Gestsdottir, S., et al. (2005). Positive youth development, participation in community youth development programs, and community contributions of fifth-grade adolescents: Findings from the first wave of the 4-H study of positive youth development. *Journal of Early Adolescence*, 25(1), 17–71.

Lerner, R., Wertlieb, D., & Jacobs, F. (2003). Historical and theoretical bases of applied developmental science. In R. M. Lerner, D. Wertlieb, & F. Jacobs (Eds.), *Handbook of applied developmental science: Vol 1. Applying developmental science for youth and families: Historical and theoretical foundations* (pp. 1–28). Thousand Oaks, CA: Sage.

Li, Q. (2007). New bottle but old wine: A research of cyberbullying in schools. *Computers in Human Behavior*, 23(4), 1777–1791.

Livingston, S. (2004). Media literacy and the challenge of new information and communication technologies. *The Communication Review*, 7(1), 3–14.

Luehrmann, A. (1981). Computer literacy: What should it be? *Mathematics Teacher*, 74(9), 682–686.

Luehrmann, A. (2002). Should the computer teach the student, or vice-versa? *Contemporary Issues in Technology and Teacher Education*, 2(3), 389–396.

Muthén, B. O. & Muthén, L. K. (2007).MPlus 4.1 [computer software]. Los Angeles, CA: Muthén & Muthén.

National Research Council Committee on Information Technology Literacy. (1999). *Being fluent with information technology*. Washington, DC: National Academy Press.

Palfrey, J. & Gasser, U. (2008).*Born digital: Understanding the first generation of digital natives*. New York: Basic Books.

Papert, S. (1980). *Mindstorms: Children, computers and powerful ideas*. New York: Basic Books.

Papert, S. (1993).*The children's machine: Rethinking school in the age of the computer*. New York: Basic Books.

Partnership for 21st Century Skills. (2011). *Framework for 21st Century Learning*. Washington, DC: Partnership for 21st Century Skills.

Piaget, J. (1953). *The origins of intelligence in the child*. London: Routledge and Kegan Paul.

Putnam, R. (2000). *Bowling alone: The collapse and revival of the American community*. New York: Simon & Schuster.

Resnick, M. (2008). Sowing the seeds for a more creative society. *Learning & Leading with Technology*, 35(4), 18–22.

Resnick, M., Martin, F., Sargent, R., & Silverman, B. (1996). Programmable bricks: Toys to think with. *IBM Systems Journal*, 35(3–4), 443–452.

Ribble, M., Bailey, G., & Ross, T. (2004). Digital citizenship: Addressing appropriate technology behavior. *Learning and Leading with Technology*, 32(1), 6–12.

Scales, P., Benson, P., Leffert, N., & Blyth, D. (2000). Contribution of developmental assets to the prediction of thriving among adolescents. *Applied Developmental Science*, 4(1), 27–46.

Scales, P., Benson, P., & Mannes, M. (2006). The contribution to adolescent well-being made by nonfamily adults: An examination of developmental assets as contexts and processes. *Journal of Community Psychology*, 34(4), 401–413.

Schrock, A. & boyd, d. (2008). *Online threat to youth: Solicitation, harassment, and problematic content* (An Internet Safety Technical Task Force report). Cambridge, MA: Harvard University, Berkman Center for the Internet and Society.

Spitzberg, B. (2006). Preliminary development of a model and measure of computer-mediated communication (CMC) competence. *Journal of Computer-Mediated Communication*, 11(2), 629–666.

Subrahmanyam, K., Greenfield, P., Kraut, R., & Gross, E. (2001). The impact of computer use on children's and adolescents' development. *Journal of Applied Developmental Psychology*, 22, 7–30.

Theokas, C. & Lerner, R. (2006). Observed ecological assets in families, schools, neighborhoods: Conceptualization, measurement, and relations with positive and negative developmental outcomes. *Applied Development Science*, 10(2), 61–74.

Tsai, C. C., Lin, S. S. J., & Tsai, M. J. (2001). Developing an Internet attitude scale for high school students. *Computers & Education*, 37, 41–51.

Turner, J., Sweany, N., & Husman, J. (2000). Developing the computer interface literacy measure (CILM). *Journal of Educational Computing Research*, 22, 37–54.

Williams, D. (2006). On and off the 'Net: Scales for social capital in an online era. *Journal of Computer-Mediated Communication*, 11(2), 593–628.

Part II

Identities in Flux and in Play

Introduction Part II: Identities Unleashed

Brian J. Foley

No. 2: "Good day, Number Six."
No. 6: "Number what?"
No. 2: "Six. For official purposes, everyone has a number. Yours is number 6."
No. 6: "I am not a number, I am a *person*."

From The Prisoner, television show, 1967

In modern society, each of us carries around dozens of different types of identification. There are obvious forms like our driver's license and credit cards as well as physical traits like our fingerprints, retina, and, of course, our face. We also remember passwords or secret handshakes that are ways to indicate that we belong or deserve access to something. The purpose of all these forms of identification is to establish our identity to people and systems that control the resources we need. Unlike a door key, which provides access through a physical interaction with the lock, our cards and passwords provide access to things through our identity. We gain access to resources such as bank accounts and Web sites that we have previously attained by simply identifying ourselves. The numbers and accounts that we use are sometimes described as our identity, and we are told to guard it carefully against theft. But there is another identity that we have. Our personal identity: the thing that describes who we are, not simply our name but also our character. The word *identity*, from the Latin *iden* meaning "the same," is used in many ways, but includes these two related but clearly distinct ideas: (1) a set of characteristics by which a person is recognizable in different instances and (2) the persistent essential character of a person. The first definition describes identity from an external perspective. It is something that can identify an individual from a group. In contrast, the second definition provides a more personal and qualitative and often internal perspective. Each type of identity plays a key role in social behavior and learning in everyday life. But in a virtual world, the rules and roles of identity are different.

Dual Identity

The use of identification plays an important part in society; it provides access to our resources and enables authorities and others to give appropriate rewards and punishments for behavior. The motivation that people have to get a reward like a college degree and the threat of punishments like a traffic ticket are only possible if the appropriate people can be identified. Identification is both utilitarian and potentially authoritarian as it can track an individual person across space and time and connect the person to the information unique to them. We are identified by our names or by the many numbers we are assigned that connect to records in various databases. The database might include information about a person's status, history, privileges, and might include some data that is unique to the person (e.g., a driver's license photo). Despite this information, the rise of "identity theft" shows how easy it can be to disconnect the numbers from the actual person they are meant to identify.

Identity theft is a serious problem because criminals can steal resources and have their bad behavior linked to another person, but the victim does not actually lose his or her identity – one's "real" identity is different from the various records about them. When we think of a person's identity, it is far more than a number. This is the second type of identity, the one that dominates the psychological and sociological literature. Our perception of others and of ourselves, the *personal identity*, entails our physical embodiment, personal history, and a complex web of affiliations to individuals, groups, activities, and ideas. Many have noted that personal identity is neither singular nor fixed but is something that both develops over time and is context specific (Erikson, 1963; Marcia, 1993). Although a personal identity may be difficult to describe, it is clearly not something that can be stolen. Our numbers, fingerprints, and other identifiers play a small role in our self-concept, but their existence and use in society do affect our behavior.

Personal identity is a key concept in of all types of social science and philosophy. It is thought to play a key role in moderating behaviors from interactions with others (Tajfel & Turner, 1986), interactions with authority (Huo, Smith, Tyler, & Lind, 1996) and how people learn (Wenger, 1998). In education, the degree to which students identify themselves as part of a larger community of practitioners can add authenticity and motivation to learning. Educators have tried to use identity to improve student learning but creating educational experiences in which students are encouraged to adopt a target identity (Barton, 2003; Brown & Campion, 1994; Rogoff, 1990). While these environments have been successful, some students resist taking on the new identity. Barton (2003) describes one student, Kobe, who is interested in learning but refuses to participate because he has a reputation as being anti-school. Taking on a new identity would clash with part of his existing one. We have learned from these and other studies that personal identity is not something easily manipulated.

The two versions of identity, identification and self-concept, serve very different purposes. Identification is primarily utilitarian in nature while self-concept is fundamental to our thinking and behavior. Both are drawn into question as people go from the everyday regular world into the virtual world[1].

Virtual Identities and Social Capital

Because online experiences have become increasingly rich and engaging, they enable new ways of being (Heudin, 2004). In order to participate in online activities, people are required to create a virtual identity that may or may not correspond to their regular identity. Without the constraints of biology, one can create a virtual identity of any age or gender or, if the site allows, can take the identity of a wizard or alien. The choices that we make in creating the virtual identity depend on the type of interactions we expect to have on the site. On a social networking site one might create a virtual identity that matches his or her regular identity in order to connect with old friends. But on other sites one might choose to provide little information so as to remain anonymous. Each creation of a virtual identity provides an opportunity to create a new version of one's self that may or may not be identified with the regular identity and that may or may not match our personal identity.

When people log onto a site to animate their virtual identity as an alien, their virtual personal identity would seem to change, presumably their regular personal identity is not that of an alien. But this change is not complete because it is still the person who makes decisions for the virtual identity. Gee (2003) describes this as a "projective identity" in which a person must

---

[1] Rather than debate whether virtual worlds are "unreal," I use the terms "regular" to describe the world that we all in habit and "virtual" for worlds that some engage online.

"project one's values and desires onto the virtual character" (p. 55). The behavior of the virtual identity may be different from the regular identity as a person acts in character, but the conceptually and emotionally it is still the person with the controls making the decisions.

Freedom to take on a role like a wizard is an important difference between the regular and virtual worlds, but the freedom from identification is an even more important difference. Because many virtual identities are not linked in an obvious way to the regular identity of the person controlling it, there are limited consequences for online behavior. As Turkle (1984, 1995) and others have noted, the resulting freedom provides both dangers and opportunities. When people are anonymous they have less incentive for good behavior and less incentive not to engage in bad behavior. Anonymity has been associated with negative and even anti-social behavior (Zimbardo, 1969). This association has been supported by anecdotal reports on anti-social or behavior online (Dibble, 1993; Turkle, 1995) including a new term, "griefers," to describe online players who cause intentional harm to random players (Dibble, 2008). Anonymous situations can have some positive effects as well. Studies of computer-mediated communication indicate that people have a tendency to disclose more personal information and to engage in more intimate interactions than in face-to-face communication (Spears, Lea, & Postmes, 2007).

While anti-social behavior often catches the attention of the media, the situation online is in fact not so dismal because there are motivations for people to behave in positive ways. Online behavior is regulated by the desire to build and maintain reputation and relationships: to increase social capitol (Resnick, 2001). Just as we carry identification to access resources attained over time, a virtual identity gains access to virtual resources. An obvious example would be the experience points that a role-playing game (RPG) player may have obtained over several months. But the discussion board poster who has developed a reputation for insightful commentary also has something to lose. This is the sort of social capitol that a virtual identity can accumulate – and put at risk if he or she starts behaving in ways that go against community norms. Maintaining and increasing this social capitol is important activity for both the real and virtual identities (Ellison, Steinfield, & Lampe, 2007). These identities are not well described as being anonymous because they are known in the virtual world. Online reputations are developed through personal interactions in much the same way is offline. Steinkuehler (2005) describes how players in the game Linneage get reputations as "beta vet" based on their history of success in the game. Gee (2002) describes how players in the game EverQuest risk a reduction in their online status if their player is killed in the game. Such a reduction is cause for great concern as the identities are a product of many hours of "play."

The development of a virtual identity is very different from biological development. New users can be ignored or closely scrutinized if they appear not to understand the norms of the world (Boostrom, 2008). Behavior is easily monitored because of the extensive documentation of online activities. In many virtual worlds, records are kept of users scores, achievements, and online discussions. Sometimes the game play itself can be recorded for others to view. These detailed and often public accounts of behavior make it much easier to learn about another user's reputation. Many virtual environments create explicit indicators of the reputation by summarizing past behaviors such as the level of a player in an online game or the "top reviewer" rating on Amazon. All of this documentation serves to make it easier to assess another user's identity and heightens the consequences for each interaction. But this is mediated by the ancillary nature of the online identity. A person can easily create a new account and a new online identity and begin again.

The combination of freedom and the ability to create and recreate identities with the desire to for the virtual identity to gain social capital encourages people to experiment with virtual identities. Each virtual identity provides a chance to succeed within the system. Much like an artist working on a scratch pad, the user creates an identity that can easily be discarded but might be retained if it turns out to be of value. As users try different virtual identities, these experiments have an important side effect: learning. With each virtual identity, the user gains knowledge and experience. This knowledge may be specific to the virtual world such as how to get a high score, or they may be learning things of general value such as collaboration or leadership skills.

Learning and Scratch Identities

The freedom to create identities and develop them for a time allows users to explore identities in ways that were impossible before. Turkle's (1995) book *Life on the Screen* explored many of these ideas long before the modern multiplayer games and online communities that we see now. She accounts how one user of an online community creates four separate identities so he can experience the community in different ways, sometimes playing multiple roles simultaneously on separate windows (p. 13). Each identity allowed him to participate in the community in a different way and explore what the identity is like. Research on identity play shows how common it is for online users to pose as alternate identities online (Bruckman, 1996; Subrahmanyam, Smahel, & Greenfield, 2006; Valentine & Holloway, 2002; Valkenburg & Peter, 2008). Lenhart, Rainie, and Lewis (2001) reported that in their survey, almost a quarter of adolescents who used instant messaging indicated that they had pretended to be someone else. More recently researchers have begun to ask how these environments and the resulting identity play could be leveraged to support learning and development.

What sorts of identity play are likely to be productive? Gee (2002) argues that most in-depth interactions with online worlds or games involve significant learning of symbol systems (semiotic domains) and representations for that environment. This type of learning can help users develop islands of expertise (Crowley & Jacobs, 2002) that improve overall literacy skills. Shaffer (2006) argues for creating "epistemic games" in which students take on the identity of a professional in an area they are learning (e.g. city planner). Epistemic games provide opportunities for participating in complex environments and take on the identity of a participant in the community. Identity is more directed (students have fewer choices) than the play seen on most online sites.

A few projects have been successful at implementing directed identity play for the purpose of learning. Shaffer (2006) provides several examples of epistemic games in mathematics, science, urban design, and journalism. Bers (2001) showed how an online community enabled disabled students to participate in activities that many students take for granted. Clarke, Dede, Ketelhut, and Nelson (2006) explored how students could take on the role of a scientific investigator in a historical context. Dodge et al. (2008) showed how a virtual environment could lead to multiple learning modes so that different students could interact in ways that were comfortable to them. Lee and Hoadley (2007) report on a project where students were tasked with creating multiple identities (e.g., cross-gender) in an online community and reporting on their experiences. In each case the students were asked to adopt an identity for the express purposes of learning about some topic. We don't know how adopting and identity in this way compares to a free choice identity. The level of identification is sure to be a critical variable to the success of this approach.

Identity play can provide an outlet for students whose participation in school is limited in some way. Imagine a student like Kobe (Barton, 2003) with a reputation as a charismatic non-participator in school who develops an interest in history. He faces a difficult decision. If he starts seriously studying and learning history, his reputation among his friends will likely be lost, and he has no way of knowing if he would succeed at history or what sort of satisfaction this would give him if he did. Such a risk would be difficult for anyone to take, but if he could participate in historical analysis through an online identity, he would be able to test this new interest without risking his status within the school. We can imagine other scenarios such as studying controversial topics (e.g., religion), going against cultural norms (men studying nursing) or working with people from opposing groups (Israelis and Palestinians). Being able to participate in a community without public identification has enormous potential as an alternative to traditional schooling.

These early attempts at instructional online identity play raise more questions than we can currently answer. There are ethical concerns about trying to manipulate someone's identity even in the service of education. But as people have and will come to embody online identities routinely – and develop new skills at identity play – these issues may fade. We also wonder how the practices and knowledge developed thought online participation will transfer to school and other situations. How do students who are immersed in a practice then reflect on their process to learn about the field they are engaged in? The differences between the free choice play described by Turkle, Gee, and others is fundamentally different from the more directed play of Schaffer's epistemic games. Whatever we learn about these issues, that both types of identity, the identification and the personal identity, remain a key factors in both learning and play even as the virtual world releases our identities from their traditional bonds is clear.

References

Barton, A. C. (2003). *Teaching science for social justice*. New York: Teachers College Press.

Bers, M. U. (2001). Identity construction environments: Developing personal and moral values through the design of a virtual city. *The Journal of the Learning Sciences*, 10(4), 365–415.

Boostrom, R. (2008). The social construction of virtual reality and the stigmatized identity of the newbie. *Journal of Virtual Worlds Research*, 1(2), 1–19.

Brown, A. L. & Campione, J. C. (1994). Guided discovery in a community of learners. In K. McGilly (Ed.), *Classroom lessons: Integrating cognitive theory and classroom practice* (pp. 229–270). Cambridge, MA: MIT Press/Bradford Books.

Bruckman, A. (1996) Gender swapping on the Internet. In P. Ludlow (Ed.), *High noon on the electronic frontier: conceptual issues in cyberspace* (pp. 317–325). Cambridge, MA: MIT Press.

Clarke, J., Dede, C., Ketelhut, D. J., & Nelson, B. (2006). A design-based research strategy to promote scalability for educational innovations. *Educational Technology*, 46(3), 27–36.

Crowley, K. & M. Jacobs (2002), Islands of expertise and the development of family scientific literacy. In G. Leinhardt, K. Crowley, & K. Knutson (Eds.), *Learning conversations in museums* (pp. 333–356). Mahwah, NJ: Lawrence Erlbaum.

Dibbell, J. (1993, December 21). A rape in cyberspace. *The Village Voice*, 38, 36–42.

Dibbell, J. (2008, January 18). Mutilated furries, flying phalluses: Put the blame on griefers, the sociopaths of the virtual world. *Wired Magazine* 16.02. Retrieved May, 12, 2009, from http://www.wired.com/gaming/virtualworlds/magazine/16-02/mf_goons.

Dodge, T., Barab, S., Stuckey, B., Warren, S., Heiselt, C., & Stein, R. (2008). Children's sense of self: Learning and meaning in the digital age. *Journal of Interactive Learning Research*, 19(2), 225–249.

Ellison, N. B., Steinfield, C., & Lampe, C. (2007). The benefits of Facebook "friends": Social capital and college students' use of online social network sites. *Journal of Computer-Mediated Communication*, 12(4), article 1. http://jcmc.indiana.edu/vol12/issue4/ellison.html

Erikson, E. (1963). *Childhood and society*. New York: Norton.

Gee, J. (2003). *What videogames can teach us about literacy and learning*. New York: Hargrove.

Heudin, J.-C. (2004). *Virtual worlds: synthetic universes, digital life, and complexity*. Boulder, CO: Westview Press.

Huo, Y. J., Smith, H. J., Tyler, T. R., & Lind, E. A. (1996). Superordinate identification, subgroup identification, and justice concerns: Is separation the problem; is assimilation the answer? *Psychological Science*, 7, 40–45.

Lee, J. J. & Hoadley, C. (2007). Leveraging identity to make learning fun: Possible selves and experiential learning in Massively Multiplayer Online Games (MMOGs). *Innovate*, 3(6), 1–9.

Lenhart, A., Rainie, L., & Lewis, O. (2001). *Teenage life online: The rise of the Instant-Message generation and the Internet's impact on friendships and family relations*. Washington, DC: The Pew Internet & American Life Project.

Marcia, J. E. (1993). *Ego identity: A handbook for psychosocial research*. New York: Springer.

Resnick, P. (2001). Beyond bowling together: Sociotechnical capital. In J. Carroll (Ed.), *HCI in the new millennium* (pp. 247–272). Boston, MA: *Addison-Wesley*.

Rogoff, B. (1990) *Apprenticeship in thinking*. New York: Oxford University Press

Shaffer, D. W. (2006). Epistemic frames for epistemic games. *Computers & Education*, 46(3), 223–234.

Spears, R., Lea, M., & Postmes, T. (2007). Computer-mediated communication and social identity. In A. Joinson, K. McKenna, T. Postmes & U. Reips (Eds.), *Oxford handbook of Internet psychology*. Oxford: Oxford University Press.

Steinkuehler, C. (2005). *Cognition and learning in Massively Multiplayer Online Games: A critical approach*. Madison: University of Wisconsin–Madison.

Subrahmanyam, K., Smahel, D., & Greenfield, P. (2006). Connecting developmental constructions to the Internet: Identity presentation and sexual exploration in online teen chatrooms. *Developmental Psychology*, 42(3), 395–406.

Tajfel, H. & Turner, J. C. (1986). The social identity theory of inter-group behavior. In S. Worchel & L. W. Austin (Eds.), *Psychology of intergroup relations* (pp. 33–48). Chicago: Nelson-Hall.

Turkle, S. (1984). *The second self: Computers and the human spirit.* New York: Simon & Schuster.

Turkle, S. (1995). *Life on the screen: Identity in the age of the Internet.* New York: Simon & Schuster.

Valkenburg, P.M. & Peter, J. (2008). Adolescents' identity experiments on the Internet: Consequences for social competence and self-concept unity. *Communication Research*, 35(2), 208–231.

Wenger, E. (1998) *Communities of practice: learning, meaning, and identity* Cambridge: Cambridge University Press.

Valentine, G. & Holloway, S. L. (2002) Cyberkids? Exploring children's identities and social networks in on-line and off-line worlds. *Annals of the Association of American Geographers*, 92(2), 302–319.

Zimbardo, P.G. (1969) The human choice: Individuation, reason, and order versus deindividuation, impulse, and chaos in Nebraska. In W. J. Arnold & D. Levine (Eds), *Symposium on Motivation*. Lincoln: University of Nebraska Press.

5   "You Can Make Friends Easier on a Boy Face": Identity Play and Learning in a Multiuser Virtual Environment

Brian J. Foley, Melanie S. Jones, Pamela Aschbacher, and Cameron McPhee

The internet continues to provide a unique media of communication. From its very beginning, media scholars have noted how each new variation on the ways that individuals and groups can communicate and collaborate online have implications for how we view ourselves (Turkle, 1984, 1995). Notably, participation in online communities provides the opportunity for people to moderate or recreate an identity (Pearce, 2009). While much of the research on internet communication has focused on adults, there is increasing interest in how online interactions influence young people's identity development. Understanding identity formation in this context has implications for how youth see themselves as learners, as technology users, and as members of a community.

This paper considers identity creation and participation within the Whyville community. The Whyville Web site (www.whyville.net) provides a complex environment with opportunities for social interaction and learning, providing its online community with tools for creating a virtual identity and for participating in community life. The site is highly popular with young adolescents, particularly among girls. As such, Whyville provides a unique environment in which to observe children's online behavior and the ways that they explore their identity. To study how users are exploring issues of identity and to determine the implications for learning in virtual environments, we use surveys, interviews, and analysis of the site logs that enable us to examine behavior on the site.

Background and Theory

Early studies of online communication focused on the differences between person-to-person and online (often text-based chatting) communication.

Person-to-person communication provides a rich source of information from body language, tone of voice, and other cues. In contrast, online communication provides a much more limited transmission, which can affect the types of interactions available (American Association of University Women, 2000). Although website-mediated interactions online are typically limited by a lack of face-to-face interaction, the variety of online settings for social interaction provides occasions for people to engage with others in ways that are not possible in face-to-face interactions.

Turkle (1995) noted that because the internet brings with it the potential for anonymity, individuals are not constrained by their appearance or past behavior, allowing them to create new identities through which they can explore multiple facets of themselves. Users can present multiple senses of self, assume identities similar to their own, or take on those of a different gender, culture, or personality. Further, because these interactions can be anonymous, the taking on of multiple forms of identities or different versions of oneself can be done without fear of face-to-face disapproval, as might occur in real life. Moreover, online identities are easily transformed should social disapproval occur, a behavior that would not be possible in the "real world."

Researchers are beginning to understand how the limitations and freedoms of online communication affect social interaction. Spears, Postmes, Lea, and Wolbert (2002) argue that the limited nature of online interactions makes group identity information more salient. Although one has limited information about the person with whom he or she is communicating, clues about the individual's group affiliations allow the person to fill in some of the missing information. Bargh, McKenna, and Fitzsimmons (2002) found that, when individuals unknown to one another were paired, either in face-to-face situations or via internet chat, those in the internet chat condition were more likely to represent their true selves than were those in the face-to-face interaction conditions. Moreover, individuals in the chat group also reported liking their partners more than did those who engaged in face-to-face interactions. Although online communication and participation in online communities is described as "virtual," it is clearly personally meaningful.

Technological developments have reduced the difference between online and in-person communication. Multi-user virtual environments (MUVEs), including both multiplayer games and online communities such as Second Life, allow users to create a visual identity (avatar) to aid communication on the site. Many sites also allow audio in addition to text-based chatting. These developments allow the online experience to mimic in person communication by providing users a feeling of "social presence" (Nowak & Biocca, 2003). Avatars can become a key element in conveying information about the user, and in some cases the choice of avatar leads the user to change his or her behavior (Yee & Bailenson, 2007).

Despite some similarity to in-person communication, online participation is still characterized by the potential for anonymity that Turkle (1984) first described. While some online communities emphasize connections to one's real-world life, others allow people to create new identities. Social networking sites such as Facebook emphasize connecting people through real-world identities. On multiplayer game sites and online communities such as Second Life people typically create new identities that lack an obvious connection to their offline lives. These new identities provide the opportunity to participate online in ways that are different from what is usually possible in the off-line world.

The literature on young people in online worlds is limited, but Bers's (2001) work suggests that identity play may provide a useful means by which young people can acquire knowledge and develop skills. Bers's description of identity construction environments (ICEs) includes several design features of internet sites that afford the positive exploration of identity and morality among adolescents. These features include opportunities to create representations of one's self, for storytelling about one's self, and for participation in the activities of a community. Critical to Bers's model are Erikson's (1968) theory of identity and Papert's (1980) constructionist view of learning. According to Erikson's theory, adolescence is a crucial time for the formation of identity, during which peer groups provide opportunities to try out new social roles. What often guides this role-playing is the perception of which roles are valued by their peers and by society as a whole. Bers's model also rests on Papert's constructionist perspective that children learn best by doing, planning, and constructing projects that they find interesting and meaningful. Bers studied how constructing artifacts for an online identity, such as a virtual home or personal narratives, helps individuals to develop their interests and relationships in a safe and supportive environment.

Some educators are exploring how online environments can provide students with experiences that afford problem solving in authentic situations. The River City project (Dede, Ketelhut, & Ruess, 2002; Ketelhut, 2007) showed how students could engage in scientific inquiry in a virtual environment. Not only did River City provide an entire town for students to explore, but it was set in the eighteenth century, a time when their emerging scientific skills would be very valuable. This alternative environment both motivated students and provided an authentic context for scientific inquiry. The Quest Atlantis project (Barab et al., 2002; Barab, Sadler, Heiselt, Hickey, & Zuiker, 2007) also utilizes a virtual world to support students' learning and development. Students in Quest Atlantis undertake a series of quests designed to address both educational standards and the development of prosocial dispositions. Students have access to the site from home as well as from school so that they can participate in the community beyond the class assignments. Studies of learning on both River City and Quest Atlantis show significant learning gains for the students and increased motivation. Dodge et al. (2008) report on how skills developed on the Quest Atlantis site were able to transfer to offline activities. Interestingly, Quest Atlantis allows users freedom to participate in many activities of their own choice, but limits them to their assigned identity (Dodge et al., 2008).

The context in which young people interact with an online community affects both the type of learning and their identification with the activities. School-based communities, such as River City, provide students with access to online worlds to explore but typically do not allow students to explore alternate identities. Schools generally require that instructors assess the participation of students, thus precluding anonymous participation. This does not afford the same types of behavioral freedom of an anonymous site, but it does allow instructors and researchers to assess students' learning and behavior.

Online communities that are accessed outside of school provide more freedom as well as additional learning opportunities, albeit non-academic learning. Sites such as Neopets, Club Penguin, Habbo Hotel, and Whyville allow young people to construct their own identity and to participate in the community. Identities on these sites are not linked to off-line identities (particularly when a user's avatar is a penguin or a hamster), so users have the freedom that anonymity provides in their interactions on the site. Similar to popular sites for adults such as Second Life, these sites enable users to try out an online identity in the context of a rich environment of activities and social interaction.

In terms of learning, non-school sites are closer to so called "free-choice" learning environments such as museums and clubs (Falk & Dierking, 2002; Schauble, Leinhardt, & Martin, 1997). Unlike formal learning environments, free-choice learning involves voluntary participation in activities in which the user is interested and that have meaning. Research on informal learning environments and museum learning, in particular, is characterized by the free choice of the participants to engage in the activities. Choice has implications for the motivations of the learner and the potential impact on the learners' views of themselves (Falk, Brooks, & Amin, 2001). Informal learning activities such as those offered in after-school clubs or summer camps may have a greater impact on students' identity formation than traditional classrooms do (Banks et. al., 2007).

Learning in informal settings is also characterized by social interaction in the learning environment (Schauble et al., 2002). Many online environments, however, provide both the choices and the social experiences seen in other free-choice environments, as well as some unique benefits. Gee and Hayes (2011) describe how fan-based or hobby-based sites, which they call "passionate affinity spaces," allow users to interact with one another based on a shared interest when they may have little in common otherwise in terms of age, geographic location, or life experience. Ito and colleagues (2010) find that while many youth initially join social sites because of existing social ties (i.e., their friends are already members), such users often go on to create social ties online with other members they did not know previously. Online environments can also provide greater access that allows users to engage for more than a few hours at a time, and can provide freedom to explore without the social pressures that are inherent in users' off-line identities. Bruckman (2000) describes how the online environment MooseCrossing enabled two girls to spend an entire weekend collaborating online using a combination of synchronous and asynchronous chat and sharing.

Online communities also have great entertainment value. Millions of adults participate in multi-user games and communities, and the sites directed at children are growing alongside those of adults. The success of River City and Quest Atlantis have established that these sites can provide rich learning experiences through a formal classroom or semi-formal setting, but informal learning online is more difficult to assess. The Whyville website provides a great opportunity to explore this type of learning.

Whyville

Whyville is an online multi-user environment for young people that, although it has a number of educational activities, is generally not connected to schools. Young people log into the site after school hours, making the site more of a free-choice environment. Started in the late 1990s by developers interested in science education, the site has grown dramatically. With millions of registered users and tens of thousands of active users at any time, the site has become an important destination for young

Figure 5.1. Visual style of Whyville.

people. Whyville has remained independent of corporate influence, while other sites, such as Club Penguin and Neopets, have been bought by large corporations who use their popularity to advertise merchandise. Whyville also has been an important resource for researchers looking to understand the behavior of young people online. Numerous studies of the Whyville community have been conducted on the site over the past decade (Foley, Jones, McPhee, & Aschbacher, 2002; Kafai, 2010; Kafai & Giang, 2008; Kafai, Feldon, Fields, Giang, & Quintero, 2007) including a special issue of *Games and Culture* (Fields & Kafai, 2010a, 2010b; Kafai, Cook, & Fields, 2010; Kafai, Quintero, & Feldon, 2010; Lemke, 2010).

Whyville shares many of the features of other online sites, including the ability to chat with other users, participate in individual and group activities online, create an avatar and home, and participate in site management functions. It is one of the few sites for young people that allows them to type messages to one another (although the text is filtered). One of the aspects of Whyville that sets it apart is the visual style of the site (Figure 5.1). The environment is a mostly two-dimensional world with cartoonlike characters that are whimsical without being childish.

The Web site is designed as a virtual town. The Whyville Square is lined with buildings, such as Dr. Lelia's, where users can meet and chat about science; the Getty Museum, where viewers can see images of the artwork that are in the actual museum; and City Hall, where users can learns about city rules and events. Members of the Whyville community, known as "Whyvillians," are identifiable through colorful cartoonlike avatars. The avatars are generated by combining face parts that can be purchased in the "mall." There is an active economy for face parts, most of which has been created by users on the site. There also are activities such as virtual science experiments (e.g., ice skater spin), online games (e.g., checkers), home construction, and monitoring of the diet of one's avatar. Users can transport themselves to various hangouts on the site to meet new people or to connect with friends. In addition to the bubble chat, users can communicate via one-on-one chatting ("whispering"), site messages ("Y-mail"), and bulletin board postings. Users can also write articles for the site newsletter, the *Whyville Times*.

Whyville is successful at engaging a large community of adolescents. At this writing, there are over 6 million registered users, with hundreds of thousands of users logging in each month. A 2002 survey found that more than 80 percent of the users were ten to fifteen years old, with approximately two-thirds of these users identifying themselves as girls (Foley et al., 2002). This demographic is particularly important due to the need to interest girls in science and technology. On a typical day, tens of thousands of games are played on the site, which include some sophisticated explorations of topics such as rocketry, ballooning, and marine biology.

As with any voluntary learning environment, Whyville needs to engage users and remain popular to stay viable. The activities on the site reflect both a desire to educate and entertain. Similar criticisms have been made of museums, which often need to balance generating excitement and promoting learning (for a discussion, see Roberts, 1997). As an enticement to get users to engage in some of the more educational activities, the site offers rewards (called "clams," the unit of currency on the site) to play games. Users can spend their clams on other activities such as constructing a house or improving their avatar. These activities are some of the most popular, which encourages more game play. Most of the game playing is not truly free choice because users need to play games to earn clams and thus fully participate in other aspects of the site. For some users the science activities resemble "requirements" more than choices (Foley et al., 2002).

Previous studies of Whyville describe a dynamic social environment for tweens. One of the initially striking features of the site is the predominance of girls on the site. Foley et al. (2002) estimated that 68 percent of the users were girls, possibly drawn by the social nature of the site and the ability to design their look and participate in the administration of the community. Research by Kafai and her colleagues explored many aspects of the site including designing avatars (Kafai, Fields, et al., 2010), the role of race on the site (Kafai, Cook, et al., 2010), design of houses (Tynes & Kafai, 2003), the games that are played on the site (Fields & Kafai, 2010a) and the cheats that some users develop (Fields & Kafai, 2010b). Together these studies provide a rich description of the ways in which young people are interacting on the site.

Two Studies of Whyville Identities

We describe two studies of how young people interact on the Whyville site and to assess the learning potential of these environments. First, a survey of more than 200 site users concerning why they were interested in Whyville and what they found there (Foley et al., 2002). Second, we explore how the site users respond to participatory simulation. Both studies address aspects of Whyville users as participants in the online community and learners in the informal, social, and information-rich environment.

Survey of Whyville Users

In a typical community, conducting a survey can be fairly straightforward, but interacting with people online is more complicated. We were concerned that obtaining informed consent from parents would be an obstacle to the participation of the users who were minors. Parent permission would require users to talk to their parents about what they do online and to reveal their names to the researchers. Thus, to recruit survey participants, we submitted an article to the site newspaper, the *Whyville Times*, introducing the study. Three researchers on this project introduced themselves to the Whyville community as "Whyologists" and were easily identifiable by the Whyologist beanie hats that they wore while on the site. We also created the Whyology Center, where users could learn more about the survey, sign up for participation, or simply hang out. To sign up, users needed parents to fax a signed consent form with a phone number that we could use to verify the signature. As an added incentive, online users were offered a reward in clams for their participation in the survey. Despite this incentive, the parents of only 219 online users (116 girls and 59 boys, ranging in age from 8 to 19), who subsequently completed the survey, returned the consent forms. From this group, we were able to recruit eight users to participate in an online focus group to further explain their relationship with Whyville.

The survey group included many people who were experienced Whyville users. To get the perspective of site "newbies," we also recruited some students at local sixth- and eighth-grade classes who had never been on Whyville to try out the site for two months. These students also completed the survey and a few participated in focus-group interviews. Neither of these groups is particularly representative sample of the site's users, but they do provide a range of views and attitudes of the site participants.

Overall, we collected three types of data for the study: the online survey of Whyville users, the transcript of the focus groups composed of experienced and new users, and the online writing on the site (primarily from the *Whyville Times*). The survey included questions related to experiences with computers and technology, features of the Whyville site, creation of online identities, attitudes about school, and interest in science. Questions in the focus groups centered on issues related to identity, perceptions of other users on the site, and general impressions of the Whyville site.

Survey responses illustrated the ways in which the sites users identify with the site and some of the social groupings that have emerged on the site. We were particularly interested in how users developed their online identities and what these identities meant to the users. We organized their responses around several topics: why Whyville, online participation, avatar appearance, multiple identities, and Whyville and the real world.

Why Whyville?

The users in the survey come to Whyville for a variety of reasons. While Whyville users generally do not join the site with the intention of exploring and constructing their identities, much of the site's appeal appears to come from those design features that contribute to this process. For instance, many users report being drawn to the real-world simulation aspects of the site, be it the virtual economy, owning and decorating a house, or participating in an online community. When asked, "What made Whyville sound interesting to you?" most responses included some reference to these features. The following are examples of typical responses (all quotes *sic*):

- The fact that you could dress yourself up and earn clams. And I also think it is a good way ta learn how ta manage money. lucky007 Girl age 12
- I joined Whyville because it sounded like a lot of fun. It would be a good place to talk to alot of different people. I like that u can make your own face and get a house. flyguy813 Boy age 15

- My bff told me about it. She said that Whyville is a wonderful place to explore and discover yourself. She also told me that you can make lots of new friends, build your own house and start a family! puppypals Girl age 11
- I heard about the games you can play, the clams you can earn to buy things and how you can create your own person. dawnck Girl age 12
- Because I was looking on Yahoo for building my own house, and whyville popped up, and I knew that you could build your own house and chat!! That is why i joined! Emma200 Girl age 15

It is interesting that these young people were so interested in adult type behaviors such as having money and building a house. This correlates with Subrahmanyam and Greenfield's (1998) descriptions of the characteristics of typical girl play. Two of the quotes explicitly state identity building ("discover yourself" and "create your own person").

Online Participation

Participation is the core of an online community. How users participate in both the prescribed and emergent activities describes their role within the community. On a site the size of Whyville, multiple communities coexist within the larger community. These groups are based on offsite activities (e.g., skateboarding) or onsite participation. One user described her typical day on Whyville:

> I go on Whyville like 3 times a week and I check my mail and I go to that little mall place and buy parts for my face. And then I like sell parts and stuff in that little auction to get more clams. Then I try to find the little alien and the ship but they all land in weird places and I can never finish that. And oh, then I go to that little slide place with the pool and I talk to different people. (girl, 14)

Chatting is an extremely common activity among "Whyvillians." As indicated in Table 5.1, over 70 percent of users engage in chat "most of the time" that they are logged in to Whyville. Users socialize even more through the site's e-mail program, Y-mail, with over 60 percent of users sending or receiving Y-mail on a regular basis. Redesigning one's avatar is also a very popular activity among the users. The avatar design tool (called "Pick Your Nose") allows users to add features such as "face parts" that can include things like clothes and skateboards to their appearance. Features can be created with a drawing program or purchased from other users

Table 5.1. *Percentage of Users who Participate in Each Activity "Most of the Time"*

Activity	Girls (*n* = 160)	Boys (*n* = 59)
Chatting	72%	75%
Face design (pick your nose)	79%	59%
Science activities	25%	37%
Y-mail	63%	68%
Reading the Whyville Times	28%	31%

Table 5.2. *User Behavior Related to Participation in Official Whyville Community Activities*

Percentage of Users Who	Girls (*n* = 160)	Boys (*n* = 59)
Write articles for the *Whyville Times*	16%	10%
Create and sell face parts	43%	41%
Post on the discussion boards	33%	34%
Own a house	23%	17%
Share or rent in someone else's house	33%	20%
Donate face parts (Grandma's house)	89%	81%

using clams. This activity is very popular – more so among girls than boys on the site (79 percent to 59 percent).

Beyond chatting, users can participate more deeply in the Whyville community through activities such as posting on the site's bulletin boards, reading or writing an article for the *Whyville Times*, designing face parts, and building a virtual house. The simplest of these is to donate unwanted face parts to Grandma's house (for detail, see Fields & Kafai, 2010b). Table 5.2 presents a breakdown of the participation in such activities. As seen in the table, over 80 percent of the users surveyed had donated face parts. Other activities includes building a house or writing for the newspaper. Girls were more likely to be involved in building houses (56 percent compared to 37 percent of boys). Only a few of the users had written for the paper, but almost half of the users stated that they intended to write something (47 percent of both boys and girls). This suggests a desire to have significant involvement in the community, because the *Times* is the primary voice of the community. Bulletin boards are another form of written communication on the site. Posting on them is fairly common according to the survey but was not mentioned in the focus groups. We noted that very little discussion takes place on these boards, which tend to be dominated by new users' requests for help with games and getting clams.

In addition to site-prescribed roles, such as homeowner, journalist, scientist, and clothing designer, many social roles and activities have emerged from the users themselves. For instance, because Whyville is essentially a community of adolescents, "dating" is prevalent on the site. Often you will see users asking around for a "BF" or "GF." We asked users about their participation in these types of activities as well. Our results indicated that 63 percent of users (57.5 percent of girls and 77.9 percent of boys) state that having a boyfriend or girlfriend on the site is at least "somewhat important."

Some Whyville users have instituted what they call "beauty contests," whereby several users' (usually girls') avatars are judged by another user. Sometimes prizes are given to the winner in the form of clams. Appearance is definitely a key factor in social acceptance on the site, whether it is to appear fashionable in beauty contests or to be identified with a particular community. To increase their acceptance and gain popularity, users devote a lot of time enhancing the look of their avatar. However, users still run the risk of being rejected by others on the site, as revealed in a focus-group interview with sixth graders ("I" indicates an interviewer comment).

> *B*: They all base you on how you look.
> *G1*: But it's cool because you can be someone different online.
> *I*: Does it bother you that it's all based on how you look?
> *B*: Because they don't give you a chance sometimes.
> *G2*: I walked into the disco once and someone said, 'You're such a freak.'

This type of appearance-based alienation is a topic written frequently about in the *Whyville Times*. While users participate in this social system, many also question the morality of engaging in it. As one *Times* writer asked, "Face Parts: the basis behind them and their impact on society. Do the parts themselves make you ... or break you? ... Is the Face Mall the thing that shapes us into our roles on Whyville?" (Whyville user TIKE, boy, age unknown, July, 2002). Another *Times* writer stated,

> Many people complain that we put too much pressure on appearance in Whyville. It's so important that you look good. But how come nobody mentions that we're perfectionists when it comes to appearance in reality? It's important to be skinny in reality. It's important to be tall in reality. It's important to have gleaming white teeth in reality. This is important, and that's important, too. Or so they try to convince us. (Whyville user Giggler01, girl, age unknown, April, 2003).

Lemke (2010) points out that the beauty contests are based on avatars in which the users have far more control than their everyday appearance. Avatar appearance is a demonstration of skill – but is also dependent on having financial resources to purchase face parts. The need for face parts motivates users to participate in activities in which they can earn clams. Whyville users participate in the economy because only with clams are they able to design their avatar, buy parts for their houses, and engage in similar activities. Possession of currency creates a social structure that the users must learn to navigate. Longtime users sometimes accumulate large sums of clams (one user claimed to have over 40,000), which they can use to help others and to curry favor with gifts of clams.

Similar to most online communities, there is the social distinction between the longtime users and the newbies. New users typically spend more of their time observing and participating in the easy aspects of the community. The long-time users often complain (in the *Times* and on bulletin boards) that the newbies are a nuisance, while the newbies complain that they are ignored by the more established users. Despite the complaints, this is a stable distinction that rewards users who persist on the site and who lose their newbie status. The newbie–old-timer relationship is also an example of legitimate peripheral participation (Lave & Wenger, 1991) sustaining a community even when individual users come and go.

Avatar appearance.

" ... however you decide to create your face, it reveals your identity" (Whyville user Bluejello, girl, age unknown, *Whyville Times*, Feb, 2002)

Given the importance that many Whyville users place on appearance, the design and evolution of one's avatar was an important topic of discussion in the focus groups. As is often the case in real life (especially for this age group), for some users, the manipulation of identity on Whyville is a conscious act, as illustrated by the preceding quote from the *Whyville Times*, while, for others, it is such an intrinsic part of participating in Whyville that it goes unrecognized. Either way, it is clear that the creation and use of one's avatar is significantly tied to users' ideas about themselves and social conformity (or nonconformity). When we asked users how their Whyville face compares to their real-life appearance, the majority of responses focused on specific features (e.g., "my hair is different," "I have blue eyes"), but a few users (7 percent) made reference to their Whyville look being closer to an ideal. Only 8 percent stated that their Whyville face was the same as their appearance in real life, indicating that, in one way or another, most users *are* playing with image, appearance, and personae while on the site.

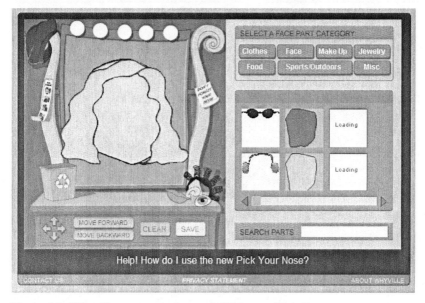

Figure 5.2. Whyville avatar creation tool: "Pick your Nose."

The following are comments that users made about their appearance in response to the question, "How does your Whyville face look different from you?"

- It's the person I've always wanted to look like blond hair blue eyes u know. (Girl, 13)
- Well, I have dirty blonde hair, brown eyes, zits, braces, and a weirdly perportioned body, like most teenagers! (LOL) :) (Girl, 13)
- 1st of all i don't have blue hair. the whyville face is what i want to look like but my mom won't let me. (Boy, 13)
- Well different color hair, different color eyes, different features, and different attitude and style. (Girl, 14)
- I don't think i'm that pretty as i am on whyville. (Girl, 12)

Although users can change their image in smaller ways, such as changing their hair color and jewelry, many users continually change their appearance drastically, often taking on the stereotypical looks of different social groups. About a quarter of the users identified their look in terms of groups such as "skater," "gangster," or "punker" (Figure 5.3). These real-life groups are not particularly relevant to activities on the site, but they allow users to identify with a real-world community. The group identification is a label that indicates a set of attitudes and interests of the group and the person

Figure 5.3. On-screen avatars of various social groupings on the site.

who chooses to affiliate with it, allowing users to connect with like-minded people online.

Through their avatar's image as well as their behavior on the site, users can immerse themselves in these identities without the potential risks associated with becoming part of these groups in real life. Other users let their avatar reflect their mood rather than their affiliation:

> I wear whatever I feel like that day – like if I'm sad and stuff, I make myself look like a gothic person, if I am happy, I put myself in white. (Girl, 13)

Trying on these identities online allows adolescents to learn how well different characterizations map on to their "true" self, without getting pigeonholed into a certain stereotype, which can often be difficult for young people. Further, they are able to learn the social acceptability of different personae, without the risk of isolation and marginalization from their real-life peers.

Multiple Identities

Not only can users change the appearance of their avatar; they also can develop alternate identities through the creation of several accounts on the site. The only restriction is that each account must have a separate e-mail. Many of the users in the survey reported having multiple accounts, with girls (60 percent) doing this more often than do the boys (41 percent).

Approximately one-quarter of users stated they have three or more identities (girls, 28 percent; boys, 19 percent). Some users take advantage of this possibility by developing several different identities through which they can experience different social interactions. In addition to trying on different roles for the purpose of figuring out which ones fit best, users are able to experiment with identities that are usually difficult to take on in real life, such as the opposite gender. During the online focus group, one girl explained:

> At first I wondered how hard it was to be a boy here. I mean, the girls chase them around asking for dates and stuff. It must be annoying, and I was right, and plus, it is easier to make friends on a boy face. (Girl, 14)

Thus, this online role-playing not only mimics real-life identity play, but it is also unique in that it allows users the opportunity to negotiate social spaces entirely differently than they ever could in real life. That such exploration could have important implications for later socialization is plausible. Kafai, Fields, and Cook (2010) note that a key reason for multiple identities on Whyville is that users can earn more clams.

Whyville and the Real World

> Is Whyville like reality? … when I sit down at my computer … I am still stuck with being, well, me. I am still the same person sitting at my computer. But all of a sudden, I look different. All of a sudden I am talking to these people who know nothing of the "real" me, and therefore the "me" that I am in Whyville can be someone totally different (Whyville user Giggler01, girl, age unknown, Dec, 2002)

It is important to understand how users' activities on Whyville inform and are informed by who they are or see themselves to be in real life. Although we did not ask about users' personality on the survey, this is a topic that has been written about in the *Whyville Times* and was discussed in the focus groups. Several users expressed the idea that *Whyville* tended to appeal to "less popular" or shy kids. One user explains:

> The popular ppl think this site blows … id say yes, this is a good place for an unpopular person, because they can be anyone they want to be … (Girl, 14)

During a focus group interaction with 8th grade girls, users delved more into the psyches of their fellow users:

> *I*: What kind of people go on Whyville? Like what do you think they are like in real life?

G1: I think they're totally different.

I: Why do you think they're different though?

G1: I think people go to Whyville to get acceptance.

G2: I agree. I think they over-exaggerate who they are to make people like them more.

I: Why do you think they do that?

G2: Appearances matter. People just don't approach you because they know your Personality; they approach you because you're attractive, because of your looks. So they don't go I think they have a nice personality and go talk to you, they go oh, they're cute, nice smile.

Not surprisingly, several of the people in our online focus group told us that they were not part of the popular crowd in school. One said that she was quiet in real life but not on Whyville:

> Because on here, if I make a mistake, it doesn't matter, I won't get teased for it the next day. (Girl, 14)

While users can take on new and different roles online than they generally can in real life, this is only one of many complex ways that being part of this online experience helps adolescents to explore and develop their identity. Notably, adolescents' participation on Whyville works to construct who they are in real life. As discussed earlier, it is possible that learning to navigate the Whyville social dynamics, and negotiating within an established social structure gives users increased confidence in dealing with the same issues that they encounter in real life.

Further, as users participate in the various activities offered in Whyville, they grow increasingly comfortable with computers, the internet, and science in general. The following responses to the question, "How has Whyville changed the way you think about computers or science?" show enthusiasm for science with some users while others seem to ignore it:

- i like going on the computer a lot more (Girl, 16)
- it has changed the way i think about computers cause i never used to go on the computer cause there was nuthin to do but now i can go on whyville and talk to my friend who just moved (Girl, 11)
- I think it shows me that there are so many things to learn about. It also shows me that learning on the internet can be incredibly fun. (Girl, 14)
- I think more of science and know more about both of them. (Girl, 19)
- I like computers a lot better now, and I understand them better, science is more fun! (Boy, 11)

- Whyville has showed me different ways to look at websites and science. I haven't really changed except for going on the computer a whole lot more! (Girl, 14)
- no not really to be honest (Boy, 13)
- It hasn't really changed anything because before I knew a lot about computers. (Girl, 13)

Survey results revealed that the majority of the users are enthusiastic about technology, with 83 percent indicating they like computers "a lot." Moreover, users average 3.46 years of computer experience, and more than half (52 percent) are able to design their own Web pages. With respect to attitudes toward science on the site, one-third of users are more interested in science after their experiences on Whyville.

Science Learning on Whyville

Since its inception, Whyville has had a goal of improving young people's understanding of, and interest in, science. As a result, many of the activities on the site address science concepts in one way or another. Online activities such as the Spin Lab, the Rocket Launch, Smart Cars, and many others have a science theme. But causal observation on the site revealed only limited discussion about science among the users. Both the user survey and a study of a science event provide more detail on the users' attitudes and practices in science.

In the survey, we asked users in which of the science activities they were experts. Users ranged from those who did not feel expert on any activity (18 percent) to a pair of users who were expert on every activity (1 percent). On average, users felt they were expert on 2.9 ($SD = 2.4$) science activities. This figure represents a significant amount of science learning from an informal learning environment. The one activity that girls were more engaged with than were boys was the Solstice Safari. This activity is the only one (at the time of the survey) in which users collaborate to solve a problem.

We asked users how they learned to be experts on these different activities. Most users cited the written instructions (69 percent) or trial and error (14 percent), but a few received help from others (12 percent). This response suggests that students are not spending time discussing the games on the site. As such, they are not taking advantage of the social environment to learn to use the site or to learn about science. This matches our observations that there is little discussion of science topics on the site, which motivated a follow-up study, described in the following. Nevertheless, users

Table 5.3. *Source of Science Learning*

Percentage of Users Who Learn "A Lot" of Science from	Girls (*n* = 160)	Boys (*n* = 59)
Science classes at school	70%	58%
Friends and Family	14%	13%
Trying things themselves	25%	34%
TV shows or movies	24%	44%
Books or magazines	24%	31%
Whyville	33%	49%
Other Web sites	5%	17%

felt that they were learning a great deal from Whyville. When we asked how much science they learn from different sources, Whyville was ranked second, behind school, but before television, trying things by themselves, books, and friends and family (Table 5.3).

Participatory Simulation: Why-pox

In an environment with many science activities, users have an opportunity to explore science and discuss it with their peers. This opportunity has great potential for helping young people develop their identity as scientists. But according to the survey, only a few of the users viewed themselves as scientists on Whyville, and there was very little chat about science or even discussion about the games themselves. One explanation for the lack of science discussion on the site is the individual nature of many of the science activities. Since the experience is not shared, there is little reason to talk about them.

In an effort to create a more shared science experience, Whyville management instituted a participatory simulation of disease spread called "Why-pox." This innovative activity has been the subject of several studies (Foley & Kobaissi, 2006; Kafai et al 2007; Kafai, Quintero, et al., 2010; Nuelight et al. 2007). We then wondered whether young people will take on a learning identity when faced with a relevant and dynamic science event.

Previous analysis of Why-pox showed that users were able to transfer some of their experiences and learning about disease to the discussion of Why-pox, but they also introduced a number of non-biological mechanisms in their thinking. In a study of a class who joined Whyville to experience Why-pox, Nuelight et al. (2007) showed students making learning gains through the experience, but noted that the classroom discussions moderated by the teacher may have played an important role. Kafai et al. (2010) analyzed the chat data from a later Why-pox outbreak and found that the pox had an impact on life on the site that could have implications for how users view science.

During the Why-pox outbreak, spots begin to appear on the infected users' faces, who would occasionally sneeze when chatting (the word "Achoo" would appear in their text). Both the spots and the sneezing got worse for a few days and then faded after about seven days, after which the user was immune to Why-pox. Because the disease affected some of the most important aspects of users' virtual identities, their appearance, and ability to chat, Why-pox seemed the ideal approach for focusing the user's attention on science. The Whyville Center for Disease Control (WCDC) allows users to learn about disease in several ways, including the use of disease simulators and discussion forums.

While the analysis of the WCDC provides some indications of how the users responded to Why-pox this does not provide a clear indication of the impact of the disease on social behavior on the site. To get a more complete picture of the impact, we examined chat logs from the site before and during a Why-pox outbreak. The chat data (over 100,000 chat comments per day), combined with the Why-pox–specific bulletin boards, and user-written articles from the *Whyville Times* provides a clearer picture of Why-pox. The chat transcript contains an immense quantity of data, of which only a fraction are relevant to Why-pox or science. Analyzing the chat data required "data mining" to assess the science-related discourse (Foley & Kobaissi, 2006). The bulletin board posts were coded according to the type of comment made by the user (e.g., proposed a hypothesis, reported results of a simulation, responded to another post).

Why-pox Participation

Prior to Why-pox, discussion of science on the site was extremely rare. The analysis of chat in the three days before Why-pox started showed that few chat comments involved science. Of 2,400 coded comments, only 3 (0.125 percent) were rated as being related to science (counting words related to disease showed only 0.014 percent). This matches our observations showing that science is not a common topic of conversation on the site. The logs from the next few days show that Why-pox succeeded in generating more science-related discourse. It took about a week for the number of cases to increase to the point where it was apparent. Figure 5.4 shows

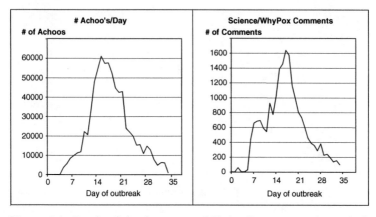

Figure 5.4. Graph of the frequency of "Achoo" comments for each day of the outbreak. *Source:* Taken from Foley & Kobaissi (2006).

the percentage of sneezes ("Achoo") in the chat transcript. By day 16, as the epidemic reached its peak, the percentage had risen to more than 44 percent of all chat comments. Users' comments about disease and immunity (counting the frequency of a list of twenty-eight science words) also rose to 1.05 percent of all comments, about seventy-five times the pre–Why-pox rate but still a relatively small part of the conversation.

The majority of the Why-pox–related chat focused on the experience of having or getting the disease. Users wanted to know how one could catch it, what one could do to avoid it, and how to get rid of it once infected. In the thirty days, we identified fifty-three extended discussions of science topics. Here is an example, which shows users reacting to Why-pox and beginning, at a superficial level, to try to understand its behavior (intervening unrelated comments by other users have been removed):

    User59 I have the disease!
    User28 me too
    User84 look i dont have y-pox
    User28 Did you change you clothes recently?
    User28 Achoo
    User84 i just did
    User28 That is how I think people are getting them

The Why-pox outbreak made disease epidemiology a relevant subject for all the users on the site. Those who were interested in learning more could participate in WCDC activities. This structure is similar to what Schauble et al. (2002) calls a funnel approach. A gallery in a museum is seen to provide access to different topics at a superficial level, but "narrower and deeper" activities are available for those who are interested. One level of participation could involve simply reading the WCDC pages and, perhaps, running one of the simulations. To become more involved, users could attempt to answer at least one of fourteen questions posed by city management. Posts on the discussion boards demonstrate the deeper level of participation.

The posts on the WCDC bulletin board provide more evidence of students' engagement with science. The prompts on this board asked users to provide an assessment about Why-pox (e.g. When will the epidemic peak?). Responses were coded to identify the type of post (e.g. respond to prompt, ask a question, off topic, etc.) and the source of data (warrant) for any scientific assertion (claim). The bulletin board included 3,060 posts from 1,698 unique Whyville identities. While most users posted only once some became active posters (140 users posted 4 or more times), including one user who made 38 separate posts about Why-pox. The extent of collaboration and the quality of the science inquiry evident in the posts varied greatly. More than 56 percent of the posts provided some evidence for the conclusions made in their posts. The WCDC simulations (e.g., Figure 5.5) were the most common source of evidence (41 percent of all posts), but others used experiences on the site (11 percent) and real-world experiences (3 percent) to support their conclusions. Some of the posts demonstrated sophisticated analysis of the simulator data:

> When only one person per day is infected the disease draws on alot longer but as you increase it to 2, 3, 4, etc. the infection rate rises and more people are catching the disease more quickly. This probably happens because the disease is getting more exposure and therefore has a greater opportunity to spread. The peaks on the graphs also happen earlier – this also makes sense for the same reason. (Whyville CDC BBS, day 10)

Despite instances of scientific thinking as in the above quotation, few users participated at a very deep level. Only fifty-two users responded to half of the questions. Given the number of users on the site during this time (>30,000 unique users during that time). Since this version of Why-pox, the simulation and the WCDC materials have been changed in an effort to create more opportunities for scientific thinking (Kafai, Quintana, et al., 2010).

Identity and Why-pox

Why-pox was designed to use people's online identity as motivation to engage in science inquiry around the spread of a disease. The marks on

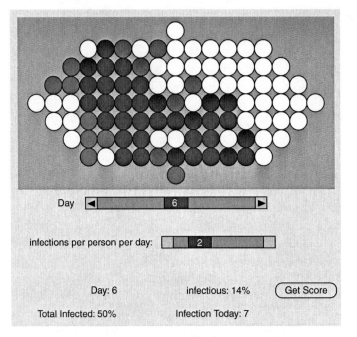

Figure 5.5. Screenshot of the WCDC infection simulator.

people's avatars were highly disruptive for many users. Writers for the
Whyville Times weighed in on the outbreak with over twenty articles about
Why-pox during the first thirty days of the disease. Writers articulated
several reactions to the new phenomenon on the site. Their reactions
focused on understanding what is happening ("is this a computer virus?"),
the appearance of the spots on people's avatars, and social behaviors such as
appropriate behavior around infected people. Many of the articles ranged
across several different aspects of the Why-pox:

> WhyPox aren't good! I once wanted them, but not any more – they're
> infectious and if I get them more people will get them too! So always stay
> alert and away from people with pox. I'm not saying that you can't talk to
> your friends on Whyville if they have pox, just stay a fair distance away
> from them … (*Whyville Times*, Day 14)

The hope was that this would drive users to the WCDC where they would
investigate further and learn about disease transmission. The chat transcripts show a number of different reactions (data do not include the identity of speaker in chat comments):

- I AM GUNNA COMPLIAN! THIS STUPID POX ISN'T REAL MY GAWD – Achoo – i'm gunan MAKE city hall disinfect me – Achoo – Achoo…I HATE POX! I DUN DESERVE IT – My perfect face,life,everything …ruined. [several sequential comments by one user without response]
- whyville is to get away from reality. not bring war and disease here!

These comments show a sense of annoyance with the pox as disturbing what they see as an idealized environment. They suggest that students see Whyville as an artificial environment where they can design their "perfect face, life, everything."

U2: how do you get it?
U2: do you just log in, and you have spots on your face?
U1: I don't know… to learn more you have to CDC on the bus menue
U2: whisperto-U1: it looks disgusting
U1: I'm gonna go to the CDC …..ok?? I'll brb

Here two users talk about the Why-pox and one decides to go to the WCDC for some answers. However, the WCDC does not have easy answers, but instead presents questions and simulators for users to try to figure them out. The promise to "brb" (be right back) is not compatible with the WCDC activities.

U3: did u read in the times we get a higher salary AND free whypasses if we figure out stuff about the y-pox
U4: i know how u get the pox
U5: if ppl sneeze on u
U3: did u guys read the times?we get a higher salary AND free why-passes if we figure out stuff about the pox
U3: but once i sat next to katie and i never got 'em
U6: it is spread
U4: ok tiff has the pox and she said dat she came on yville and she had the pox and it says achoo by itself lol
U3: really?omg i dont want the pox
U6: me either
U4: it makes u look ugly
U5: **falls asleep**
U3: *poke*> wake up this is a serious meeting>
U3: cuz we want a higher salary and whiypasses

U3: i'm not "epidemic person" LoL~i can't figure out stuff
U3: We'll WoRk As A TeAm =) [no response]

This transcript shows one user trying to motivate others to participate as a group in order to gain clams and WhyPasses (membership in the WhyClub part of the site costing a few dollars a month). Despite the rewards, the other members do not seem interested in participating in the activities – one even emotes falling asleep. The users' reactions suggest a playground mentality where discussing school-type subjects is not "cool." To maintain their identities social standing, they must disavow interest in these topics. Even the motivated user, U3, states that he or she is "not 'epidemic person'"[sic]. The norms for discussion on the site seem to work against the goals of the Why-pox simulation and help explain the low participation rates. Even though the epidemic does affect users' avatars, the need to fit in to the group and maintain social standing is stronger than are the incentives to engage in the activity. This reaction has more in common with the conversations of students on a playground than an intellectual environment like a museum or school.

Future Trends

Since its founding in 1999, Whyville has helped pioneer the development of virtual worlds and multi-user games for young people which have become an important part of cyberspace. Multi-user Web sites have become the norm for the internet. Organizations from television shows to universities have created online communities for their members and fans to participate in. These environments seek to provide a virtual space for people with common interests to interact and increase their identification with the organization.

Whyville remains innovative is its attempt to use multiuser space to engage young people in an intellectual identity. It has been on the forefront of developing activities such as the Why-pox that take advantage of the things most precious to the online user – his or her identity and avatar. At any time, users can log out of Whyville and leave their online identity behind. This freedom allows young people to separate their online identity from their everyday lives, thus providing increased freedom of choice about their activities to the point where they can explore activities that would be risky off-line. An example of this are the users who switch genders online to explore what life is like with a "boy's face." By inserting Why-pox into the social environment, Whyville has found a way to tap into the energy that users put into their identities and use that to motivate learning.

The ability to choose has important consequences for social development and learning activities on the site. Research on free-choice learning in environments such as museums and clubs shows that choice enables young people to participate more deeply in activities that can become more meaningful that school learning (Falk & Dierking, 2002). The act of choosing to participate helps to define one's identity as a learner and a member of a community. Online environments like Whyville provide even greater opportunities for choice because users may not be restricted by social pressure from peers. These users' choices online say a great deal about how students explore the freedom of the online environment. The constructive activities online seem to be the most engaging for the users. Writers for the *Whyville Times* can be labeled as poets, creative writers, concerned citizens, activists, or community helpers. As creators of face parts or homes, users present themselves to their fellow citizens as successful business owners, fashion consultants, or design experts. Whyville users also engaged in the informal social activities, including those focused on their creations. The spontaneous beauty contests provide a way for users to present their creations to the community and to develop shared standards.

The creative output of the Whyville community is impressive, but that says little about the ability of an online community to provide a learning experience for specific content. Although participation in the science activities on Whyville was high, the lure of clams was a key motivation. The lack of discussion about the games on the site suggests that they are not something that the users thought were interesting. It was believed that Why-pox would encourage users to engage in scientific deduction because it was both novel and disruptive of the normal behaviors online. Unlike museums, where science conversations often include many questions, answers, and discussion about science topics (Allen, 2002), Whyville users rarely had significant conversations on science topics or even Why-pox. The limited participation suggests that the logical deduction approach of the activities was not something that users are likely to choose, despite the interactive simulations. Users do not seem to view the construction of a scientific explanation as being similar to the construction of a face or a home – or at least it does not seem appropriate topic for the users. In contrast, science museums create a science-centric atmosphere where visitors expect to be focused on science.

Conclusion

The need for software that could be used by large numbers of people spurred the development of the field of computer-human interaction and user interface engineering. Similarly, the need to develop virtual worlds that support users' identity development and creativity is creating a need for social environment engineering. Cases like Whyville provide a starting point for understanding the role of the activities and reward structure in helping structure the resulting online community. Clearly there is a demand for online experiences that allow people to try out different identities and practice living in their virtual skin.

These environments may also become a tool for learning as well. Education is evolving to be less focused on the classroom and more connected to many different ecologies (Collins & Halverson, 2009). Whyville is less encouraging in this regard – evidence of deep learning is difficult to find even when sparked by innovative pedagogy such as Why-pox. But social-learning engineers may find that new sites that build on the engaging identity-play environment of Whyville may be able to also nurture a community that values things like scientific explanations or expository writing. The design of the site clearly plays a role in the users' behaviors, but we don't yet know how to create an informal online environment that will engage all users in significant learning.

References

American Association of University Women. (2000). *Tech-savvy: Educating girls in the new computer age*. Washington, DC: Author.

Allen, S. (2002). Looking for learning in visitor talk: A methodological exploration. In G. Leinhardt, K. Crowley, & K. Knutson (Eds.), *Learning conversations in museums* (pp. 259–304). Mahwah, NJ: Erlbaum.

Banks, J. A., Au, K. H., Ball, A. F., Bell, P., Gordon, E. W., Gutierrez, K. D., et al. (2007). *Learning in and out of school in diverse environments: Life-long, life-wide, life-deep*. Seattle, WA: The LIFE (Learning in Informal and Formal Environments) Center.

Barab, S., Sadler, T., Heiselt, C., Hickey, D., & Zuiker, S. (2007). Relating narrative, inquiry, and inscriptions: A framework for socioscientific inquiry. *Journal of Science Education and Technology*, 16, 59–82.

Barab, S., Thomas, M. K., Dodge, T., Goodrich, T., Carteaux, B., & Tuzun, H. (2002). Empowerment design work: Building participant structures that transform. In P. Bell, R. Stevens, & T. Satwicz (Eds.), *Proceedings of the Fifth International Conference of the Learning Sciences (ICLS)* (pp. 531–532). Mahwah, NJ: Erlbaum.

Bargh, J. A., McKenna, K. Y. A., & Fitzsimmons, G. M. (2002). Can you see the real me? Activation and expression of the "true self" on the Internet. *Journal of Social Issues*, 58(1), 33–48.

Bers, M. U. (2001). Identity construction environments: Developing personal and moral values through the design of a virtual city. *The Journal of the Learning Sciences*, 10(4), 365–415.

Bruckman, A. (2000). Situated support for learning: Storm's Weekend with Rachael. *Journal of the Learning Sciences*, 9(3), 329–372.

Dede, C., Ketelhut, D., & Ruess, K. (2002). Motivation, usability, and learning outcomes in a prototype museum-based multi-user virtual environment. In P. Bell, R. Stevens, & T. Satwicz (Eds.) *Proceedings of the Fifth International Conference of the Learning Sciences (ICLS)*. Mahwah, NJ: Erlbaum.

Dodge, T., Barab, S., Stuckey, B., Warren, S., Heiselt, C., & Stein, R. (2008). Children's sense of self: Learning and meaning in the digital age. *Journal of Interactive Learning Research*, 19(2), 225–249.

Erikson, E. H. (1968). *Identity: Youth and crisis*. New York: W. W. Norton.

Falk, J. H., Brooks, P., & Amin, R. (2001). Investigating the role of free-choice learning on public understanding of science: The California Science Center LASER Project. In J. H. Falk, E. Donovan, & R. Woods (Eds.), *Ways free-choice science education: How we learn science outside of school* (pp. 115–132). New York: Teachers College Press.

Falk, J. S. & Dierking, L. D. (2002) *Lessons without limit: how free-choice learning is transforming education*. Walnut Creek, CA: AltaMira Press.

Fields, D. A. & Kafai, Y. B. (2010a). Knowing and throwing mudballs, hearts, pies, and flowers: A connective ethnography of gaming practices. *Games and Culture*, 5(1), 88–115.

Fields, D.A. & Kafai, Y.B. (2010b). "Stealing from Grandma" or generating cultural knowledge? Contestations and effects of cheating in tween virtual world. *Games and Culture*, 5(1), 64–87.

Foley, B., Jones, M. S., McPhee-Baker, C., & Aschbacher, P. A. (2002). *Designs that work for girls: Analyzing the design of a Web site popular with girls*. Paper presented at the International Conference of the Learning Sciences, Plenary Session, Seattle, WA.

Gee, J. P. & Hayes, E. (2011). *Language and learning in the digital age*. New York: Routledge.

Ito, M., Baumer, S., Bittanti, M., boyd, d., Cody, R., Herr-Stephenson, B., et al. (2009). *Hanging out, messing around, and geeking out: Kids living and learning with new media*. Cambridge, MA: MIT Press.

Kafai, Y. B., Feldon, D., Fields, D., Giang, M., & Quintero, M. (2007). Life in the times of Whypox: A Virtual epidemic as a community event. In C. Steinfeld, B. Pentland, M. Ackermann, & N. Contractor (Eds.), *Proceedings of the Third International Conference on Communities and Technology* (pp. 171–190). New York: Springer.

Kafai, Y. B. (in press). Of monsters and sick computers: Children's folk conception of a computer virus. *Journal of Science Education and Technology*.

Kafai, Y. B., Cook, M. S., & Fields, D. A. (2010). "Blacks deserve bodies too!" Discussion and design about diversity and race in a tween virtual world. *Games and Culture*, 5(1), 43–63.

Kafai, Y. B. & Giang, M. (2008). Virtual playgrounds. In T. Willoughby & E. Wood (Eds.), *Children's learning in a digital world*. Oxford: Blackwell Publishing.

Kafai, Y. B., Quintero, M., & Feldon, D. (2010). Investigating the "why" in Whypox: Explorations of a virtual epidemic. *Games and Culture*, 5(1). 116–135.

Ketelhut, D. J. (2007). The impact of student self-efficacy on scientific inquiry skills: An exploratory investigation in River City, a multi-user virtual environment. *Journal of Science Education and Technology*, 16(1), 99–111.

Lave, J. & Wenger, E. (1991). *Situated learning: legitimate peripheral participation.* Cambridge: Cambridge University Press.

Lemke, J. (2010). Lessons from Whyville: A hermeneutics for our mixed reality. *Games and Culture*, 5(2), 149–157.

Nowak, K. & Biocca, F. (2003). The effect of the agency and anthropomorphism on users' sense of telepresence, copresence, and social presence in virtual environments. *Telepresence: Teleoperators and Virtual Environments*, 12(5), 481–494.

Neulight, N., Kafai, Y.B., Kao, L., Foley, B., & Galas, C. (2007). Children's participation in a virtual epidemic in the science classroom: Making connections to natural infectious diseases. *Journal of Science Education and Technology*, 16(1), 47–58.

Papert, S. (1980). *Mindstorms: Children, computers and powerful ideas.* New York: Basic Books.

Pearce, C. (2009). *Communities of play: Emergent cultures in multiplayer games and virtual worlds.* Cambridge, MA: MIT Press.

Roberts, L. (1997). *From knowledge to narrative.* Washington, DC: Smithsonian Institution Press.

Schauble, L., Gleason, M., Lehrer, R., Bartlett, K., Petrosino, A., Allen, A., et al. (2002). Supporting science learning in museums. In G. Leinhardt, K. Crowley, & K. Knutson (Eds.), *Learning conversations in museums* (pp. 425–452). Mahwah, NJ: Erlbaum.

Schauble, L., Leinhardt, G., & Martin, L. (1997). A framework for organizing a cumulative research agenda in informal learning contexts. *Journal of Museum Education*, 22(2 & 3), 3–8.

Spears, R., Postmes, T., Lea, M., & Wolbert, A. (2002). When are net effects gross products? The power of influence and the influence of power in computer-mediated communication. *Journal of Social Issues*, 58(1), 91–107.

Turkle, S. (1984). *The second self: computers and the human spirit.* New York: Simon & Schuster.

Turkle, S. (1995). *Life on the screen: Identity in the age of the Internet.* New York: Simon & Schuster.

Yee, N. & Bailenson, J. N. (2007). The Proteus effect: The effect of transformed self-representation on behavior. *Human Communication Research*, 33, 271–290.

6 Deleting the Male Gaze? Tech-Savvy Girls and New Femininities in Secondary School Classrooms

Claire Charles

The implications of new media technologies for learning, including videogames, have been increasingly explored by educators and researchers in a world characterized by multi-literacies (Gee, 2003, 2007; Snyder & Beavis, 2004). Yet such exploration does not always consider the gendered dimensions of the opportunities for identity opened by digital technologies. Nor does it always emphasize the ways in which digital technologies might invite young people to take up gendered identities that are implicated in broader relations of power and marginalization. In this chapter, I explore the use of specific digital technologies in two secondary school classrooms in Melbourne, Australia. I explore the use of these technologies in the classroom in relation to the ways they are implicated in producing young feminine identities.

A key point of departure for this chapter is the contradictory notions around how young schoolgirl femininities are produced and regulated in contemporary commentary. Research in the field of critical girlhood studies has explored how new possibilities apparently exist for young female identity in developed, Western cultural contexts such that regulation of girlhood in these contexts is increasingly characterized around what girls *can* do, rather than what they can't or shouldn't do (McRobbie, 2007). These possibilities gather around being successful and confident within education and the workforce, and the term "girl power" is sometimes used to label these discourses of young feminine "compulsory success" and empowerment (Gonick, 2006). Yet other research points to the continued presence of old familiar notions of (hetero)sexual objectification and marginalization in young women's lives. The enduring presence of sexual harassment within school cultures is highlighted, as well as the difficulties for young women associated with achieving sexual attractiveness and desirability while at the same time avoiding labels such as "slag" (Chambers, Tincknell, & van

Loon, 2004; Renold, 2000). School researchers have shown how these discourses of heterosexuality continue to shape young women's experiences of schooling, despite increasing representations of girls' power in some cultural forms such as media and popular culture.

This chapter explores the way both these different possibilities for young feminine identity can be shaped and mediated by digital technologies in school classrooms. While it has been suggested that girls' use of new media technologies can enable them to contest and negotiate the normative notions of femininity that wider culture presents, in this chapter I explore how digital technologies in school classrooms may not engender straightforward opportunities for negotiation and resistance.

Two specific secondary classroom environments are explored in the chapter. The classrooms are both within independent, elite schools in Melbourne, Victoria, Australia, which require significant yearly tuition fees. The first classroom is a Year Ten English (Language Arts) class at a large elite girls' school, in which the young women are using Acrobat Connect Professional (ACP), online conferencing software, to discuss images of women in the media. The second classroom is a Year Eight English (Language Arts) class at a large elite co-educational school, in which students are undertaking a small unit of work on computer games[1].

The objectives of this chapter are to, first, identify key discourses of young female identity within Western educational contexts. A second goal is to chart how these discourses are mediated by digital technologies in specific secondary school classrooms. And, finally, a third goal is to consider how old stereotypes and new possibilities for young feminine identity might be constituted simultaneously through the use of digital technologies in school classrooms. The chapter thus aims to contribute to understanding of the ways in which digital technologies in school classrooms mediate young feminine identities. In particular, it aims to explore how digital technologies shape the way girls are positioned, as well as how they might position themselves, in relation to key discourses of young femininity.

Background and Theory

In this chapter I consider identity primarily in relation to young femininity. I examine key bodies of knowledge and commentary about young femininity and consider how identities for young women are mediated by the

---

[1] The research undertaken in this second classroom was funded by a grant from the Deakin University Quality Learning Research Priority Area, 2004.

presence of particular digital technologies in school classrooms. This chapter is underpinned by a theoretical persuasion toward performative notions of identity and subjectivity. I am interested in how digital technologies in two school classrooms can be understood to be implicated in the performative constitution of femininity. I draw broadly on poststructural notions of identity, and in particular, the work of Judith Butler (1993, 1997, 1999).

The gender theory of Judith Butler offers a way of thinking about gender as performatively constituted through repeated and ongoing textual practices. Now well known and frequently drawn upon in understanding gender, Butler's theory suggests that gender is performatively constituted in the very textual practices that purport to represent it. She proposes that "there is no gender identity behind the expressions of gender. That identity is performatively constituted by the very 'expressions' that are said to be its results" (Butler, 1999, p. 33). This way of thinking about gender/sexuality destabilizes the idea that sex and gender exist within individuals, causing them to behave in certain 'gendered' ways. Rather, it suggests that gendered subjects are the effect of "gendered" behaviors, rather than the cause. As AnoopNayak and Mary-Jane Kehily explain, "in contrast to the notion of a subject (the girl) producing action (putting on lipstick), Butler suggests that it is the action that produces the subject" (2006, p. 460). Thus, she argues that genders and sexualities are performatively constituted, rather than pre-existing within individuals.

Many researchers have drawn attention to the role of popular culture, including digital technologies, in mediating performative articulations of gendered identities (Ang, 1996; Buckingham & Bragg, 2004; Martino, 2000, 2001; Walkerdine, 1997, 2008). This work is theoretically diverse and offers various approaches to thinking through relationships between media and subjectivity. It is not my aim to contribute to such thinking here. Instead, I draw on the general idea that gendered identities do not pre-exist engagement with media and that they are performatively constituted and negotiated through the use of digital technologies.

The main problem that contextualizes this chapter is the question of whether digital technologies today provide girls with opportunities for being a young female outside particular notions of girlhood and heterosexuality that dominant culture offers them. Existing studies into girls' use of digital technologies suggest that girls may use such technologies to create identities outside the confines of dominant heterosexuality. They focus on how girls generate possibilities for themselves outside traditional notions of heterosexuality (Kearney, 2006; Mazzarella & Pecora, 2007; Thomas, 2004). As Sharon Mazzarella and Norma Pecora note, we have recently witnessed "a proliferation of studies on girls actively creating their own culture, and in the process transgressing dictates of normative or "empha- sized" femininity" (2007, p. 113). Girls as producers of media and culture, often with the help of new digital communication technologies, is often conceptualized by feminist researchers as a space of resistance, a space in which girls are actively making meaning. They sometimes comment that girls are enabled, by these technologies, for making meaning (Harris, 2004; Kearney, 2006), and positioning themselves outside the dominant ways in which they are positioned within mass cultural representations.

Often these studies focus on digital technologies in girl cultures[2] out- side schooling. In this chapter, however, I am interested in digital technol- ogies that have been integrated into "official" classroom curriculum and pedagogy. Thus, the students are not actively producing culture on their own terms in the research upon which I draw. Instead, they are positioned as consumers or users of specific technologies that have been selected and provided by adults within the institutional practices of schooling. In this rather different context, that remains bound by traditional hierarchies between student and teacher/researcher, I suggest that girls' use of digital technologies may not simply constitute resistance to dominant discourses of young femininity. I want to explore how digital technologies may sup- port and shape articulations of young female identity, in a school context shot through with power relations, that are rather different to those cre- ated by girls on their own terms, in their cultural practices outside school- ing. It is important to consider these school classrooms as very different contexts from girls' out of school cultural practices. Within the classroom site, digital technologies may make available particular opportunities for young female identity. These opportunities thus need to be understood in the context of broader research into young feminine identities.

Key Discourses of Young Femininity.

In this chapter I am interested in two key bodies of knowledge about young feminine identity existing within feminist research literature. The first of these bodies of knowledge suggests a set of gendered power rela- tions in which young women are marginalized and constrained – in par- ticular ways that relate to dominant discourses of heterosexuality – within education, work, and other institutions. This body of knowledge suggests

---

[2] Examples of girl cultures discussed in the literature cited are girls that form groups around textual practices such as zines and Web design.

that young women can be objectified by a "male gaze,"[3] as well as dis-advantaged or intimidated within competitive, "masculine" professions such as Information Technology. While these notions might now be considered somewhat dated, as they relate to what girls *can't* and *shouldn't* do, and how they are constrained, feminists undertaking school-based research have often observed how these notions continue to be relevant within schooling. They have explored the way girls can become objects of a male gaze within schooling and become subject to sexual harassment and violence (Kenway & Willis, 1997). The presence of digital technologies in young people's lives has recently been implicated in such concerns about gendered power relations and sexual violence[4].

Girls can also turn this gaze on each other, using it to police each other's appearance and behaviour (Renold, 2000). Some researchers have referred to this idea as an internalized male gaze (Epstein, O'Flynn, & Telford, 2003; Hey, 1997). Being constituted a "slag" is a danger for girls within dominant notions of heterosexuality, as it is boys who are supposed to be sexually active and desiring (Albury, 2002), while girls ought to be concerned mainly with protecting themselves from victimization (Fine, 2004). Furthermore, girls can be marginalized in public spaces such as classrooms. As some early studies show, boys frequently demand more of teachers' attention and time (Spender, 1982). In relation to the worlds of work and leisure, particularly in relation to new information and communications technologies, literature also has suggested that girls are on the margins, intimidated and perhaps excluded from becoming adept users of such technologies (Schott & Horrell, 2002). All these notions can be linked to normative discourses of gender (patriarchy) and heterosexuality in which girls are positioned as inferior to boys and men (Weedon, 1997).

---

[3] There is a long tradition within feminist theory that discusses an unequal gendered power relationship in which women are positioned as passive objects to be "looked at" by men who are positioned as sexually desiring subjects (Lumby, 1997; Weedon, 1997). This is often referred to as a "male gaze."

[4] See, for example, a media release from the Australian Institute of Family Studies, reporting on a research review which highlights the role of new digital technologies such as mobile phones and the internet in teenage sexual harassment: http://www.aifs.gov.au/institute/media/media081110a.html. See also the following media reports from the United Kingdom, http://www.timesonline.co.uk/tol/news/uk/article534788.ece, and from Australia, http://www.smh.com.au/news/national/gang-rape-filmed-on-mobile-phone/2007/04/04/1175366325678.html, http://www.abc.net.au/pm/content/2006/s1775589.htm, all of which report on incidents in which teenage boys filmed assaults of girls on mobile phones and then made the films available to other youth through social networking sites such as MySpace and the production of DVDs.

New Femininities?

Contrasting with notions of marginalized, objectified femininity, images of young female success and empowerment have become increasingly common in public discourse and popular culture. The ubiquity of images and representations of girls' power in contemporary cultural practices has generated much engagement and inquiry within feminist sociology, youth studies, and cultural studies. This scholarship (Aapola et al., 2005; Gonick, 2006; Harris, 2004; McRobbie, 2007) explores how girls are frequently represented across a number of cultural practices as subjects of excellence, capacity, and personal empowerment. It shows how dominant discourses in relation to young femininity have arguably shifted from a set of discourses constraining who and how girls can be toward notions about what they *can* do.

Recent feminist work has drawn attention to the exclusions that are produced, as well as the power that is maintained, through celebratory discourses about girls' success and empowerment (Gill, 2008; Harris, 2004; McRobbie, 2007). As Angela McRobbie argues, "the dynamics of regulation and control are less about what young women ought not to do, and more about what they can do" (2007, p. 721). Thus, normativity, in relation to femininity, is produced through discourses about what girls can do. This production of normative girlhood has the effect of marginalizing those who fail to live up to the "can-do" (Harris, 2004) image of young femininity.

Through images of empowerment, epitomized by pop groups such as the Spice Girls, young women are presented as moving outside the notions of marginalization that characterize much earlier feminist analysis. As McRobbie argues, consumer culture invites young women to "overturn the old sexual double standard and emulate the assertive and hedonistic styles of sexuality associated with young men" (2007, p. 732). According to this commentary, girls and young women are increasingly represented as sexually desiring subjects (Gill, 2007, 2008). Thus, young women are increasingly presented as sexually powerful, rather than sexually objectified.

This image of young female empowerment is not restricted to sexual practices and relations. It also spills over into the worlds of work and education. In these spheres, it is now often young women that are imagined to be the success stories (Ringrose, 2007). These images of young female success, for many researchers, are linked with, and supporting of, the kind of subjectivity suited to today. This is a subject that is consumable and consuming. Jessica Ringrose and Valerie Walkerdine propose that "what is happening under neoliberalism [is] an intensification of feminine as site (both subject and object) of consumption" (2008, p. 230). The neoliberal, successful girl subject should be able to consume in an appropriate manner, through achieving qualifications that will allow her to enter the professional workforce (McRobbie, 2007). At the same time, she constructs herself as an object that is worthy of being consumed, through, for example, becoming an attractive "TV blonde" (McRobbie, 2004) who will succeed in a media and communications industry in which she will be consumed by others.

Feminist critique of these images of girl power has included important exploration around the extent to which old notions of objectified hetero-femininity have really been overturned at all within popular representations of girls' empowerment and new femininities. For example, McRobbie notes that she must repetitively get "done up" and make herself into an object of a gaze (2007, pp. 725–726). Rosalind Gill (2008) explores how the regulation and surveillance of young women has moved from being objectified by others (e.g., men) toward subjecting the self to relentless scrutiny. Thus, notions of hetero-femininity, in which girls are positioned as objects to be looked at and desired, are not entirely abandoned in this new world of girl power. Indeed, in some respects, they are even more important within an image-saturated culture (Hopkins, 2002), and are merely refigured as being about individual choice and empowerment, rather than obligation.

In this chapter I am thus concerned with contributing to feminist inquiry into how familiar notions of hetero-femininity may in fact be intertwined with contemporary cultural representations of girls' power. Scholars have done significant work exploring this intersection within popular culture and media texts, but less work exploring it in relation to educational contexts, and particularly classrooms. They have sometimes constructed schooling as a site in which new femininities are (re)produced in relatively straightforward ways. Anita Harris, for example, argues that the elite girls' school is "important in the production of a new young womanhood around taken-for-granted excellence and forward planning for brilliant careers" (2004, p. 106). Yet she does not consider how embodied femininities might be produced and negotiated in this environment, or the ways in which "old" notions of objectified femininity might still exist. In this chapter I explore how old and new notions of young femininity might be interwoven through the use of digital technologies in school classrooms.

I draw on fieldwork undertaken for two separate studies, in two different secondary school English classrooms in Melbourne, Australia. In what follows I will consider each site separately, briefly outlining the distinct projects and methodologies before considering the findings in relation to the aims of this chapter.

Tapping into Girl Power: Digital Technologies and Elite Girls' Schooling

The first classroom I explore is a Year Ten English classroom at "Lyla Girls' Grammar School"[5] (LGGS), an elite, independent secondary school for girls. This fieldwork was undertaken as part of a larger study concerned with elite girls' schooling as a site for the (re)production and engagement of normative femininities (Charles, 2009). Most data for the study were generated in the classroom through team teaching activities during October and November in 2004 and 2005. Together with the classroom teacher, I developed an eight-week unit of English curriculum.

Included in the unit was an activity in which students were invited to respond to a slide presentation created with Microsoft PowerPoint depicting a series of images of women. I designed a presentation of contrasting images of women in order to generate discussion around embodied femininity. Some of them have been associated with girl power, such as the Spice Girls, Madonna, and Britney Spears. Others were chosen precisely because they were different. Grace Jones and K.D. Lang, for example, were chosen for the way they appear to transgress normative embodied femininity.

The school had recently purchased a license for the program Acrobat Connect Professional (APC)[6] for use in the classroom, during the time in which fieldwork took place. This online videoconferencing software was accessible to every student in the classroom, through the use of notebook computers that each student was obliged to purchase and take with them to every class. In November 2005 students were invited to view the embodied femininity presentation using ACP.

The slide presentation was installed onto the content pod, and a discussion took place in which students were invited to respond to questions from their computers as each image was displayed. Each student's name would appear beside the text as she typed her response into the chat pod. I was able to control the scrolling of the images as the class chatted about each one. The chat lasted the most part of a seventy-minute lesson and generated about thirty pages of transcript in total. The students' approach to the discussion was uninhibited, and they seemed unaware of a teacher

---

[5] Lyla Girls' Grammar School is a pseudonym that is used throughout the chapter.
[6] APC is a software package that can be used to run virtual meetings and interactive web conferencing, described as "a complete web communication system" (retrieved from the "launch demo" option on February 25, 2009, from http://www.adobe.com/products/acrobatconnect pro/).

presence as they expressed their reactions and thoughts regarding each image. Typing at a speed with which I could not keep up, the students demonstrated their familiarity with the nature of such technologies. Many had probably had experience with live chats, given the popularity of social networking sites.

Representing a new form of media, students learn how to manipulate and control Web-based communication software, which is designed to enable business professionals to "communicate and collaborate instantly" (retrieved February 25, 2007, http://www.adobe.com/products/acrobatconnectpro/). In this way, ACP can be considered part of the process through which LGGS girls are constituted as subjects of girl power. Students are already learning to use the communication tools of the companies for which they may well work post schooling. Through competently taking up this technology in their classroom, the students constitute themselves as tech-savvy girls endowed with economic capacity (McRobbie, 2007). They constitute themselves as subjects who can competently manipulate and use the new technologies that characterize many contemporary workplaces.

LGGS is a school in which everyday use of new communications technologies is highly normalized. Notebook computers for every student has been compulsory since the early 1990s, in stark contrast to the average government secondary school in Melbourne, where designated rooms equipped with a class set of desktop computers remain the primary means of accessing computer-based technologies for students. I argue that the normalization, and mandatory nature, of such use of new communications technologies at LGGS constitutes its students as particular kinds of girl subjects. The subject produced through such practices can be associated with girl power.

This process is one through which girls are produced as particular kinds of subjects. Poststructural theories of identity, such as that of Butler, reject rationalist notions of identity in which there is a "fully formed 'I'" (McRobbie, 2005, p. 84) that directs and controls its own gendered identity. Thus, although the girls didn't necessarily speak about themselves in terms of "girl power" or "tech-saviness" during this lesson, I argue that simply by virtue of being in the room, competently using online videoconferencing software, they are produced as subjects of girl power within such a school environment.

The digital technology, in this instance purchased and provided by the school, operates as a mechanism through which girls are expected and encouraged to position themselves as empowered subjects who can master the new Information Communication Technologies (ICT) and software packages they may encounter in the workforce. Developing competency with these digital technologies in the classroom can also be conceptualized as a rehearsal at being the working/consuming subjects who may one day draw upon the services of less-privileged women to help support their lifestyles and the demands of their careers (Ringrose & Walkerdine, 2008, p. 231). In this way, the use of APC in the classroom positions the girls in relation to key discourses of girl power.

Yet this "new" competent girl subject is juxtaposed, through use of APC, with some "older" practices associated with hetero-femininity. Students engage in "othering" practices, making other women objects of a gaze, as they use the technology. They use it as an opportunity to police the boundaries between acceptable and unacceptable sexualities and femininities. Boundaries between "too sexy" and "not sexy enough," frequently policed within discourses of hetero-femininity, are explored through use of ACP in the classroom.

Students comment, for example, about singer Grace Jones having "skanky ho eye shadow," and another suggested that Madonna is "too old to be prancing around." The same student, Shali, expressed disgust when she hears that one of the Spice Girls had allegedly been a stripper prior to her involvement in the band, typing "ew, I didn't know this stuff when I was ten." When an image of Britney Spears appears, some students could be heard describing her as "skanky" or a "slut" under their breath. One student typed "Brit = shit" into the chat pod. In a later interview, one student recalled that "everyone said slutty" when the image of Spears was shown.

This use of digital technology, within this educational context, thus operates as a practice through which old intersects with new. Girls who are perfectly positioned to take up the privileged girl power identity, continue to re-create older, more familiar discourses of objectified femininity. There is a contradiction between the school-based positioning of these girls as subjects of girl power, and the actual talk and discourse that occurs in the classroom around femininity, and icons of girl power. This suggests that, as other studies have shown (Marshall &Sensoy, 2009), girl power identity does not simply replace or "delete" earlier discourses of young femininity that involve constantly policing the boundaries between acceptability and unacceptability in relation to sexuality.

Playing with Fire: Young Feminine Identity and the Sims in the Classroom

The second school site considered here is a Year Eight English (Language Arts) classroom at a private, co-educational school in Melbourne. This research was part of a small study designed to explore the gendered dimensions of teenagers' engagement with digital culture online, and the implications of these apparent differences when translated into classroom practice in literacy curriculum organized around ICTs. Three computer games were incorporated into an English curriculum unit offered at Year Eight to a mixed group of fourteen-and fifteen-year-old students. In this section, I focus on one of these, The Sims, as an exemplar of a game popular with girls as well as boys and one that has been used in other studies exploring the utilisation of commercially produced computer games in the classroom (McFarlane, Sparrowhawk, & Heald, 2001).

A "god game" where players have the power, like gods, to create their own universe and direct the lives of the characters who inhabit it, The Sims invites players to re-create contemporary suburban life though building houses, socializing, raising a family, and getting a job. Players must look after their avatars, ensuring their health and social needs are met during play. Flanagan (2003) describes The Sims as providing "subtle yet powerful methods of enculturation by which social values, interaction styles and every day activities are practiced" (p. 1). The popularity of the game with the young people in the study, and the strong consumer and social values built explicitly into the game, made it a useful choice for a unit designed around extended textual analysis. It also made it a rich site through which to explore complexities around gender and digital media.

The unit of work was delivered by the English class teacher, with myself and the other researcher present, over a two-week period. The unit included some initial lessons that were spent experimenting with the games and learning to play. Time was then allowed for students to discuss their responses to the game in small groups, and these discussions were audio-taped by the researchers. Researchers also conducted audio-taped interviews with small groups of students as they were playing the games. This was followed by some lessons in which students were invited to produce written responses to the game, both creative and analytical. They were asked to save a short clip from their game and present it to the class via data projector and to share their analysis of the clip. Drawing on some classroom observations of students playing The Sims, interviews with students, and observations of students presenting their saved clips, I explore how the classroom space becomes a site in which old notions of hetero-femininity are juxtaposed with new notions of girl power.

While many students were not familiar with their games, one girl, Emily, was familiar with The Sims and was a highly skilled player. Emily and her friend Catherine created young female avatars with luxuriously furnished houses, and Emily was able to work out how to obtain more money than the standard amount of twenty thousand dollars that players receive to build a house. When I observed Emily and her friend Catherine playing, they had created female avatars with hip, trendy clothing, including tight trousers and midriff tops. They had created expensively furnished houses for their characters to live in. Both Gill (2008) and Harris (2004) have drawn attention to the dominance of the "midriff" in the new, sleek girl-power image of young femininity. Here, Emily and Catherine cited, and created, such an image in the construction of their avatars.

As the girls developed characters and houses, they talked to each other about what furniture to buy, and where their bedrooms would be located, thus constituting themselves as consuming young women:

> *Emily:* We can have like, massive bedrooms. I want to put mine here.
> *Catherine:* Oh, how cool is that, come on, we need to buy some furniture here, or a car.
> *Emily:* Do you want that one?
> *Catherine:* Yeah.

Emily's comments in some interviews and discussion indicated that she enjoys experimenting with the game by, for example, blowing up the characters. This demonstrates her expertise and knowledge of the game, and the opportunities for subversion built into it. In addition to blowing up characters, Emily explained to me that more money could be obtained by subverting the rules of the game:

> *Claire:* Okay, and now you're building them a house.
> *Emily:* Yes, a big house.
> *Claire:* How much money have they got? Do they get a certain amount of money or something?
> *Emily:* You get twenty thousand dollars, but we know how to cheat so you can get more money, so you can make a really cool house.
> *Claire:* How do you do that, how do you get them to have more money?
> *Emily:* Oh um, people just find out cheats and they just go around and then, yeah, so I end up with a cheat and it means you can build out of the bounds, and you get more money and you can just like move people around. It like gives the game like a totally different spin, because if you have limited money you can only make a little house.

Emily and Catherine's creative response to the game involved planning some features for an updated version of The Sims. As Emily explained, "we're just making a whole new one with more modern furniture, more clothes, and … more facilities for recreation and vacation."

Through playing The Sims in the classroom, Emily constituted herself, and the avatars she created, as girl-power subjects. She rehearsed being a consuming subject, demonstrating an ability to obtain and spend money on items such as clothing and furniture. She also developed her capacity to engage with the new communications technologies that might character-ize her future workplace. As well as simply navigating the game, Emily was capable of finding "cheats," which the other girls did not know how to do, thus breaking with a "good-girl" image that is characteristic of older, more familiar notions of young femininity.

She simultaneously cited notions of a "masculine, rational, produc-tive, worker self, and a (hetero)sexualized feminine, (appropriately) repro-ductive identity that both consumes itself into being and is the object of consumption" (Ringrose & Walkerdine, 2008, p. 230). She did this by constructing herself and her avatar as potential worker/consumer subjects and constructing her avatar in the image of an appropriately "consumable" young woman. Thus, she constituted both herself and her avatar as subjects of girl power.

Emily was the only girl in the classroom who appeared to use The Sims in this way. Other girls were either not as familiar with the game, or they were assigned to one of the other two games that were available. Nevertheless, her case is interesting, in terms of the newer discourses of young femininity that shaped her engagement with the game. In the same classroom space, however, some older, more familiar notions of hetero-normative gender relations were at work through the actions of one group of boys, which was the only male group playing The Sims. The image of a young woman who is the victim of misogyny, and a male gaze, was cited through the use of this computer game.

At the front of the classroom, with everyone watching on the data pro-jector, the group created a female avatar, trapped her in a burning house, and watched her scream and eventually die. One of the boys, Mark, explained, "Look see, I've set off a rocket. Ready? So she's [the avatar] trying to put the fire out but we're going to stop her doing that, because fires are good for her. See light a rocket. Here she goes." As the fire progressed, fuelled by the wooden furniture the boys purchased for the house, another boy, Steve, said about the avatar "let's kill her, Mark. Wake her up and then kill her!" When at last it became apparent that the avatar had died, the boys' pleasure turned to anticipation of the arrival of the Grim Reaper – "how's it going, Grimmy?" – and the ritual music and appearance of that figure that accompanies a death in The Sims.

This can be understood as playing with "older" notions of femininity in which a girl is helpless and vulnerable, the hapless object a male gaze. Once again, the construction of opportunities for young female identity within this classroom was working on two possible levels. First, at the level of the computer game, in which the female avatar was positioned as an object of misogyny and violence. Here the boys were also drawing on familiar tropes from horror films – as their teacher exclaimed at one point, "You've turned this into a horror film!" – demonstrating how familiar narratives of female-as-victim can carry over into newer forms of popular culture.

Second, within the "real" environment of the classroom, in which the young female students remained silent and quiet, as their male classmates loudly and enthusiastically laughed at what is happening in the game, dominating the classroom space, and the teacher's and researchers' attention in that moment. Furthermore, the same group of male students was far from silent when Emily and Catherine presented their clip, yelling instructions to the girls such as "Invite someone over – it's too boring!"(Mark), or "Fast-forward!" (Steve), managing to assert their presence in the classroom, even when it was not the boys' turn at the front. It's important to note that this behaviour was largely confined to the one group of boys, and within the group, the behavior was mainly initiated by Mark and Steve. These two examples, of "girl power" and of "girl marginalization," mediated by The Sims, are not representative of what the rest of the class was doing. Nevertheless, they are significant in demonstrating the kinds of constructions of young femininity that can be mediated by digital technologies in secondary classrooms.

Future Trends

More young women, particularly in middle-class settings, are becoming competent users of online technologies. These appear to be increasing in particular school environments, in this case, independent, high-fee paying schools. Thus, young women in these environments will be more frequently constituted as tech-savvy subjects within the spaces of mainstream, formal school curriculum. This will perhaps be in contrast to young women in less-privileged circumstances, who may be given fewer opportunities to constitute themselves in relation to such notions of female success within the dominant institutional practices of schooling. This new girl subject of capacity is a relational identity, reliant upon other young women who are the "failed" subjects of girl power (Ringrose & Walkerdine, 2008). Thus, digital technologies in particular school classrooms may be tied up in new forms of class (re)production.

Here it is important to distinguish between digital technologies that are endorsed within mainstream school curriculum and pedagogy occurring in classrooms, and those that constitute the "literate underlife" (Finders, 1997) of schooling, existing in the liminal spaces such as corridors between classes, and beneath desks. These digital technologies, for example, mobile telephones, are often not part of endorsed "official" curriculum and thus, they may not provide young women opportunities to constitute themselves as subjects of excellence within the dominant discourses that frame what it means to be a successful subject of education and work.

Future research possibilities thus include working with young women in less-privileged environments in order to investigate how "old" familiar femininities may still be articulated through use of digital technologies. It is important to attend to the possibility of continuity, as well as change, in the way young female identities are shaped by the presence of digital technologies in schools, and the opportunities for identity that these provide. While these technologies may well encourage girls to position themselves as subjects of girl power, they may also continue to effect more familiar gendered power relations and girl identities. More work is needed around the specificities of young women's identities in terms of factors such as ethnicity, class, religion, and location and how these factors might be constituted through, and shape, the use of digital technologies in school contexts.

Conclusion

In this chapter I have considered how digital technologies shape young feminine identities in two specific secondary school classrooms. I have taken, as the central problem contextualizing this chapter, the contradictory discourses around young femininities and (hetero)sexualities in schools today. Commentary and research increasingly draw attention to discourses of girl power, in which girls are subjects of success and excellence in education and work, as well as sexually empowered. Yet alongside this, research literature continues to highlight the prevalence of sexual harassment in schooling, and the positioning of girls as "objects" of a male gaze.

I have emphasized the importance of exploring the use of new digital communications technologies in secondary school classrooms in relation to both these discourses of girlhood. Existing studies of girls' use of digital technologies have emphasized their significance in allowing girls a potential space to explore identity outside the confines of adult surveillance. In this chapter, however, I have explored how, within a school context shot through with power relations, digital technologies may invite girls to position themselves in relation to, rather than in straightforward resistance to, dominant discourses.

Girls at LGGS are well positioned to produce themselves as subjects of girl power, through the routine, and the "compulsory" access they have to new, expensive, digital communications technologies in an elite school context. Many demonstrate the capacity to engage with the online technologies that will characterize their potential future workplaces. Thus, they rehearse their identities as economically independent, consuming young women. In addition to this, however, some older notions of surveillance and objectification of other women enters the classroom through use of this technology.

Some students in the Year Eight classroom playing The Sims also produce themselves as subjects of competency with new technologies. Emily, in particular, constituted herself as a potential working and consuming subject, as well as producing an avatar in the image of the consumable girl-power figure. At the same time, in this lively co-educational classroom, a group of boys cited more established notions of heterosexual femininity, in which a female avatar is positioned as a helpless object, rather than an empowered subject. Outside the game itself, the girls were momentarily sidelined as the boys' noisy enthusiasm claims the attention of fellow students, researchers, and the teacher.

Through these examples of digital technologies in secondary classrooms, we can see that older notions of femininity are not simply nor straightforwardly replaced by newer femininities, even in privileged school contexts. I have explored how digital technologies in these classrooms shape and mediate the way girls position themselves, and are positioned, in relation to key discourses. Thus, I have argued for the importance of attending to the role of digital technologies in shaping gendered identities in schools. I have also suggested some pathways for future research, which would need to involve investigating the ways in which the gendered identities of young women and men in less-privileged school contexts are being shaped and produced through digital technology.

References

Aapola, S., Gonick, M., & Harris, A. (2005). *Young femininity: Girlhood, power and social change*. Houndmills: Palgrave Macmillan.

Albury, K. (2002). *Yes means yes: Getting explicit about heterosex*. Crows Nest: Allen and Unwin.

Ang, I. (1996). *Living room wars: Rethinking media audiences for a postmodern world*. London and New York: Routledge.

Buckingham, D. & Bragg, S. (2004). *Young people, sex and the media: The facts of life?* Houndmills: Palgrave Macmillan.

Butler, J. (1993). *Bodies that matter: On the discursive limits of sex*. New York: Routledge.

Butler, J. (1997). *Excitable speech*. New York: Routledge.

Butler, J. (1999). *Gender trouble: Feminism and the subversion of identity* (Tenth Anniversary Edition). New York: Routledge.

Chambers, D., Tincknell, E., & van Loon, J. (2004). Peer regulation of teenage sexual identities. *Gender and Education*, 16(3), 397–415.

Charles, C. (2009). Knowing girls: 'Objectification', 'girl power' and 'girls' resistance' at school. Unpublished PhD thesis, Monash University.

Epstein, D., O'Flynn, S., & Telford, D. (2003). *Silenced sexualities in schools and universities*. Stoke on Trent: Trentham Books.

Finders, M. (1997). *Just girls: Hidden literacies and life in junior high*. New York: Teachers College Press.

Fine, M. (2004). Sexuality, schooling and adolescent females: the missing discourse of desire. In R. Gaztambide-Fernandez, H. Harding, & T. Sorde-Marti (Eds.), *Cultural studies and education: perspectives on theory, methodology and practice* (pp. 125–148). Cambridge, MA: Harvard Educational Review.

Flanagan, M. (2003). SIMple and Personal: Domestic Space and *The Sims*. In *Melbourne Digital Arts and Culture, Conference Proceedings* (pp. 1–4). Melbourne, Australia. http://hypertext.rmit.edu.au/dac/blog_archive/cat_all_papers.html

Gee, J. (2003). *What video games have to teach us about learning and literacy*. New York: Palgrave Macmillan.

Gee, J. (2007). *Good video games and good learning: Collected essays on video games, learning and literacy*. New York: Peter Lang.

Gill, R. (2007). *Gender and the media*. Cambridge: Polity Press.

Gill, R. (2008). Empowerment/Sexism: Figuring female sexual agency in contemporary advertising. *Feminism & Psychology*, 18(1), 35–60.

Gonick, M. (2006) Between "Girl Power" and "Reviving Ophelia": Constituting the neoliberal girl subject. *NWSA Journal*, 18(2), 1–22.

Harris, A. (2004). *Future girl: Young women in the 21st century*. New York: Routledge.

Hey, V. (1997). *The company she keeps: An ethnography of girls' friendships*. Buckingham: Open University Press.

Hopkins, S. (2002). *Girl heroes: The new force in popular culture*. Annandale: Pluto Press.

Kearney, M. (2006). *Girls make media*. New York: Routledge.

Kenway, J. & Willis, S. (1997). *Answering back: Girls, boys and feminism in school*. St Leonards: Allen and Unwin.

Lumby, C. (1997). *Bad Girls: The media, sex and feminism in the 90s*. Sydney: Allen and Unwin.

Marshall, E. & Sensoy, O. (2009). The same old hocus-pocus: Pedagogies of gender and sexuality in *Shrek 2*. *Discourse: Studies in the Cultural Politics of Education*, 30(2), 151–164.

Martino, W. (2000). Boys at the back: Challenging masculinities and homophobia in the English classroom. *English in Australia*, 127–128, 35–50.

Martino, W. (2001). Boys and reading: Investigating the impact of masculinities on boys' reading preferences and involvement in literacy. *Australian Journal of Language and Literacy*, 24(1), 61–74.

Mazzarella, S. & Pecora, N. (2007). Revisiting girls' studies: Girls creating sites for connection and action. *Journal of Children and Media*, 1(2), 105–125.

McFarlane, A., Sparrowhawk, A., & Heald, Y. (2001).*Report on the educational use of games*. Cambridge: Teachers Evaluating Educational Multimedia (TEEM) Department for Education and Skills.

McRobbie, A. (2004) Post-feminism and popular culture. *Feminist Media Studies*, 4(3), 255–264.

McRobbie, A. (2005). *The uses of cultural studies*. London: Sage.

McRobbie, A. (2007). Top girls? *Cultural Studies*, 21(4), 718–737.

Nayak, A. & Kehily, M. J. (2006). Gender undone: Subversion, regulation and embodiment in the work of Judith Butler. *British Journal of Sociology of Education*, 27(4), 459–472.

Renold, E. (2000) 'Coming out': Gender, (hetero)sexuality and the primary school. *Gender and Education*, 12(3), 309–326.

Ringrose, J. (2007). Successful girls? Complicating post-feminist, neoliberal discourses of educational achievement and gender equality. *Gender and Education*, 19(4), 471–489.

Ringrose, J. & Walkerdine, V. (2008). Regulating the abject: The TV makeover as site of neo-liberal reinvention toward bourgeois femininity. *Feminist Media Studies*, 8(3), 227–246.

Schott, G. & Horrell, K. (2002). Girl gamers and their relationship with the gaming culture. *Convergence*, 6(4), 36–53.

Snyder, I. & Beavis, C. (Eds.) (2004). *Doing literacy online: Teaching, learning and playing in an electronic world*. Cresskill, NJ: Hampton Press.

Spender, D. (1982). *Invisible women*. London: Writers and Readers.

Thomas, A. (2004). Digital literacies of the cybergirl. *E-Learning*, 1(3), 358–382.

Walkerdine, V. (1997). *Daddy's girl: Young girls and popular culture*. Basingstoke: Palgrave Macmillan.

Walkerdine, V. (2008). *Children, gender and video games: Towards a relational approach to multimedia*. Basingstoke: Palgrave Macmillan.

Weedon, C. (1997). Feminism and the principles of post-structuralism. In *Feminist practice and poststructuralist theory* (pp. 12–41). Oxford: Basil Blackwell.

7 Affiliation in the Enactment of Fan Identity: A Comparison of Virtual and Face-to-Face Settings

Caroline Pelletier and Natasha Whiteman

In recent years, manifestations of fan interests have increasingly attracted the attention of education researchers. The practices of media fans – the individuals and cultures that celebrate and document their relationships to diverse forms of entertainment (including video games, television, film, music and media celebrities) – have been seen to demonstrate pedagogic processes, with fans learning from each other through processes of affiliation (e.g., Gee, 2003; Jenkins, 2004; Lewis, Black, & Tomlinson 2009). What has made fans such interesting objects of study for education researchers is their productivity, which can be understood in terms of the display of skilled practices. Although fans have always produced cultural artifacts (including fan fiction and fan art), the emergence of online environments has made this productivity increasingly visible (e.g., the posting of fan videos to YouTube, discussion on fan forums, and development of online fan-fiction writing communities). Contemporary sites of fan activity thus offer a very visible model of enculturation into skilled practices, one which is often taken to stand in contrast to the equally visible "failure" of education to achieve a similar level of productive participation. For this reason, fan activity settings have been seen as housing a model of productive pedagogy that could inform both education theory and practice. The notion of affiliation as pedagogically productive has also emerged in response to Lave and Wenger's (1996) work on communities of practice, in which learning, or knowing, is the activity of participating in practices, rather than the outcome of a cognitive process of internalisation. Lave and Wenger's modelling of knowledge practices collapses the distinction between learning and the negotiation of identity within a setting, with learning defined "as the historical production, transformation and change of persons" (Lave & Wenger, 1996, pp. 145–146).

In this chapter, we build on existing studies of fans and pedagogy by exploring affiliation to media texts in two settings. Our use of the term "media text" points to our interest in how fans read and interpret media products – we are looking at how knowledge about media products is generated. The two settings we explore are an online fan site inhabited by avatars and an "off-line" classroom inhabited by teachers and students. Videogames provide a central focus in each setting: in the online fan site, activity focuses on the *discussion* of video games; in the classroom, the focus is on the *making* of games. This is not to suggest, however, that video games serve as our stable reference points. In each setting, video games emerge as contested points of reference that are configured in different ways, rather than as objects with specific, inherent kinds of attributes. In exploring the enactment and regulation of fan identity, then, we are also interested in examining the ways that video games are brought into being. Our focus is therefore on (a) how understandings of what videogames are (or should be) are articulated and (b) how affiliations to particular games titles/genres of video games are established in these settings. As we will describe, the moves involved in the objectification of games served to position participants as video game fans in different ways. This positioning was temporal and dynamic, intertwined with historical social practices in each setting, such as the negotiation of friendship and struggles over status.

The Context for this Chapter: Two Sites of Fan Productivity

We draw here from two studies of pedagogy, technology, and fandom. The first study (Whiteman, 2007) explored the career of two fan communities over a two-year period. The focus for this chapter is on data from one of these settings – Silent Hill Heaven (SHH) – a Web site celebrating the video game series *Silent Hill*. The analysis presented in this chapter focuses on the enactment of identity within asynchronous posting activity on the site. This activity is investigated in relation to the ways that site members debate the key characteristics of the *Silent Hill* games, and in doing so, align and/or distance themselves from other media consumers and other posters voicing similar and/or different positions. These positioning moves are understood as constituting the ongoing formation and maintenance of fan identities on the site. The second study (Pelletier, 2007) analyzed game-making activities in classroom settings and extracurricular computer game clubs in U.K. schools.[1] Attention is given here to the different strategies for producing a "playable" game in an after-school media production club. The game designs are treated here as constituting identity, because they signal affiliation to media texts in different ways, positioning students in relation to each other and the teachers. The chapter explores how, in this way, the designs served as an important resource by which students' identity as game makers and, as learners about games, was enacted in the classroom

There are clearly a number of differences between the empirical focus of these two studies. One main difference relates to the purpose of the sites. SHH is devoted to the promotion of fan interest in the *Silent Hill* games (and related *Silent Hill* media) and can be regarded as an example of the sort of "tight-knit, textually productive fan communities" that have constituted the focus of much fan studies research (Sandvoss, 2005, p. 30). In contrast, the setting described in Pelletier's study is not explicitly fan-centric. Rather, it is constituted by an educational focus on media literacy, with fan interests drawn in to the activity in order to sustain educational outcomes. While the focus of attention and discussion on SHH is primarily (but not solely) on *Silent Hill* games, in the school setting, a range of video game texts are recruited and privileged, and appear to inform students' game-making activities. A further difference between these studies is that the students' continued "devotion" to these texts cannot be claimed on the basis of the data collected for Pelletier's study, in contrast to the durability of participation observed by Whiteman over a two-year period.

Our exploration of the performance of fan identities within Pelletier's research setting reflects an interest in the ways that fannish attachments to media texts are articulated outside of clearly demarcated fan cultures. There is growing recognition of the importance of such work. This is not least because – as Sandvoss (2005) has argued – the focus of fan studies research on explicitly fan-centric domains leads to an overly narrow definition of fandom. Expanding the purview of such research can enable the consideration of the ways that those who "do not actively participate in fan communities and their textual productivity [...] derive a distinct sense of

---

[1] The research project on which this study was based was called 'Making Games: developing game authoring software for educational and creative use'. It was led by Professor David Buckingham and Dr Andrew Burn from the Centre for the Study of Children, Youth and Media, Institute of Education, London. Caroline Pelletier was the project manager. The project was generously funded through the Paccit Link Programme by the UK Economic and Social Research Council, the Engineering and Physical Science Research Council, and the Department of Trade and Industry.

self and social identity from their fan consumption" (Sandvoss, 2005, p. 30). Whiteman's focus on SHH – a clearly fan-centric setting – can clearly be understood to be guilty of the same bias that Sandvoss criticizes. However the moves we make between this site and the less clearly identifiable fan setting described in Pelletier's work is, we suggest, productive. As Sandvoss argues, comparing affiliation in different types of fan settings is important if we are to explore the diverse range of identifications that are established in relation to media texts. We would also suggest that this move is important for understanding the educational implications of different types of fan productivity.

A second clear difference between the two studies explored in this chapter relates to the role of technology in the constitution of each setting and the implications of this for the enactment of identity. SHH provides an example of technologically mediated online environments that provide a space "to break with pre-existing features of social identity" (Webb, 2001), whereas Pelletier's study examines a face-to-face environment (a school classroom) in which the role of technology remains highly contested (Buckingham, 2007). In moving between on- and off-line settings, we are interested in challenging the idea that the body is the legitimate host of authentic identity, an idea that remains common within debates surrounding the move to computer-mediated environments from the surety of the real world. New media scholarship has increasingly questioned the opposition between "real" and cybernetic bodies (Hayles, 1999) on the basis of the materiality of digital "representation." Our exploration of the strategies by which affinity to media objects is established, and with it identity configured in these two settings similarly does not privilege the physical body as the marker of presence and therefore opens up possibilities for exploring how forms of identity work take place within different technological environments.

In order to clarify what we mean by affiliation and identity, we start by tracing the general move we are making in drawing on a de-essentialized theory of identity. This approach figures identity as negotiated, performed, and context dependent – a view of identity which, as Stuart Hall (1992, p. 285) says, has emerged as the product of the various theoretical "de-centering influences" involved in the "dislocation" of the modern subject from its essentialized moorings, including the work and discourse analysis of Foucault on the construction of the subject and the influence of the "linguistic turn" in Lacan and Derrida. Our starting point in this chapter however is a critique of constructivist approaches to identity by Brubaker and Cooper (2000); we start here in order that we might try to sidestep the internal contradictions that have been identified within some work that conceptualizes identity in this way. We then move on to present our two studies. In the conclusion, we return to the question of how technology is implicated in the enactment of identity, and the methodological implications this has for researching this concept.

The Problem with the Concept of Identity

In their review of the limitations of the sociological concept of identity, Brubaker and Cooper (2000, p. 6) argue that in contemporary research accounts:

> [...] "essentialism" [is] vigorously criticised, and constructivist gestures now accompany most discussions of "identity." Yet we find an uneasy amalgam of constructivist language and essentialist argumentation. This is not a matter of intellectual sloppiness. Rather, it reflects the dual orientation of many academic identitarians as both analysts and protagonists of identity politics.

Brubaker and Cooper's argument has particular relevance for the field of fan studies, which often features academic fans researching fan practices. More generally, it points to a tension underpinning the concept of identity. On one hand, identity implies something bounded, continuing through time, deeply rooted, essential; on the other hand, the idea that identity is constructed suggests that it is fluid, perpetually in movement, situational and contextual. Brubaker and Cooper's critique of the concept implies that although contemporary analyses of identity start from a premise that identity is constructed, they end up looking for some other phenomenon than the process of that construction – something beyond it, which underpins it, or which is a result of it. Methodologically this can be seen when the analysis of interview data (for instance) goes beyond the data to inscribe the intentions of research informants from their spoken words. In other words, whilst studies of identity may focus on a *process* (of construction), their argumentation, or conclusions, often pertain to something more akin to a *condition* or state (or that which is constructed). This tension can perhaps be detected in the move to pluralize "identity," to talk about "identities" in order to avoid the problem of reification. The idea that there are "identities," rather than an identity, still implies that identity is a property of an individual, an attribute that they have, or "construct." As Brubaker and Cooper argue, "this tendency to objectify 'identity' deprives us of analytical leverage. It makes it more difficult for us to treat 'groupness' and 'boundedness' as *emergent properties* of particular […] settings rather than as always already there in some form" (2000, p. 28). In Brubaker and Cooper's account then, "groupness," or community, is not the sum total of a group of entities (individual identities) but the movement of affiliations and oppositions constitutive of a setting.

The problem that Brubaker and Cooper identify can arguably be recognized in the tendency by educational researchers to treat games as fixed entities that provoke the formation of distinctive types of fan communities (Whiteman, 2008a; Pelletier 2009). When the pedagogic productivity of fan communities is attributed to the quality of games, these communities are understood to be organized around a shared understanding of what a game consists of. From this perspective, fan communities appear relatively stable over time, with fans moving gradually from peripheral to more expert forms of participation. This account of learning in fan communities tends to reify games by treating them as static objects whose properties can be known and thus learned. This fails to take into account the move from the materiality of the media product as a thing, to the ways that it is brought into being through its use and reception. Accounts of learning that treat games as products tend to reify identity, because fans are perceived to gradually acquire knowledge of that product – in other words, a problematic methodological distinction is made between the game, and ways of knowing the game.

Brubaker and Cooper's critique has extensive implications for studying the relationship between education and technology. One of the reasons, it could be argued, why "identity" has become such a prominent concept in the literature on young people, learning, and technology is because of the desire to recruit identities from other contexts for the purposes of education. The debate on "serious games" for instance is infused with a desire to use people's motivation and skill in playing digital games for the ends of education and training. This endeavor can be situated within a long tradition in education to recruit children's popular interests and activities (or "identities") to teach a curriculum. The concept of identity, in this argument, substantiates a model of learning in which learning is a property of an individual or group – a property or condition that can then move across different contexts. Brubaker and Cooper's argument that identity should not be treated as a (constructed) condition, but investigated methodologically as an emergent process, threatens the logic by which a child, in "constructing an identity," also constructs individualized or group-based knowledge. Taking their critique on board does not mean denying the value of education, but it does challenge the methodological basis on which analyses of educational processes can conclude that practice is re-packaged as "knowledge" and stored or transferred via the medium of "identity."

A De-Essentialized Theory of Identity

Although Brubaker and Cooper (2000) advocate dropping the concept of identity, it might be possible to address their concerns by articulating a de-essentialized concept of identity that avoids certain problems with the logic of constructivism. As we have described, their critique focuses on the slippage, in empirical accounts, from analyzing identity as a process of construction (within a setting) to analyzing identity as a construct (the attribute of a person). This slippage can be avoided by refraining from treating data as pertaining to something other than what it enacts: in effect, this means treating identity as a process of symbolization, rather than as something behind this process, or as its outcome. To say that identity is a process of symbolization is to argue that it has no ontological status apart from the various symbols that constitute it. This conception of identity means treating the articulation itself as the basic unit of analysis rather than as something outside it: in other words, treating signifying practices as constituting identity, rather than "representing" or "constructing" identity. This is not to suggest that identity is "only" discourse, or that everything is textual. Rather, it is to put forward an analytical strategy in which a sign or statement is analyzed in its appearance, rather than as a social reality that hides something else behind it (identity in the form of social class, intention, and so on) (Andersen, 2003).

This approach puts emphasis on the materiality of symbols with which meaning is made. Rather than technology "influencing" or "impacting" on identity (as if identity was something other than a process of symbolization) technology can be treated as a resource for symbolization. This shifts our focus from analyzing how people construct their identities *with* technology, to analyzing how identity is manifested digitally, or technologically.

In the two studies presented in this chapter, we explore the manifestation of identity in two settings in which video games constitute the central focus of activity. We examine how the authenticity of video games is evaluated and the principles that are applied for signifying and/or recognizing a text as a game in these settings. These articulations involve affiliating moves toward different objects of fan interest and relational positioning in difference to others. We are interested in how these positions are secured and/or challenged in these settings and how identity emerges not as other to this positioning, but as the movement of this positioning.

Affiliation in the Enactment of Fan Identity in an Online Setting

Our first point of reference in exploring the configuration of fan identity in different domains is a recent sociological study of two online fan communities. The study was based on data gathered during a two-year observation of the public forums of two sites: the television fan site City of Angel (COA) and the video game fan site SHH (for details of the study, see Whiteman, 2007; Whiteman, 2012) – our focus here.

Online since November 2002, SHH is a busy, fan-produced Web site devoted to the *Silent Hill* series of survival horror video games. In 2007, at the end of Whiteman's study, the site had 6,492 registered users. During the time that the study was conducted, the site contained a range of content including information about the *Silent Hill* series (FAQs [frequently asked questions] and guides relating to the individual games, information on characters, and links to other *Silent Hill* fan sites) while also housing forums devoted to the discussion of different topics (including separate forums for each *Silent Hill* game, the *Silent Hill* film, a forum for general discussion and a forum for discussion of game-play issues).

SHH as a Site of Pedagogic Activity

The study of SHH can be seen as part of a growing academic interest in the configuration of educational practices in popular culture domains and an even broader interest in the "wider ecology of education" (Sefton-Green, 2004): the "informal" learning that takes place outside of formal educational institutions. Some of the activity examined on the site involved easily "recognizable" examples of teaching and apparent learning (including the provision of game-play support, see Whiteman, 2008a). The study also approached participation on the site as constituting pedagogic activity, examining, for example, how members "learned" to be members of these sites. The analysis focused on the strategies involved in the maintenance of community relations in the setting, including the negotiation of social relationships, the related patterning of identification and engagement with the fan objects and the ways that these moves were regulated and policed.

Empirically, the focus of the study was on written interactions on the bulletin boards of these sites (the analysis of SHH presented in the study was based on a sample of 140 threaded discussions from the forums of the site, a total of 4,092 posted messages). In contrast to the focus on substantive, "textual productivity" of Pelletier's study (the "textual production that can circulate among – and thus help to define the fan community"; Fiske, 1992, p. 30) the focus of this study was therefore on what John Fiske has termed the "enunciative" productivity of audiences – communicative productivity relating to, for example, talk and dress surrounding media texts. On sites like SHH however, this talk is rendered in textual form and thus is able to be published and circulated within the cultures, thus suggesting a hybrid form of productivity enabled by new technologies.

The Construction of Identities of SHH

A central aspect of the study's focus in looking at this communicative productivity was exploring the configuration of identity within posting activity on the site. The interest here was not in the configuration of off-line identities as online personas, but instead in the ways that identity emerged within positing activity. The analysis focused on the points at which (and manner by which) identity was articulated, fixed and contested on the sites.

One point of interest was the formation of individual avatar identities as constituted by the accumulation of individual utterances authored by one user as well as the selection of avatar images and usernames. While the study's focus was on talk, the multimodal resources available on the sites were clearly significant in respect of the formation of avatar identities.

A range of identity cues, for example, was available to members SHH from which to construct online personas (as discussed in Donath, 1999). Members chose a username that was supplemented by a range of supporting descriptors typical on online forums; the date they joined the site, their posting numbers and related titles and their location. These cues included image based avatars or animated gifs. The information provided might be more of less "realistic" – locations cited, for example, included "Ontario, Canada" and "In the Swedish fog, that slowly merges with the otherworld." Such naming also served to reflect particular emphases in interest; many had gendering connotations. The formation of online identities through use of such cues, enabled the creative construction of online personas (Turkle, 1996) in this setting.

Despite the possibilities for schizoid and creative identity play, however, the site demonstrated a more conservative expectation that participants maintain consistent identities on the forums over time. The activity demonstrated expectations of authorial coherence – that usernames were unified and authorship consistent. This was despite evidence of moments of identity confusion on the forums when usernames emerged as having been chosen by more than one "person." This consistency was such that it was possible to get to know the "personalities" of individual avatars (the characteristic posting style, positions, opinions etc.), and to be surprised when they behaved in unexpected ways, or for the researcher to be confused when avatars with different usernames appeared to "be" someone else. Such uncertainty is visible in a post where one member of the site attempts to pin down the identity of another poster:

> I don't remember you... but it looks like you are an older member... As am i. is this a different name or were you just not active? either way.. welcome..

This example demonstrates both an awareness of the uncertainties of the environment and attempt to establish a stable point of reference in respect of the identity of the addressed, an attempt to know to whom the poster is speaking. (For further discussion of this consistency and confusion, see Whiteman, 2007).

Alongside this interest in the construction of individual avatar identities, the study also explored how notions of being a fan of *Silent Hill* games were established within the daily flow of utterances within forum activity. The approach taken in exploring this aspect of the posting activity on the site was informed in part by fan studies writing that has examined the relational construction of fan identities in different contexts; work that has been strongly influenced by Bourdieu's writings on cultural distinction (see Hills, 2002; Sandvoss, 2005; Williamson, 2005). Drawing from Bourdieu's work on the strategic construction of cultural identity, fan studies researchers have examined the marking out of distinctiveness and difference from others in terms of taste within and between fan cultures, and between fan and non-fan interests; Matt Hills, for example, has argued that fans' "tactical appropriations of media theory" (2004, p. 139) – which, he suggests, attributes authority to members of fan communities – serves to "monitor, and maintain, [fans'] valued cultural distinction(s) from non-fans" (p. 141).

This sort of positioning was evident on SHH in discussion of the relationship between *Silent Hill* and *Resident Evil* – another, better known, survival horror videogame. In 2006 a post on the site announced that *Silent Hill* had failed to make a Web site's list of the "200 Greatest Videogames," but *Resident Evil* had. Why had *Resident Evil* (RE) been listed, but *Silent Hill* (SH) ignored? In the resulting thread of responses to this question, posts demonstrated very similar readings of the relative status of *Silent Hill* and *Resident Evil*. This can be seen in the following exchange between three posters that illustrates the marking out of similar positions:

"Silent Hill isn't as popular as we all would like. I must admit that although it is extremely satisfying to maul a nurse with the emergency hammer, the action does not size up to Resident Evil. I believe one reason Silent Hill 4 was more action oriented was to appeal to gamers who were familiar with RE and wanted another fun survival horror to play. What most people don't see is there is much, much more to Silent Hill than just another good survival horror game. It is what goes on beneath the action that makes it stand apart, and few people see this."

"I agree. I think RE was more hollywood than Silent Hill, no doubt. Fast paced, no so hard puzzles, and lots of bang bang action with lots of noise. I'm pretty crazy about RE myself, but I really do prefer SH to it. I also think that majority of RE players prefer to have everything out in the open for the taking as opposed to SH where you have to work to progress in the game. But I like both very much."

"Yea dude, in other words RE is for dumb people who cant understand the art of SH, ppl look at me weird when i call SH art, and sum ppl just look at me weird cos they dont know what it is. IM happy to find ppl who know and play silent hill. i can talk about it for hours."

SH does have that beneath the action with that history stuff, all RE is "oh man, i dropped teh virus, WERE ALL ZOMBIES NOW! FIND THE CURE!" And SH is more like "hey a locked door, i need to find a key, but ill read sum newspaper articles along the way and find out more about the town, which is really not a town, but it is a town, and its related to me, and these monsters dont exist, a little girl wants to take over my daughters soul or what not, ooh look a shiny pipe, and oh shit kill the nurse. Hey oh look, theres a picture on the wall, and a dead guy hanging over a bucket... gross... oh look more monsters, let me pull out my gun that i found in the trash shoot that i had to drop a case of soda in so that it would drop...OH LOOK THE KEY!"

"Hmm..i dont know but thats what i think, a little rambling, but i tihnk SH is a kind of slippery slope, unlike RE as you guys have sed, to the point. SH, even if it is a game, is for the more intelligent people. ive really gotten stumped on some ofthe puzzles and it took me to get out the pencil and paper to figure it out."

Certain ideas about what *Silent Hill* "is" are assumed, voiced, and reinforced in these posts. These moves present *Silent Hill* as offering particular type of experience that goes 'beyond' action, with *Resident Evil* providing a potent point of reference for defining *Silent Hill* in difference to other games and texts. *Resident Evil* is "more Hollywood" presenting "everything out in the open for taking" and "to the point" – more user-friendly (easily) accessible, less challenging, more superficial. In contrast "SH does have that beneath the action with that history stuff," the game offers "a slippery slope" and "you have to work to progress in the game." Such positioning characterizes *Silent Hill* as requiring particular effort and offering depth and quality. While the first post acknowledges some affinity toward *Resident Evil* ("I'm pretty crazy about RE myself") – which is not picked up on by the respondent – the posts also demonstrate negativity toward some of the trends that *Resident Evil* represents as a game.

These posts illustrate how discussion of the relationship between the *Silent Hill* and *Resident Evil* series establishes "us against them" alliances; here, positioning those on the forums as "good" media consumers ("intelligent people") in relation to de-legitimated others ("ignorant" people). Such positioning is important because it involves the establishing of differentiations to external agents ("majority of Resident Evil players") that simultaneously establishes alliances between the participants on the site through the voicing of similar positions. Such moves establish the identity of fans in relation to other media consumers, and define *Silent Hill* in relation to other media texts. Whilst there are recognisable differences in the voices of individual avatars here – through the use of language, and references to skills – there is a common imagining of "others" against which the fans are united (in difference). Similar ideas emerged in discussion of the *Silent Hill* movie the following year, where fans were to voice fears that the mainstream audience wouldn't understand it because of its "deep" story line. While these moves have implications for what participants constitute good video games to be, these points of emphasis also serve to establish *Silent Hill* fans as possessing "sophisticated" identities – configuring them as gamers that can interpret, handle and deal with the challenges of the *Silent Hill* games.

Just as the names and images that construct avatar identities on SHH can be regarded as taking on meaning through oppositional positioning (in relation to other possible selections), discussion of *Silent Hill* and *Resident Evil* on the site demonstrates the relational construction of identity. We can see within these extracts moves to establish both individual avatar identities ("I'm pretty crazy about RE myself, but I really do prefer SH to it") whilst also attempting to fix a sense of group identity in relation to the denigrated other ("majority of RE players"). As the preceding example suggests, this positioning served to establish alliances on the forums of the site. However, differences also emerged within posting activity, founded on the voicing of very different stances in respect of the fan object.

Such moves were common within discussion of what made an authentic *Silent Hill* game. Wranglings over the essential nature of *Silent Hill* emerged frequently as a topic of discussion during the study but particularly during periods in which new material was released – such as the controversial release of the fourth *Silent Hill* game in 2006 (see Whiteman, 2008b) and the release of the *Silent Hill* film in 2007 – points at which affiliation to the series was often tested.

The frequency of this wrangling was because, while *Silent Hill* provided a central anchoring point for the activity of the site, its significance was continually debated and contested. This negotiation of the "authentic" canon text is commonplace within fan cultures. In the classic early fan studies text *Textual Poachers*, for example, Jenkins (1992, p. 97) describes how episodes of the television series *Star Trek* were assessed by fans in relation to different criteria, including "general criteria applicable to any classical narratives," but also (and more often) evaluated "against an idealized conception of the series," a "program tradition" that he described as being "abstracted from the sum total of available material" and providing "consistent criteria for evaluating each new addition." On SHH such abstraction was contested and debated within publicly visible social interactions within the day-to-day activity of the site. Like the moves described by Jenkins, the debate on SHH over the authenticity of *Silent Hill* texts involved the negotiation of what *Silent Hill* is or should be in relation to an abstracted understanding of what the games "are." As in the discussion of *Silent Hill/Resident Evil* described earlier, these understandings emphasized certain aspects of *Silent Hill* – establishing moves to fix and pin down the distinctive characteristics of the series.

During the pre-release activity surrounding the *Silent Hill* film, for example, rumors spread within online fan activity that the film was to feature a key *Silent Hill* monster (Pyramid Head) from *Silent Hill 2* alongside a character from the original *Silent Hill* game (Harry Mason). Depending on your reading of the meaning and significance of Pyramid Head (itself the focus of much debate), the uniting of these two characters had the potential to represent a significant violation of the canon. For this reason, these rumors provoked the voicing of hostility toward the film adaptation, as demonstrated by the following post:

> If the climax looks like being Harry vs. Pyramid Head, I'm also out. And demanding a refund.

The reference to leaving the cinema ("I'm also out") and calling for a refund – represents a complete rejection of the new *Silent Hill* material, one provoked by the violation of the canon. The criterion for evaluating this new material here suggests a privileging of, and concern with, the logic of the canon, which should be maintained. In response, however, another post presents an alternative and very different response to the potential appearance of Pyramid Head:

> The above in bold would officially make Silent Hill the BEST movie EVER. Suffice to say that if Pyramid Head appears anywhere in the movie, I will buy it on DVD.

In contrast to the concern with the logic of the canon text, this post focuses on the pleasure of seeing Pyramid Head on the screen; this monster is presented as a potent attractor of this fan's interest. Such moves show how fan sites do not constitute homogenous sites of allegiance to media texts, suggesting instead the ways that affiliations are established in respect of different aspects of the object of fan interest and serve to establish distinctions between fans. Announcing an affinity with, or distancing move from, the character of Pyramid Head in this way is another example of the positioning strategies by which the identities of individual posters are established on the forums. As with the discussion of *Resident Evil* and *Silent Hill* described earlier, the meaning of these relational moves in respect of this character is context specific, tied into struggles over legitimacy and authority within the site (is it appropriate to privilege Pyramid Head, for example?). The significance of such preferences therefore emerges within the play of identifications with different aspects of the games. This play demonstrates the complex nature of identity work on the site: the way that the utterances that bring the object of fan interest into being also establish the identities of individual members.

Affiliation in the enactment of (fan) identity in a face-to-face setting

The second setting that we will examine is an after-school game-making club in a co-educational U.K. secondary school that ran as part of a research project called "Making Games." The club ran for six weeks, and met once a week for an hour, although on two occasions, students attended for the whole day. The club was led by researchers and one of the school's teachers, and was attended by eight thirteen- to fourteen-year-olds. Its function was to teach, and research, media literacy within a more "informal" setting than classroom-based courses. Attendance was voluntary, and there was little whole-class teaching. Affiliation to video games was enacted in this setting in students' talk, but also importantly, in the production work that students generated.

This work consisted of software files, created using a game-authoring tool[2] developed for the project. These files were videogames, but bore limited resemblance to the commercial games discussed on SHH. They were made using non-professional tools and were not published or complete. The students' games might not be recognized as such by outsiders to the project on an initial play-through, because they often consisted of, for example, strange groups of objects gathered together according to an unfamiliar logic that emitted unexpected and strange noises when clicked, with images suddenly filling the screen, and scores increasing or decreasing for no immediately obvious reason.

Our approach to the enactment of video game fan identity in respect of these complex texts focuses on how students' production work is signified as "game," or, in other words, the basis on which the work realizes a claim to be recognizable as a game. In the previous section, we examined how SHH posts established versions of what *Silent Hill* is or should be. Here, similarly, our analysis of students' production work pays attention to negotiations of what games are and/or should be. This is realized in the way that production work is evaluated, categorized as like and/or unlike the object of fan interest. In both the after-school club setting and SHH, therefore, we analyze fan identity in terms of the way in which affiliations are established in relation to media texts. In this section, this affiliation is enacted in the way production work becomes "readable" as text (or becomes a game) in the setting.

The Game-Making Club as a Site of Pedagogic Interaction

The club organizers' pedagogic strategy involved asking students to play each other's games on a regular basis and give feedback to each other on how the game "played." This strategy was intended to enable students to produce "legible" texts without having been formally taught the conventions of game design. The rationale here was that by regularly getting feedback as production work developed, students would develop understanding of how other people "read" their game – how they navigated its three-dimensional space and interpreted puzzles and challenges. They would consequently make games that others could read and/or play – in other words, texts that were "literate."

Analysis of students' production work suggests that this pedagogic strategy gave rise to very different, and competing, ideas about what made game "playable". The different versions of playable texts can be interpreted

---

[2] The tool is now called MissionMaker

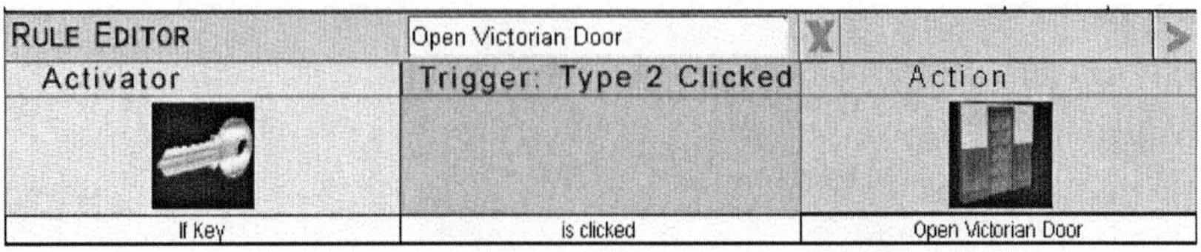

RULE EDITOR	Open Victorian Door	✗	➤
Activator	Trigger: Type 2 Clicked	Action	
If Key	is clicked	Open Victorian Door	

Figure 7.1. Game makers make rules by deciding which entities with which properties to put into the software's three-part rule system.

in relation to the conditions under which play happened in the club, with game making and game play taking place alongside each other – in contrast to the play of commercial games. Students' games were "playable" in specific ways, and by specific people, for instance, by a student's friend who had similar interpretations of a game title. It is in this respect that production work can be read as enacting fan identity, because it situated people in relation to each other, including some and excluding others from play.

Resources for the Enactment of Identity

The identity work that characterized the club emerged from the resources students engaged with in their production work – and, namely here, the game-authoring software. This supported the creation of three-dimensional, first-person games. It consisted of a selection of ready-made entities, such as rooms, corridors, doors, objects that the player character can pick up, media files (image or audio files), scoreboards, and so on. These entities were assembled and configured by the game maker. In other words, the emphasis was not so much on game makers producing the raw materials for representation and interaction, but on assembling ready-made entities and specifying (through a form of object-based programming) the relations between them. This specification constituted the game's rules. For example, "if the key is clicked, the door opens."

The word "rule" here covers two overlapping elements: the logical rules according to which the game is created (as shown in Figure 7.1), and the rules of the game established in play (for instance, winning involves killing all the evil aliens).

Two Contrasting Conceptions of What a Game Is/Should Be

In order to demonstrate the different ways that production work was symbolized as "game" in this setting, we focus on two pieces of production work.

Figure 7.2. The "Egyptian areas" in Simon's game.

The pieces are not representative, but demonstrate some of the processes by which production work was implicated in positioning in the setting. The first game – authored by Simon – foregrounds genre conventions that distinguish games from other media texts. The second game – by Jak – consists of images and sounds sourced from the internet. It foregrounds technical effects: logical rules that demonstrate programming and technical dexterity. The two games suggest different conceptions of what makes a game playable. These two versions competed with each other in the club, because they were legitimized as symbolizing "game" in relation to different sources of authority: in the first instance, the teachers and, in the second, a "real" game designer who assisted with running the first session of the club.

Simon's Game: Playability as the Re-Enactment of
Genre Conventions

The first couple of rooms in Simon's game offer explicit instructions, framing these rooms as the game's "training level." For instance, upon entry of the area shown in Figure 7.2, a sound recording is played, recorded by Simon: "To kill robots and remove obstacles in the Egyptian areas you need

Figure 7.3. A robot in Simon's game that is made invisible (or "killed") when the "sword," shown here in the player's inventory, is waved above its head.

the sickle sword. Use it to remove this blockade. The sword is hidden." The statement describes the sword in terms of its general properties, with a particular incidence of when these properties apply pointed out. The recording identifies the meaning of this incidence (removing a blockade, shown as Figure 7.3) as well as subsequent incidences of using the sword and the consequent effects.

This explicit induction into the game semiotics stops after the first couple of rooms. This splits the game into two halves, a training level and the main part of the game – with the latter characterized by the absence of explicit instructions and hints as to the meaning of events. However, the challenges that constitute "the training level" do not recur in the rest of the game. There is, for example, only one obstacle in the Egyptian areas that the sword can clear, despite the use of the plural in the instructions quoted earlier ("To remove obstacles …"). Also, challenges in the rest of the game – such as ascertaining the significance of certain sounds – are not anticipated in "the training level." The training level is thus not matched to subsequent challenges. Perhaps unsurprisingly, no one in the club completed Simon's game without asking him for assistance after the first couple of rooms.

In discussions with Caroline, Simon stated that his game was inspired by the video game *Silent Hill*, which, as we saw in postings from SHH, is often presented by fans as offering a complex and challenging game experience. When other members of the club gave feedback which indicated that the game was too difficult to play, Simon responded by arguing that the other students were clearly inexperienced, in other words, incapable of solving the puzzles he had devised, and also overcome in games like *Silent Hill*. The difficulty other students experienced in playing his game was treated by Simon as a sign of his own superior gaming experience.

Several moves here can be interpreted in terms of the enactment of fan identity. First, there is the design of complex puzzles. It is the complexity of these puzzles that Simon stated made his game like *Silent Hill* – it was not, for instance, similarity in story line or setting that tied Simon's production work to *Silent Hill*. Second, there is the justification for maintaining the complexity of the puzzles in terms of the inexperience of the other club members. These two moves enact a fan identity that emphasizes affiliation to a media text on the basis of a certain kind of complexity and also superiority over other, less-knowledge players – a move which repeats what we observed in parts of SHH.

In Simon's game, a further move can be interpreted in the light of the emphasis placed on "genre conventions" by the teachers/researchers, who stated repeatedly, and on the basis of their media studies–informed conception of literacy, that students should make their work legible/playable precisely by re-articulating such conventions. The training level can be read as a reference to a genre convention. Its function as a convention is however undercut, in that it does not introduce players to subsequent challenges. This positions Simon's game as literate – because it accords with the teachers' definition of literacy – while preserving its complexity: It remained unplayable by other student players. The success of this design strategy was affirmed by the teachers/researchers, who congratulated Simon on the sophistication of his game. The unplayability of Simon's production work was thereby treated, by teachers and other students, as a characteristic of other students' lack of experience, rather than, for instance, a fault with this work.

The emphasis on genre conventions in Simon's production work is also seen in the arrangement of weapons and enemies. The location of these elements suggests an increasing level of difficulty: As the weapons get bigger, so do the enemies and obstacles. The final weapon in the game is a mine, which blows up a reinforced door. When Simon demonstrated his game on the classroom whiteboard to the rest of the group in the final session of the club, he emphasized that the section involving the reinforced door was "really cool," and paused to ensure everyone was watching. He then demonstrated "blowing up" the door, by waving the mine in front of it. It did not seem to be clear to others in the group, including the teachers and researcher, why this event was "really cool" – at least, there was little reaction despite the buildup of expectations. This may have been because "blowing up" the door required the same actions, and thus same level of skill, as overcoming all the other "challenges": waving the weapon in front of the enemy to make it invisible. The sequence therefore works as a symbol of an increasing level of difficulty at a visual level (bigger weapon means bigger challenge), but not in terms of playing skill. Simon's designation of the final challenge as "really cool" suggests an emphasis on the visual signification of genre conventions; the function of such visual signs within play is however neglected. So, just as the training level does not offer training relevant to playing the rest of the game, so the sequencing of weapons/enemies does not realize increasing difficulty.

Interpreting these characteristics of Simon's production work in terms of the enactment of identity points to the way in which the production work realizes a claim both to literacy and to fandom – fandom of a text whose specificity is its complexity, or one might also say its unplayability by non-fans. The production work meets the teachers' criterion for legibility and playability, because it demonstrates understanding of "genre conventions"; the fact that others in the class could not read such conventions appropriately signified the exclusivity and sophistication of Simon's fan knowledge. In other words, identity is enacted on the basis of demonstrating knowledge of media texts that remain unknowable or unplayable by others in the club. This design strategy secured Simon a reputation as the most expert player – for instance, other students as well as the teachers and researcher often turned to him for design advice.

Jak's Game: Playability as Method of Production

In contrast to Simon's production work, Jak's production work consists of images, sounds, and three-dimensional entities with loose semiotic associations. They are organized primarily, it seems, to sustain certain spectacular effects, including the effecting of complex logical rule structures, and the incorporation of images and sounds sourced from the Web. To take an example of this, a door in Jak's game opens when two objects are placed in a specified location. The rule structure can be expressed as follows: *If* the die *and* the stick of dynamite are placed in front of the door, *then* the door opens (see Figure 7.4).

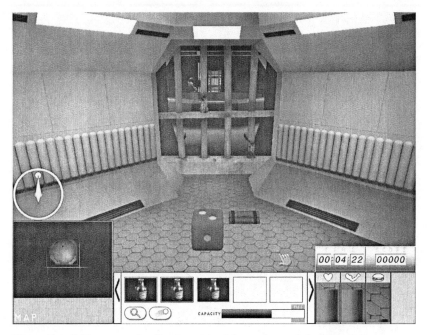

Figure 7.4. Jak's game – the die, the stick of dynamite, and the locked door.

This logical structure is relatively complex because it requires the combination of two elements to produce one effect. The teachers/researchers were not aware at the time that this type of logical structure was technically possible. Jak learned how to produce it following a conversation with one of the developers of the game-authoring software, who had contributed to the running of the club's first session. Once Jak had established that the developer had worked on "real" computer games, including ones Jak had played, he spent most of the first session asking him about his work, as well as how to use the software to achieve certain effects, notably "killing," "blowing things up," and doing cut-scenes.

In subsequent sessions, Jak was told on several occasions by club members that they could not work out how to open doors in his game, and so consequently could not progress through the game. The club members stated that they could not work out the logic by which objects in the game were related; for instance, the logic that links together a die, a stick of dynamite, and a door. Such elements are not conventionally related in game texts. Jak did not address this "problem" (i.e., from the perspective of the other members of the club, including the teachers/researchers) until the last session, when Caroline asked him to use more conventional associations (for instance, a door opening with two keys, or with the stick of dynamite only).

There is a clear contrast here in the design strategies of Simon's and Jak's production work. Rather than foregrounding genre conventions, Jak's game valorizes a certain logical complexity, informed by Jak's conversation with a "real" game designer in the school club. Whereas Simon's production work is legitimized as "game" in reference to expert game players as well as the teachers/researchers' conception of literacy, Jak's production work is legitimized as "game" in reference to his interaction with a game producer – one who had more experience of making (real) games than did the teachers/researchers. Jak's knowledge of certain logical structures allowed him to teach the other students in the club ways of using the software that the teachers/researchers did not know. His attention to logical structures thus introduced a competing curriculum into the club, one which emphasized software usage and which devalorized genre conventions.

What is at issue here is not whether Jak's production work is more, or less, literate that Simon's in developmental terms; rather, the two instances of production work suggest different strategies for symbolizing "game" and for enacting fan identity in the classroom. Jak's production work enacts a fan identity precisely on the basis of its affiliation with a "real" game designer, and its disaffiliation with the teachers/researchers. One could argue that it frames fandom of games in terms of its (fandom's) opposition to school-based structures of authority and knowledge – in strong contrast to Simon's production work.

After the first session, Jak spent a significant amount of time searching the internet for images and sounds, and inserting them into his game. To take one example: After Caroline asked Jak to provide an ending for his game, the following image (Figure 7.5) was inserted into the production work:

The image is iconic of one of the *Star Trek* films. When Jak demonstrated his game in the final session of the after-school club and Figure 7.5 appeared on screen, the other students asked whether the player character had been successful in the mission or not, to which Jak replied positively. Jak was then asked what happened if the player was unsuccessful – a question which suggests that the other students did not know whether to interpret the image as a sign of "winning" or "losing." Jak replied that the same image and explosion sound appeared anyway. The image does not signify the state of the game at its end point therefore (which had been the point of providing an "ending," in Caroline's request to Jak); its value, it seems, is that it brings an instance of a "real" media text into Jak's production work. The authenticity of Jak's production work is not signified

Figure 7.5. The image that appears at the "end" of Jak's game.

in relation to genre conventions therefore, but in relation to images and sounds sourced from "real" media texts (i.e., commercial, rather than curricularized).

When Jak showed his game on the classroom whiteboard in the last session of the club, there was much joking and laughing among the other students. When Jak stated that, in one location, the player has to place a bottle of beer in front of a door in order to open it, Simon interjected: "If the crew are that stupid as to make a key which resembles a bottle of beer they deserve to die." Simon's comment makes fun of Jak by rejecting the latter's claim that what makes a game is a particular technical process, rather than genre conventions. The exchange emphasized that the strategies realized in both pieces of production work were competing ones, vying for viability in the club. Although Simon's claims to expertise were not always acknowledged, his game's re-enactment of genre sequences won the teachers/researchers' approval, as well as that of other students: The unplayability of his game was interpreted as a symbol of his superior playing experience and knowledge of games. Jak's game, on the other hand, became a joke among all the other members of the club; its unplayability became, in this setting, a symbol of illiteracy.

One benefit of examining this data in the light of the concept of fan identity is that it permits a re-evaluation of what was being learned in the after-school club. Although the teachers'/researchers' pedagogic strategy emphasized playability, the two games analyzed here were "unplayable" without the designers' running commentary, which indicated how the production work should be interpreted and navigated. In this respect, the pedagogic strategy failed to realize its aim. Analysis of the design strategies however suggests that the problem cannot be adequately described in terms of poor implementation, students' cognitive incapacity or lack of understanding of the activity's purpose. Rather, in the context of students playing each other's games repeatedly, design strategies emerged that gave occasion for the symbolization of identity in relation to competing points of identification: the teachers/researchers, versus the "real" game designer. As with SHH, therefore, the play of identifications led to different aspects of games being emphasized and brought into being in the production work.

Tying the two studies together: Technology, pedagogy and identity

In this chapter we have drawn on a de-essentialized theory of identity to examine the enactment of video game fandom in two settings. These settings – the online fan community and the face-to-face club – were selected because of our interest in the performance of fan activity within sites with contrasting material configurations. Our analysis has focused on the enactment of identity in two forms of digital texts: postings and "amateur" games. We have treated these texts in the same way, as "utterances" – to use the Foucaultian term – which materialize identity. This approach has implications for conceptualizing the significance of fan productivity and sites of fan-based interaction for educational practice, because instead of focusing on how fans learn *from* games, or on how fans learn *about* games in a community of practice, our approach has traced different articulations of what games *are*.

The first study looked specifically at an online community organized around the imagined fan object of "Silent Hill" and examined how different and conflicting conceptions of what *Silent Hill* is/should be enacted identity on the site. The study presents a different view of online video-game-based communities than has sometimes featured in educational literature that focuses on the homogeneity of "informal" communities of practice – a homogeneity made possible by any presumption that there is consensus about what the object of fandom consists of. It is on the basis of a presumed consensus that "informal" fan communities can appear more productive pedagogically than formal education.

The second study similarly noted the contestations about the object of interest in an "informal" school setting – an after-school game-making club. In this setting, positioning was realized in claims about how students' production work was like/unlike commercial games, as objects of fan interest. The study echoes arguments about the situated nature of literacy and learning (Buckingham, 1993), by highlighting the ways in which production work aligned students with competing conceptions of what makes a game playable – an argument that is concerned with the authenticity of texts as games in a school setting.

In both settings the work of enacting identity was thus realized in similar ways. This similarity emphasizes the continuity, rather than difference, between how the settings function pedagogically – as sites of teaching and learning – with conceptions of what games "are" constituted as alliances with, and oppositions to, points of authority.

We started this chapter by presenting Brubaker and Cooper's argument that constructivist accounts of identity did not always manage to avoid its reification, often maintaining a methodological commitment to treating identity as the property of a person rather than as an emergent property of a setting. This contradiction – this slippage between utterance and author – is something that we have tried to avoid in this chapter. This is because we have not extended our analysis beyond our data – the posted utterances, the game texts, and the interactions observed during the club sessions. It is important to recognize however, the difficulty of avoiding the slippage that Brubaker and Cooper (2000) identify. Such slippage was also, as we noted, central to the way in which data was generated in the school setting. The notion that identity is the property of an individual is central to institutionalized education practices; such a notion shores up the view that knowledge is also the property of an individual. Future research on games and learning might however be enhanced by exploring the scope of a different notion of identity, one which foregrounds the movement of positions around what games are. This helps us to re-imagine how we might think of fan productivity as educational.

References

Andersen, N. A. (2003). *Discursive analytical strategies: Understanding Foucault, Koselleck, Laclau, Luhmann*. Bristol: Polity Press.

Buckingham, D. (2007). *Beyond technology*. Cambridge: Polity Press.

Buckingham, D. (1993). *Children talking television: The making of television literacy*. London: Falmer Press.

Brubaker, R. & Cooper, F. (2000). Beyond Identity'. *Theory and Society*, 29, 1–47.

Donath, J. (1999). Identity and deception in the virtual community. In M. A. Smith & P. Kolloch (Eds.), *Communities in cyberspace* (pp. 29–59). London: Routledge.

Fiske, J. (1992). The cultural economy of fandom. In L. Lewis (Ed.), *The adoring audience: Fan culture and popular media* (pp. 30–49). London and New York: Routledge.

Gee, J. P. (2003). *What video games have to teach us about learning and literacy*. New York: Palgrave.

Hall, S. (1992). The question of cultural identity. In S. Hall, D. Held, & T. McGrew (Eds.), *Modernity and its futures* (pp. 273–316). Cambridge: Polity Press.

Hayles, K. N. (1999). *How we became posthuman: Virtual bodies in cybernetics, literature and informatics*. Chicago: University of Chicago Press.

Hills, M. (2002). *Fan cultures*. London and New York: Routledge.

Hills, M. (2004). Strategies, tactics and the question of Un lieu Propre: What/ where is 'Media Theory.' *Social Semiopics*, 14(2), 133–149.

Jenkins, H. (2004, February 6). Why Heather can write. *MIT Technology Review*. Online at http://www.technologyreview.com/Biztech/13473/page1/.

Jenkins, H. (1992). *Textual poachers: Television fans and participatory culture*. New York: Routledge.

Lave, J. & Wenger, E. (1996). Practice, person, social world. In H. Daniels (Ed.), *An introduction to Vygotsky* (pp. 143–150). London: Routledge.

Lewis, L., Black, R., & Tomlinson, B. (2009). Let everyone play: An educational perspective on why fan fiction is, or should be, legal. *International Journal of Learning and Media*, 1(1), 67–81.

Pelletier, C. (2007). *Learning through design: Meaning and subjectivity in young people's computer game production work*. PhD thesis, Institute of Education, University of London.

Pelletier, C. (2009). Games and learning: What's the connection? *International Journal of Learning and Media*, 1(1), 83–101.

Sandvoss, C. (2005). *Fans: The mirror of compulsion*. London: Blackwell.

Sefton-Green, J. (2004). Literature review in informal learning with technology outside school. (Nesta Futurelab Series, Report 7). Online at http://www.futurelab.org.uk/research/reviews/07_01.htm last accessed 10/6/2005.

Turkle, S. (1996). Who am we? *Wired*, 4.01. Online at http://www.wired.com/wired/archive/4.01/turkle.html last accessed 1/10/2006.

Webb, S. (2001). Avatar culture: Narrative, power and identity in virtual world environments. *Information, Communication & Society*, 4(4), 560–594.

Whiteman, N. (2007) *The establishment, maintenance, and destabilisation of fandom: A study of two online communities and an exploration of issues pertaining to Internet research*. PhD thesis, Institute of Education, University of London. http://homepage.mac.com/paulcdowling/ioe/studentswork/whiteman.html.

Whiteman, N. (2008a). Learning at the cutting edge? Help-seeking and status in online videogame fan sites. *Information Technology, Education and Society*, 9(1), 7–26.

Whiteman, N. (2008b). Homesick for Silent Hill: Modalities of nostalgia in fan responses to *Silent Hill 4: The Room*. In L. Taylor & Z. Whalen (Eds.), *Playing the past: History and nostalgia in videogames* (pp. 32–49). Nashville, TN: Vanderbilt University Press.

Whiteman, N. (2012). *Undoing Ethics: Rethinking Practice in Online Research*. New York: Springer.

Williamson, M. (2005). *The lure of the vampire: Gender, fiction and fandom from Bram Stoker to Buffy*. London: Wallflower Press.

8 Navigating Life as an Avatar: The Shifting Identities-in-Practice of a Girl Player in a Tween Virtual World

Deborah A. Fields and Yasmin B. Kafai

There is a long-standing tradition of studying play and games from the perspective of understanding how children come to participate in the practices, norms and artifacts of the larger communities in which they live (Corsaro, 2005; Goodwin, 2006; Opie & Opie, 1985; Piaget & Inhelder, 1969; Sutton-Smith, 1986; Thorne, 1993). In the last two decades, much of children's play and games has moved into virtual spaces in form of digital toys, video games, and virtual worlds. Virtual worlds such as Neopets, Habbo Hotel, Toontown, Barbie Girls, Webkinz, and Whyville among others offer digital publics, or meeting spaces, and game activities for thousands of concurrent players who create avatars as their virtual counterparts. While virtual worlds are popular among millions of children, we know little about how players join these communities and how and why they engage in different activities.

In this chapter we study how one girl learned to participate in what was for her a new setting of play – a virtual world called Whyville.net with an emphasis on science education, populated by over a million young people ages eight to sixteen. Girls in particular have become prominent players in virtual worlds, a trend counter to many early observations that documented the absence of girls and women in gaming and technology at large (e.g., Cassell & Jenkins, 1998). The study of virtual worlds as play spaces then allows us to continue a conversation about gender and gaming to understand better "which games [girls] play, why and with whom, and whether they take advantage of in-game opportunities to generate, not just consume game experiences" (Kafai, Heeter, Denner, & Sun, 2008, p. xviii). Further, because Whyville is a new social world for kids who participate, it provides a unique opportunity to study identity construction, or how participants on Whyville shape and are shaped as certain sorts of people through interaction with others (Gee, 2000/2001).

Our study is situated between interests in girls' participation in virtual worlds and identity construction – how girls establish who gets to be whom through play. This chapter is part of a larger study of different aspects of learning in the virtual world of Whyville that included over six hundred participants in Whyville, twenty "tweens" (young people be*tween* childhood and teenage years roughly ages ten and twelve) in an after school club, and forty tweens in two sixth-grade classes (eleven to twelve years old). In prior research we studied different aspects of learning and participation in Whyville: issues in avatar representation, ethnicity, learning science, cheating, and learning from peers across social settings including the classes, the club, and Whyville (see Feldon & Kafai, 2008; Fields & Kafai, 2010, 2009; Kafai, Cook, & Fields, 2007; Kafai, Feldon, Fields, Giang, & Quintero, 2007). While these studies provided much information about general trends in tweens' participation in Whyville, we wanted to understand how individuals learned to participate in Whyville and how they established themselves in that social world.

To begin to study this we developed a case study of one twelve-year old girl, Zoe[1] or bluwave within Whyville, who participated in all of the contexts of our larger project: Whyville, the after-school club, and one of the sixth-grade classes. We knew a few things about her participation from the club and the class, such as that she was an early "expert" in Whyville from whom other kids sought help with games and trading parts for avatars. However, beyond these observations, easily revealed in video data, we knew little about how she became a core participant in Whyville and what her participation in that virtual world was like. How did she develop expertise in Whyville? Were there changes in how she acted in relation to others in Whyville, or was there a single, linear trajectory of participation? How did she face dilemmas related to representation, ethnicity, and cheating that we identified as common issues of participation from the larger study?

Like other researchers before, we wanted to examine aspects of her play and participation that for us were previously unseen or unrecognized, largely because of methodological challenges in investigating an individual's participation in the virtual world. In our prior studies of Whyville we had relied on video and field notes of the club to help us learn about dynamics and social interaction there (Kafai, 2008), sometimes supplemented by focused digging into logfiles and chat data of kids' interactions surrounding a particular practice (Fields & Kafai, 2009, 2010). Or, to understand broader dimensions of participation in Whyville, we searched Whyville's

---

[1] Pseudonyms are used for both names and usernames to protect confidentiality.

weekly newspaper and performed quantitative analyses on the logfile and chat data (e.g., Feldon & Kafai, 2008; Kafai Cook, et al., 2007). In order to understand Zoe's participation and identities in Whyville, we *qualitatively* studied logfile data to track her navigation and chat interactions over a six-month period. In the following sections, we outline our theoretical framework of identities-in-practice, the methods and data sources that we used to examine Zoe's participation, and findings about her changing identities, or identities-in-practice, in Whyville.

Theories of Identities-in-Practice

Ever since Lave and Wenger (1991) argued that learning is situated and that learning means becoming a different person with respect to a local community of people, the concept of identity has played an important role in understanding learning in sociocultural educational research. To put it in their terms, "learning involves the construction of identities" (Lave & Wenger, 1991, p. 53). From this perspective, when one learns, it is not just learning a body of abstract knowledge but learning how to be and to act and to believe within a particular group or community of people. This idea of identity construction as learning differs from the more traditional psychological approach to identity as a developmental achievement of adolescence popularized by Erikson (1968) in the 1940s and 1950s. In contrast to Erikson's view that youth must accomplish and commit to a certain notion of themselves, one that exemplifies some continuity of self, the sociocultural perspective sees identity as a continual negotiation between oneself and the world. "Being recognized as a certain 'kind of person,' in a given context" (Gee, 2000/2001, p. 99) is accomplished through interaction and activity. So from this "sociocultural" viewpoint, to which we refer in the rest of this proposal when discussing "identity," studying identities offers ways to make sense of a person in relationship to other people and capture the intersection of the individual and the social.

In order to emphasize the continual negotiation of individuals within local communities and contexts, a number of researchers have begun to use the more specific term "identities-in-practice" (Barton, Tan, & Rivet, 2008; Holland, Lachicotte, Skinner, & Cain, 1998; Leander, 2002; Vadeboncoeur, Hirst, & Kostogriz, 2006). A practice theory of identity tries to account for the ways that a person's identity is both stabilized and changed during the course of interaction – how a social situation defines or constructs how a person is perceived through practice and how an individual may disrupt such construction through their actions (Leander, 2002; Wortham,

2004). Considered as a productive convergence of cultural-historical activity theory and theories of social space, identities-in-practice are considered to be "historical, produced in activity, and unable to be analytically separated from activity" (Leander, 2002, p. 204). Researchers within this line of thinking demonstrate how identities are created in the moment through interaction, albeit layered over time. It is this specific theoretical framework of identities-in-practice that we draw on in describing one tween-aged girl's changing participation in the virtual world of Whyville. This lens of "identity" is useful for our case study because we are particularly interested in how she was perceived and how she acted in relation to others on Whyville. In large part because of the data available to us regarding her participation in that community (logfiles and chat records), we focus on her identities-in-practice as revealed in her activities and textual interaction rather than a self-reflective sense of who she is. To better understand the context in which this takes place, we describe the virtual world of Whyville. net in more detail in the next section.

The Virtual World of Whyville

Whyville.net is a massive, free virtual world (in 2005 at the time of the study it had 1.2 million registered citizens) that encourages youth ages eight to sixteen to play casual science games in order to earn a virtual salary in "clams," which they can then spend on buying and designing parts for their avatars, projectiles to throw at other players, and other goods such as cars and plots of land. The consensus among Whyvillians is that earning a good salary and thus procuring a large number of clams to spend on face parts or other goods is essential for fully participating in Whyville (Kafai & Giang, 2007). Social interactions with others are the highlight of life in Whyville for most players and consist primarily of Y-mailing (the Whyville version of e-mail) and chatting on the site. Chat takes place in dozens of public and private locations in the virtual world of Whyville, where players are visible to each other on the screen as floating faces, typically with shoulders and chests as seen in the picture of the Beach in Figure 8.1. Although Whyville has dozens of locations where citizens may float around and chat with each other, some locales are more densely populated than are others and serve as places to meet people, including the Beach, the SunRoof, and the Mall. Other locations, because they require the insider knowledge of teleporting to get there, are not commonly known to new citizens or "newbies". These spaces are less densely populated and include the Moon, Mars, and Saturn (see Fields & Kafai, 2009, for how newbies learn to teleport). Still

Figure 8.1. The Beach on Whyville.

other locales serve as niche locations for special interest groups such as
GeekSpeak (where avatars with darker brown skin tones hang out), Sector
Y (Goths), and WhyHouse (anime/cartoon cats and dogs).

Since player-created faces are the primary representation of one's presence on Whyville, how one looks is very important. Looks also demonstrate
a player's tenure on Whyville and relative experience level; new players
have fewer clams, and their looks generally show this because cheaper face
parts are perceived as less attractive (Kafai, Fields, et al., 2007). There are
four ways to acquire face parts – collecting donated, cheap, parts from
Grandma's, buying them from Akbar's Face Mall, having a friend donate a
specific part, or trading face parts at the Trading Post. Although Grandma's
serves as the first place most new citizens frequent to obtain face parts,
the limited face parts obtained there are generally looked down upon by
more experienced players. Akbar's is a collection of stores selling face parts
created by Whyvillians and sold for clams – better looking face parts are
often more expensive. The Trading Post consists of over forty rooms where
individual pairs of Whyvillians can trade their face parts for another's face
parts or clams.

While Whyville is the primary setting of our research, we also draw on
data gathered in a school where youth played on Whyville in two different contexts. In early 2005 we set up an after-school club where twenty-
one tweens in the fourth through sixth grades (nine to twelve years old)
came to play on Whyville for an hour most days after school. While the

club began as a quiet place, it quickly became loud and lively as participants learned the site and began to shout advice to each other, arrange parties on Whyville, chat, throw virtual projectiles at one another, and critique each other's avatars (Kafai, 2008). Most youth were new to Whyville, so learning to participate in the site was a common (if tacit) goal. Club members eagerly displayed their knowledge of the site by offering advice and answering questions, such as how to create a good look or throw a projectile. The second context in which students played on Whyville were the two sixth-grade classes at the school For the most part, students' activities on Whyville were more structured during the class to facilitate their learning about a virtual virus, Whypox (Kafai, Cook, et al., 2007; Kafai, Feldon, et al., 2007; Kafai, Fields, et al., 2007). For this reason most of our analysis on social interaction concerns the club because we were interested in free choice participation in Whyville. The girl chosen for the case study presented in this chapter participated regularly in both the club and one of the sixth grade classes.

Background: Virtual Worlds and Identities

Much has been written about technology and identity from Sherry Turkle's early work (1986, 1995) to more recent studies (Black, 2006; Boellstorff, 2008; Lam, 2000; Leander & Lovvorn, 2006; Taylor, 2006). In creating avatars, representations of oneself in virtual spaces, and participating in virtual spaces, often one cannot be known outside of how one decides to portray oneself through visual representation, written chat, and perhaps an online profile. There is thus an opening to create a new identity "from scratch," or at least to choose which aspects of one's self will bleed into one's virtual persona. This provides opportunities to convey who one is in ways that one cannot in other social worlds because of one's unchosen body and local culture or to be someone very different in behavior or looks – avatars are "not just placeholders for selfhood, but sites of self-making in their own right" (Boellstorff, 2008, p. 149). In one sense this allows for a "second self" (Turkle, 1986) different from one's normal everyday self with people in "meat space" or "real" life. Further, because many virtual worlds have large populations in conjunction with the relative anonymity they provide, they provide unique opportunities to find an affinity group with a specific shared interest or develop oneself in ways not allowed in other social worlds. For instance, Black (2006) and Lam (2000) found that English language learners who were often viewed from a deficit model of achievement in their schools could construct identities of proficiency in online multicultural communities of fan fiction and pop culture.

Still, there are a number of challenges that people face when joining virtual worlds and trying to become a recognized member in them. Simply because one can design a look or an avatar from scratch does not mean that this is easy to do. For instance, in both the more adult-oriented virtual world of Second Life as in the tween-populated virtual world of Whyville, participants may design and sell parts for avatars including clothes, hair, accessories, or even different kinds of heads and bodies. However, the tools for doing so are challenging to use and most participants buy parts from others, making them reliant on whatever virtual income they have (Boellstorff, 2008). In Whyville as in other virtual worlds, this creates some degree of social stratification because what are considered to be better-looking face parts are usually much more expensive. Portraying different ethnicities is another issue in creating an avatar in both Second Life and Whyville. In both sites, while any skin color and even different kinds of species are available to wear (anime animals are a niche population in Whyville, while in Second Life round balls of light or furry baby animals have had their moments of popularity), whiteness is the default look as it is in other virtual sites (Boellstorff, 2008; Nakamura, 2002). In Whyville, over 90 percent of the clothing available comes with peach-colored skin, making it difficult to have much of a wardrobe if one's avatar is African American, Latina/o, Asian American, or even Goth (white skin) or Pixie (purple skin) (Kafai, Cook, et al., 2007).

Social interaction and ethics are other issues faced by new members of virtual worlds. In a site with over a million participants, how does one begin making friends? How much of one's real-life self ought one to share? When is it okay to pretend to be another gender or another age or simply lie? Researcher dana boyd (2007) has argued that places like Whyville are the new digital publics, places where adolescents can engage with each other without explicit adult supervision. Tweens are a particularly interesting age group because they are transitioning from childhood into adolescence. It is the time when they become interested in the opposite sex and explore this interest in talking, reading, and flirting with each other. Chat rooms and virtual worlds like Whyville allow tweens to experiment with various aspects of flirting without revealing their real-life identities or violating the boundaries established within their peer groups (Thorne, 1993). In our following documentation of the life of one girl player's avatar, we were able to draw on our understanding from several years' worth of research on these topics and hundreds of hours of our own participation in the virtual world to understand her activities in the broader context of the virtual world of Whyville.

Methods

Data Collection and Analyses

The study of Zoe/bluwave focused on observing the identities-in-practice of one tween girl in a virtual world. Although supplemented by field notes, videos, and an interview from the after-school club and the classes, the primary data in constructing this case study were logfiles of every click, public chat, and private whisper statements made by one girl over the course of six months. Making sense of logfiles qualitatively, especially longitudinally following one person over several months, is challenging and unusual and represents one of the goals of this chapter. Some researchers have used logfiles selectively over a short period, for instance, two girls over a few days (Bruckman, 2000) or a small group during a few class periods (Clarke & Dede, 2007). Others have done extensive *quantitative* analysis of log-files (e.g., Williams, Yees, & Caplan, 2008) or analyses of social networks (Ducheneaut, Yee, Nickell, & Moore, 2006). Perhaps the most common *qualitative* use of logfiles is to collect and analyze chat (Nardi, Ly, & Harris, 2007), but collection of chat has generally been limited to whatever place the researcher virtually inhabits at a given time.

We began by choosing Zoe/bluwave, one of the club members who we thought had a fairly high participation rate in Whyville based on her interactions in the club. We first created minute-by-minute summaries by isolating her logfiles and going click by click through the data. Then we condensed these into short daily narratives that noted patterns and innovations in participation. Each line of her logfiles contained her username, a time stamp, her location in Whyville, and if applicable, chat or whisper text. In all there were over 54,000 lines of text in bluwave's logfiles. To create the minute-by-minute summaries, we sampled the days she was on Whyville, selecting the first seven days and then alternating every five or six days to ensure breadth of days of the week in our sample. In all we analyzed thirty-five days during her first two months on Whyville from January to June 2005. In the final interpretation of Zoe/bluwave's activities, we also took into account video, field notes, and interview data from the club while looking for consensus or discrepancies between her activities and "ways of being."

Limitations and Ethics

Although documenting Zoe/bluwave's logfiles and chat in this way illuminated many aspects of her participation in ways that were hidden to us before, this method provides far from a perfect picture of her activities. First, chat files sorted by username only give us one side of the conversation. We are left to guess at what others were saying or when she switched from talking from one person to another by bluwave's responses. Occasionally if we thought she was with someone else participating in the study from school, we would look at that specific moment in time and sort by usernames from school participants, isolating the people in the same room with her and documenting a fuller conversation; unfortunately this turned out to be very rare. Second, we do not have all of her online data. For instance, we did not collect photos of her changing avatar or a spatial record of her movements within particular spaces on Whyville. As one might imagine from the picture of the Beach (Figure 8.1), avatars move around in Whyville, and much can be signified by relative proximity. Many people move next to each other when whispering on Whyville, embodying the closeness of a private conversation. We also did not collect ymails because these were deemed to be more personal than live chat. Thus, we have not documented who she ymailed, how often she ymailed specific individuals or the content of ymails. While we know how much time she spent ymailing and can often infer who she ymailed based on the order of activities (talking to someone, saying she would ymail him or her, and going immediately to ymail), we have very limited knowledge of this practice that lent itself to more enduring relationships. Ymail is generally used to keep in touch with already established friends because it does not contemporaneously depend on finding someone on Whyville. Finally, this is an analysis of one girl's participation in a particular virtual world for a limited amount of time at a certain period in the development of that virtual world. Although we can identify certain common trends in participation and what may be some exceptions in the life of our case study, both Zoe/bluwave and Whyville have changed over the past four years since the data were collected, and we wish to underscore that neither she nor Whyville should be considered static or as limited to our description in this chapter. Also, these data were analyzed several years after her actual participation in early 2005; thus, we were not able to check our interpretations of her activities with her (member checking).

This final issue brings up questions about the ethics of our online research (Kraut et al., 2004), namely, collecting and analyzing an individual's logfiles and chat without being able to discuss them with Zoe/bluwave herself. We collected the data with full knowledge of parents and the related Institutional Review Board approval. Students signed a separate assent form agreeing to be a part of the study and knowing that they could stop data collection or review videotapes at any time. We know from conversations recorded in field notes and video that kids in the club discussed that Whyville leaders could see all of their chat and that they looked for behavior and chat that went against the rules of the site such as sharing phone numbers or related personal information, using inappropriate language, or scamming others. When the leaders of the club or teachers of the classes became aware of behavior that they considered troublesome (such as prodigious flirting by the boys), they discussed this with students, reminding them to act on Whyville as they would if their parents were looking over their shoulders. Of course, as often happens in research, the participants became familiar with having video cameras around the club and acted similarly with regard to our collection of logfiles.

In the rest of the chapter we use Zoe's username "bluwave" when describing her Whyville activities and "Zoe" when describing interviews or after-school club activities rather than using the cumbersome Zoe/bluwave throughout the chapter. While in some ways these two names could be considered synonymous, in Whyville she was only known by her username. She inhabited this self-chosen name, giving "bluwave" a reputation among others who put her into their address book as a friend or recognized her when she entered a room in Whyville. In Whyville one's username has much more enduring power for recognition than how one looks, because looks can frequently change while usernames are immutable[2]. In line with discovering how she acted and in some way who she was in Whyville, it seems appropriate to talk about her as bluwave in relation to that social space. Because this chapter is focused on how she learned to participate in Whyville, especially those aspects of her identity that were unknown to us from prior studies, we predominantly refer to her as bluwave except at the beginning of the next section where we describe what we knew about her before we delved into the logfiles qualitatively and chronologically.

Findings

A Brief Introduction to Zoe

Zoe was a twelve-year-old, sixth-grade, African American girl at the time of the study. In addition to being a regular club participant, she participated in one of the two sixth-grade classes that played on Whyville. In the club she

---

[2] Unless one opens a new account, in which case the person must reintroduce him- or herself to friends so that they know who the person is.

Figure 8.2. A re-Creation of bluwave's Whyville look.

was one of the first members to learn inside gaming practices on Whyville such as teleporting and throwing projectiles (Fields & Kafai, 2009, 2010), and she often taught others how to do things on Whyville, such as trading face parts. In fact, what she said that she most liked about Whyville in an interview three months into her life on the site was the social opportunity to hang out with friends and the financial side of life: "almost like a real everyday life, because you get a salary … and you can raise it by play-ing games or selling parts." In her interview she described her choice of username as "I first wanted 'angel,' they were all gone, even with all the numbers," and then she chose something that shone and sparkled "so I can shine." We created the pseudonym "bluwave" to mirror the shining of her original username. The theme of angels and shining came up again as she described her avatar sometimes appearing as an angel with wings (halos and wings are commonly available on Whyville) and wearing a T-shirt with her sister's name on it that she designed. She often put on an "I'm so bored" arm when she had nothing to do. We have made a re-creation[3] of what she may have looked like on Whyville with the halo, wings, and "bored" arm (see Figure 8.2).

[3] Although we have a verbal description of her avatar, we do not have an original screen-shot. Because this was pilot research into participation in virtual worlds, we simply did not collect everything that in retrospect would have been helpful.

Zoe was not only one of the quicker learners of the club, she was also one of the core 7 percent of participants on Whyville. Across our 595 participants in the larger study, representative of the population of Whyville as a whole, bluwave was in the top set of participants, the group that participated most regularly and intensely on Whyville (Fields, Giang, & Kafai, 2008).

In constructing a case study, deciding which parts of a person's life, even a virtual life, to describe is difficult. There is a strong temptation to be sensational, but culture is "lived out in the mundane and ordinary" (Boellstorff, 2008, p. 72). For this reason we have tried to pay attention to patterns and phases of participation, activities that took precedence at different times. Of course, we also have particular questions about how bluwave established one or more identities on Whyville and how these related to what we knew of her from the club and her self-description. In other words, we have an interest in seeing things that we did *not* know about from her participation in the club. So in the following sections we briefly describe daily patterns of activity sustained over the course of her time in Whyville; how she became an "insider" in a primary area of activity, the Trading Post; a shift in her avatar design relating to ethnicity and her engaging in flirting; and a period of scamming other Whyvillians. As we describe various aspects of her participation and identities, we also attempt to illuminate aspects of Whyville that are important to understanding her avatar's life.

The Daily Life of bluwave as an Avatar

Early on bluwave took up what is probably a very familiar pattern of Whyville participation: logging on to Whyville, checking ymail messages, checking her bank statement, adjusting her look using a feature called "Pick Your Nose" and then alternating between socializing and earning clams, perhaps with a shopping break at Akbar's Face Mall. Earning clams is accomplished by playing science games[4], profiting from the trading of face parts, or designing and selling face parts, the latter of which is quite difficult and is usually taken up after several weeks of participation (Kafai, Fields, et al., 2007). Bluwave gradually built up her salary by finishing several levels of science games, going through periods of heavier and lighter play of these games; she played salary-raising games more regularly during weeks 1 through 3 and 6 through 8, with a dip in participation during

---

[4] For a detailed analysis of most science games present when bluwave played them in 2005, see Aschbacher (2003).

weeks 4 and 5. In creating her avatar, she began with donated parts from Grandma's supplemented with parts from trading at the Trading Post or shopping at Akbar's Face Mall. After her first two weeks, she completely stopped going to Grandma's and relied solely on shopping and trading. This in itself was a move toward higher competence in Whyville in what might be considered an important move toward a socially acceptable look since parts from Grandma's are generally ill-esteemed (Kafai, Fields, et al., 2007).

In building her social life, by the end of her first week bluwave had already started a regular practice of browsing social areas in Whyville, jumping from space to space until she found a suitable place to try to make friends. Once she made a friend (usually at the Trading Post or in a highly populated area of Whyville like the Beach), they would often go to a quieter location to chat and would follow up the acquaintance by ymailing each other. It is intriguing that bluwave made friends by hanging out at the Trading Post. Although the entryway to the Trading Post is crowded with people making trades, based on our observations it is not common as a place to search for friends. By the end of her first week, she had added flirting to her regular social agenda of making friends, discussed later. Some of her most frequent comments to others were compliments on looks, insults about looks, requests for information, or answers to questions. If someone insulted her, she often found creative ways to bypass the chat filter and curse back at the offender, such as using asterisks ("bi***") or misspellings ("bioch"). Most of these patterns are typical of some of the population in Whyville, though bluwave was one of the more intense and regular players on the site.

A Quick Adaptation to Whyville Trading

One of the places where bluwave spent extensive amounts of time in Whyville was the Trading Post. In the after school club, Zoe was one of the first members to teach others how to trade on Whyville, and she often solicited others to go to the Trading Post and trade with her. In her final interview, she said that one of her favorite parts about Whyville was trading as it related to the financial exploration she enjoyed on Whyville. How did she figure out how to trade well and what were her activities at the Trading Post?

Bluwave first went to the Trading Post on her second day in Whyville. In her first seven days, bluwave spent over twenty hours on Whyville, and 38 percent of those (or almost 8 hours) were at the Trading Post, where

Table 8.1. *bluwave's Changed Discourse of Trading*

Day 3	Day 6
you have anything else?	u lik
let me see!!	a barrette for your hair
some clams	HI!
okay, ill trade the pokadot hair pin for the clams	25??
ill trade the clamz for the hair	Kk
do you hav any oter hair?	how about 20
let me see!	
yes..the first one looks cool!!!!	
wanta trade	

she quickly learned to trade parts. There was a significant learning curve as within that first week she dramatically changed the way she negotiated trades. At first she spoke in long phrases such as "does anyone want a head?" or "okay, ill trade the pokadot hair pin for the clams." But by the end of her first week she had adapted to a shortened, more precise language that fit her trading interests. Consider the differences between the two different trading exchanges on day 3 and day 6 in Table 8.1. These two trade negotiations are indicative of bluwave's trading conversations in the first three days and in the last two days of her first week. In contrast to the early part of her first week, by day 6 she started with a shorter invitation to trade ("u lik"), having put up a barrette for trade, probably the same polka-dot hairpin discussed on day 3 as it is a common newbie part. She had a sales pitch, "a barrette for your hair." Instead of saying that she wanted clams, something she had realized was more versatile than face parts, she simply listed a price ("25??") and followed quickly with a markdown, "how about 20." She also used shortened spellings and language more commonly used in Whyville, "u" for you, "lik" for like, "Kk" for okay.

The change in discourse shown in Table 8.1 demonstrates part of bluwave's new ability to negotiate trades. She also changed her pattern of participating at the Trading Post from having longer conversations with Whyvillians in a given room in the Post to cycling quickly from room to room saying, "u lik?" or "got any clamz?" and quickly moving on to another room if she did not like the answers. This probably made better use of her time, allowing her to see more people in a shorter amount of time and quickly gather whether they had clams or they were interested in anything she had. All of these changes of participation exhibit her learning the "big-D" Discourse of Whyville, "ways of thinking, acting, interacting, valuing, feeling, believing, and using symbols, tools, and objects in the right places and at the right times" (Gee, 1999, p. 13) as well as the appropriate language terms or little-d discourse, demonstrating that she has learned something about being a Whyvillian (Steinkuehler, 2006). Interestingly, bluwave did not simply use the Trading Post for accumulating wealth and getting good face parts. She made her first friends there, experienced rejections of friendship based on her looks, and apparently learned what was considered ugly and "hot" on Whyville. Related to looks and friendship, the Trading Post was also one of the places where she most defined herself in relation to ethnicity.

The Challenge of Representing Race

Creating a good (or acceptable) look on Whyville can be more challenging than one might think. There are many different reasons for choosing a particular look: being like one's "real" self, having something that one cannot have in real life (thick lips or a haircut parents would not allow), displaying an affinity for something, wearing something popular, or just creating an aesthetic piece (Kafai, Fields, et al., 2007). One thing is certain: Without a good look, some people will probably make fun of a user. Zoe described some of her changes in looks on Whyville as a response to social critique of her look:

> The first time [I changed my look] I was a newbie and I had like a complete face and [other Whyvillians were] making fun of me, like, 'Oh you newbie face, you need to buy clothes that the girls wear on.' And then I changed my look to another complete face that looks like me and then after that I didn't look a lot like me.

Based on her interview, we can tell that the first look Zoe created for bluwave was a face that was already completely drawn, often sold as a "newbie face" for those who could not afford separate eyes, eyebrows, nose, and mouth. Apparently her first face did not have a body, though her other later faces did. Interestingly, Zoe described each face in relation to whether it looked like her or not. In what ways in particular did her avatar resemble her own physical appearance? Bluwave's online activities give us a perspective on what she meant by that.

Even in her first week bluwave began to pursue an African American look on Whyville. We see this in her requests for shirts that matched her dark-skinned head beginning on day 4 (January 14): "does anyone hav any african-american t-shirts???" In Whyville, all clothing comes with necks, so

Figure 8.3. An example of a mismatched head and body.

an African-American T-shirt is a shirt that has a dark brown neck and arms. One fashion faux pas is to have a neck that does not match one's head – it is something of a jarring look (see Figure 8.3). Our previous research documented inequities in the percentage of face parts that have non-peach skin, whether dark brown, lighter brown, olive, or yellow – in fact, there are even fewer non-peach bodies than there are non-peach heads (Kafai, Cook, et al., 2007). Bluwave seems to have struggled with these imbalances in her efforts to obtain dark-skinned bodies to match her head.

Bluwave's efforts to be black on Whyville came to the fore at the Trading Post. Often she would respond to someone's offer of a trade by saying, "no i'm not white," (January 16) as an explanation for why she was not interested in certain proffered parts presumably with peach skin colors, or ask, "do u have any black ones?... no! not that kind of black! african-american" (January 18). Although she solicited "black" face parts, apparently many Whyvillians did not interpret her request in terms of ethnicity and skin color but in terms of clothing colors. By her twenty-second day in Whyville, bluwave shifted from eagerly soliciting dark-skinned face part to apologizing for only having African American parts when she began a trade. For instance, she responded to a trading request by apologetically framing her selection of available parts as limited to African American parts: "2 tell u the truth...i don't hav the type of stuff... do u mind if it's

Figure 8.4. SpinGeek or the "Black Place" on Whyville.

african-american?" (February 1). The following day (February 2) she suddenly shifted from trading African American parts to only dealing in Latino
parts, probably meaning a lighter shade of brown – something more easily
obtained than the darker brown more commonly interpreted as African
American on Whyville. This change in skin color is likely what she meant
in her interview when she described her third look as not "a lot like me"
because this coincided with the second time she changed her look. There
are other ways of being or associating with African-Americans on Whyville
besides having a dark brown color of skin. The location SpinGeek (see
Figure 8.4) is known as the "black place" in Whyville. Bluwave began hanging out in SpinGeek at the end of her first week on Whyville, January 18
and went there quite frequently from February 13 to the end of our data
collection. Bluwave's interactions at SpinGeek commonly included asking
for names of specific face parts, soliciting friendships, flirting, and ban-
tering compliments and insults back and forth. It seems to be the place
she most frequented for getting names of face parts, particularly Latino
ones – not surprising since it probably was and remains the most likely
place for her to find other darker-skinned avatars like herself. Both of these

developments – bluwave's changing her avatar from African American to Latina and coming to frequent a particular social space in Whyville – represent shifts in her development as a Whyvillian. She adapted for better or worse to the availability and socially constrained acceptability of looks and found a local hangout.

Although in our prior research we identified inequities in face part availability in Whyville, we did not have any hints from club members or from *The Whyville Times* articles that the tweens were frustrated by the difficulties of obtaining non-peach skin parts. Nowhere in any of our interviews did Zoe or other African American, Asian American, or Latina/o tweens reference ethnicity in describing their looks. Similarly in our analysis of *Times* articles tweens never expressed personal frustrations at unavailability of darker-skinned face parts – they only spoke out in general about the inequities and called for designers to take up the call to design more face parts for African Americans and Latinos (see Kafai, Cook, et al., 2007, for descriptions of these face parts). Zoe provides one clear case of a tween who was frustrated in her enduring attempts to express her ethnicity in her avatar's looks through darker skin tones. Certainly not all of her avatar's looks were related to a virtual representation of physical looks; haloes and angel's wings were hardly part of her "real life" look though they were certainly part of her narrative about herself as angelic and shining. But her effort to find darker-skin-toned face parts is an example of a concerted effort to connect an ethnic identity across spaces. It also demonstrates one way that she moved to more central participation in Whyville, adapting to a skin color that was higher in demand so she could continue her trading and adapt her look to one interpreted as more acceptable.

Contradictions in Flirting

Flirting is a common practice on Whyville but in the case of bluwave we were surprised by her flirting activities because of the discrepancy between observations collected in the club and her chat logs. The age group that participates on Whyville (eight to sixteen years old) may have something to do with the frequency of practice of flirting as youth this age tend to engage in "anticipatory socialization" (Kafai, Fields, & Searle, 2010), imitating the flirting practices that they observe in older youth and on popular media. The general pattern of Whyvillian flirting consists of soliciting members of the opposite sex in a crowded, populous area and following-up with individuals who respond positively in a quieter, less populous area[5]. Most "relationships" do not appear to last beyond a short conversation or occasional ymails. Although flirting is common in Whyville, in our after-school club, none of the girls publicly flirted. While we had over a hundred accounts of male club members discussing girlfriends, coming up with pick-up lines (usually something like "u r hot"), or shopping for things to give their girlfriends, only the boys engaged in these activities. In fact, though the girls teased the boys about their invented pick-up lines and even gave them advice about flirting, they generally showed disdain for flirting activities. One club participant, Briana, summed her opinions up this way: "Whydating is whack!" Some of the girls' disdain for flirting might be attributed to the mild reprimand one of the leaders gave to club members midway through the club regarding flirting on Whyville. Yet much to our surprise, when we started going through the logs minute by minute, we discovered that bluwave and other girls flirted on a regular basis in Whyville. This was startling to us because girls' flirting was never captured in the field notes or videos.

Bluwave's flirting began on her fifth day in Whyville (January 15) when she started asking, "r u single" and "wanna hook up?" Later on other common lines were "a/s/l" (age, sex, location – a common form of communication in dating adds) or "u r hot." Her efforts became a bit more sophisticated over the next few days, and on her eighth day (January 18) she described to some school friends on Whyville that "i almost hav a boyfriend… because he told me to y-mail him… all he has to do." In other words, a flirtation resulted in a boy asking her to ymail him, and all he had to do was reply back to seal the deal. All of these interactions are typical of the casual flirtation that is frequent on Whyville (Kafai, Fields, et al., 2010) and bluwave's adoption of these practices could be considered a sign that she was trying out some of the ways that Whyvillians socially interact.

Bluwave's flirting changed over the months she inhabited Whyville. Several weeks into her participation, she demonstrated agency in her flirting by using her age to encourage or discourage potential suitors. If she wanted to turn away someone who was flirting with her she said, "im way too young 4 u… i'm just 12," (February 1), and if she wanted to encourage a flirtation, she would lie about her age, claiming she was thirteen years old living in Los Angeles. The following is one of these encounters (February 13):

[5] We are currently pursuing in depth systematic analyses of flirting in Whyville. See Kafai, Fields, and Searle (2010).

do u think i'm hot???

13/f/la

...

r we bf and gf?

kk

whymail me

In this incident bluwave asked for feedback on her looks ("do u think i'm hot???") and gave her age/sex/location where she lied about her age by saying she was thirteen as well as saying that she was from Los Angeles[6]. Then she confirmed that they were boyfriend and girlfriend ("bf and gf") and asked her new boyfriend to ymail her, the main way to make a relationship more long lasting in Whyville. These sorts of conversations happened regularly through the course of her second and third months on Whyville. However, during her fourth and fifth months bluwave's flirting became less frequent. Other practices also changed. For instance, she went to the Trading Post less often and instead took up playing checkers. She seemed to invest in friendships that lasted longer, and her occasional flirtations changed from the simple solicitation-confirmation-ymail pattern (described previously) to more enduring relationships with longer conversations.

Considering how much flirting takes place in Whyville, it should not be surprising that one of the core players participated in that practice. If she was figuring out how to participate in the Whyville culture, to become an insider, then it was almost inevitable that she would at least experiment with flirting. Indeed, as she became a more established member of Whyville, bluwave's flirtations changed from shallow pick-up lines to more extended conversational friendships. Yet we would not have been aware of either her flirting or the shift in her flirting practices without the minute-by-minute case study analysis of the first six months of her Whyville life. The detailed qualitative analysis revealed the incongruity between her

---

[6] In saying "13/f/la," bluwave was saying that she was 13 years old, female, and from Los Angeles. In Whyville, saying the city or state that one is from is acceptable in chat standards. Giving out more specific information such as the name of one's school, addresses, or phone numbers are not allowed. Before they can chat, all users must pass a chat test confirming that they understand these privacy rules, and Whyville both blocks more specific information in chat, searches for violations, and reprimands users who violate these rules by taking away chat privileges for a time.

practices in the club versus in Whyville, and the longitudinal aspect of the analysis uncovered the change from less to more enduring relationships in her socializing on Whyville. These methods revealed another aspect blu-wave's shifting identities-in-practice as well.

Scammer!

On February 21, six weeks into her life in Whyville, bluwave began using the Trading Post in a new way – to scam or fraud other Whyvillians out of their clams for the next fourteen days. It began after she herself was scammed. In the main lobby of the Trading Post, where Whyvillians mill around trying to identify people to trade with before moving on to a specific Trade Room, some Whyvillians broadly solicited people who wanted their "clams doubled." Bluwave expressed interest in this and followed them to the designated Trade Room (#48), but on find-ing out the details she at first expressed skepticism (see the following quoted conversation). After pressing the soliciting Whyvillians, "r u a scammer?? TELL THE TRUTH," she agreed to their methods, which consisted of one person (bluwave, the victim) putting all her clams up in a one-sided trade while the others put nothing up for trade. After the other party left his or her seat (giving the illusion of the trade ending), bluwave was told to press "agree" to complete the trade, thus giving all of her money to the scammers. Bluwave's side of the conversation appears in the following:

2:53 p.m.	Trade Room 48
	O SRRY
2:54 p.m.	i don't beleive u!!!!
	WAIT
	r u just gonnin on his side>>>>>
2:55 p.m.	fine
	r u a scammer?? TELL THE TRUTH
2:56 p.m.	fine ill do it
	get back in the chair ill do it
	soo what am i supposed 2 do?

After following the instructions, bluwave checked her bank statement and realized that all of her money was gone. Then she went immediately back to the Trading Post where she begged time and again for people to donate five clams to her (the amount charged for each trade) – she was so bereft that she could not even trade face parts! She actually found the culprits who tricked her, confronted them with their actions, and briefly followed them to their Trade Room to try to stop the next victim from falling prey to their scam. The "<<<<" in the following conversation were used to point directly at the culprit (bluwave probably went to the right of the culprit and used the arrows to point left at the culprit, then moved to the other side and pointed again at the culprit).

3:13 p.m.	Trading Post Lobby	
	U GUYS SCAMMED ME!!!!!!!!!	
3:14 p.m.	Trade Room 1	
	y did u scam me??	
3:15 p.m.	Trade Room 48	
	<<<<don't do it shes a scammer	
3:16 p.m.	i did it and i got my clamz scammed>>>>	

Shortly after this she gave up on trying to disrupt their scam, and after finally succeeding in getting someone to give her five clams unconditionally, she began to try the same scam on others.

Over the next two weeks, bluwave consistently tried to get unsuspecting Whyvillians to fall for the "clam doubling" scam as it is known among the Whyville designers. This involved going to densely populated areas on Whyville like the Beach and the Trading Post Lobby and asking people, "do u want ur clamz doubled?" If someone expressed interest, she directed him or her to a specific trading room and told the person, "put up all of ur clamz plz," then instructed him or her, "ok when i get out of the chair press the agree." From a chat frequency count, we know that she used the word "doubled" over two hundred times, demonstrating persistency in her scamming activity, though it did not continue past two weeks. In a single day (February 25), she actually recruited for her scam thirty times in ninety minutes and got six people to go to a trading room. We know that she completed her scam at least once and probably enough times to keep her continuing at it for a time. The following is the account of when she successfully completed her scam:

11:44am	The Moon
	do u want ur clamz doubled?
11:45am	rm 49 at the trading post kk
	Foyer, TradeRoom 49
	...
	put up ur clamz plz
11:48am	ok when i get out of the chair press agree the typ
	all clear?

11:49am   leave
          Index, tradeResult, oneMail, delete, records, userDetails
11:50am   records, userDetails, index 2x, bankStatement

In this conversation, bluwave began by recruiting a victim for her scam on the Moon with her typical solicitation, "do u want ur clamz doubled?" When the person responded positively, bluwave directed the person to Trade Room 49, then went there herself. A couple minutes later the person arrived and bluwave directed the Whyvillian to put all of his or her clams up for trade "put up ur clamz plz," then said to press "agree" when she left her chair. Bluwave then left her chair ("leave") and immediately went to check the result of the trade ("tradeResult"), checked her ymail, and looked at someone's profile on City Records (perhaps her victim's?), then checked her bank statement. Because there was a trade result, we know the trade went through. That bluwave checked her bank statement afterward is another confirmation that she successfully obtained the Whyvillian's clams.

Scams are not infrequent on Whyville, though they are strongly discouraged and warned against by both the designers and local citizens[7]. Along the range of cheating practices in Whyville, from making guides for science games to identity theft (stealing people's passwords and accounts), scams are on the unethical and fraudulent side and certainly not publicly condoned (Fields & Kafai, 2007). There are regular ymail warnings against giving out one's password and newspaper articles alerting citizens to the latest clever innovations in scamming. In some ways, Zoe's scamming could be seen as part of her efforts to be an insider on Whyville and in one sense it demonstrates her growing expertise in Whyville. She was a victim and then became a perpetrator; she imitated the practices of others in an effort to become rich (a common value in Whyville). It is also one other way that her Whyville life was tied to her frequenting of the Trading Post and her interests in the financial opportunities in Whyville. Not surprisingly, it is not something she discussed in her interview at the end of the after-school club. She did acknowledge in the interview that she had a few other Whyville accounts – a common way to earn more money on Whyville (the first author even did this to earn enough for her first Whyville car), though she did not describe the way that she persistently begged people to give her accounts that already had high salaries – an activity she carried out about

---

[7] If discovered, Whyville will punish or even erase the account of the perpetrators. Yet it does not appear as though bluwave ever reported the individuals who scammed her, nor did the individuals she tried to scam seem to report her.

the same time that she began scamming people. Both of these activities, seeking multiple Whyville accounts and scamming others, are indications of bluwave's move toward being a Whyville insider, building up experiences with practices that were common on the site, including scamming. But her adoption of the questionable practice of scamming was also temporary, lasting only two weeks. Bluwave's identity-in-practice as a scammer was temporary, lasting only two weeks of the six-month duration of our study.

Future Trends

Our case study of Zoe/bluwave's shifting identities-in-practice during her first six months of life in Whyville makes several contributions to the research of identities in virtual worlds. It is clear that no activity alone provides a comprehensive account of her time on Whyville, and many of her activities should be seen in the context of the larger Discourse(s) (Gee, 1999) functioning in Whyville. She adapted very quickly in learning the language and practices of trading as well as the values of earning money, creating a good "look," and making friends and boyfriends. She also changed over the course of her first six months of Whyville life. We cannot say "who" bluwave was except in the context of her practices at a given time; thus, we talk about her identities-in-practice as shifting.

Another important contribution our study makes is in the area of methods. By systematically and qualitatively delving through her logfiles and chat over six months, we were able to demonstrate how bluwave's participation changed rather than categorizing her into a number of stereotypical bins such as "core" player, girl, tween, or African American. Our data and analyses also enabled us to go beyond self-report in understanding her identities, a traditional limitation of many studies that depend on surveys or interviews. In fact we were able to identify surprises if not contradictions between her activities and interview from the club and her participation in Whyville that would have been missing had we only studied one data source or site.

There are limitations to our study. It is only one tween girl that we studied, and we know that she was exceptional in that she was one of the top 7 percent of Whyvillians in terms of her relatively heavy participation in the site (Fields, Giang, & Kafai, 2008). Currently we are conducting similar case studies of five other tweens from the after-school club to expand our understanding of the range of participation of different tweens in Whyville (Giang, Kafai, Fields & Searle, in press). Yet while these case studies are illuminating regarding identities-in-practice, they do not offer much help in understanding practices in Whyville as a whole (we depended on other studies to explicate those). We also were not able to ask Zoe for her reflection on her activities in Whyville because of the length of time between the data collection and this particular analysis.

Earlier we mentioned the potential of virtual worlds for exploring one's identities in the vastly populated spaces of online spaces. As the case of Zoe/bluwave demonstrates, there is the potential for changing "who one is," yet there are also limitations. On one hand, she was not able to take on whatever identity she wanted in Whyville, as in the case of her efforts to appear African American through a dark brown skin tone demonstrates. On the other hand, she seemed to be able to change how others interpreted her rather quickly. For instance, she shifted from regularly scamming Whyvillians to not scamming at all, and there appears to be no trace of stigmatized behavior toward her regarding this. Yet in sites where an established group of people interacts with a person regularly, such as a classroom, people cannot easily shift the identities others bestow on them (see Wortham, 2006, for an excellent example). If Zoe had tried out cheating or scamming behaviors at her school, she likely would not have been able to drop this identity as quickly as she did on Whyville.

Related, this case study also revealed some of the ways that identities from different social worlds could connect or be separate. Zoe/bluwave faced conflicts in the discourses and cultural models operating in the club and in Whyville. Some of her "real-life" identities-in-practice seeped across those two social spaces and others did not. Zoe's interests in finance, her strong ethnic identity as an African American, and her idea of herself as sparkling and angelic did seep into Whyville through her participation in the Trading Post, the visual representation of her avatar, and her adoption of SpinGeek (the "black place") as a regular hangout. But she faced large discrepancies of values regarding common (if sometimes discouraged) practices on Whyville such as flirting and scamming in contrast to social norms in the club and school. Beach, Thein, and Parks (2008) argue that we need to study "how adolescents' allegiances to social worlds shift in terms of adopting or rejecting the discourses and cultural models operating in these worlds" (p. 282). Our study has begun to explore this in noting bluwave's changing practices in flirting and scamming, ones that suggest she eventually rejected some of the cultural models operating on Whyville and embraced others. As part of her becoming a more central participant in Whyville, we might interpret her activities as trying on different practices and keeping some while discarding others. This is not meant to say that social practices in the club and Whyville were dichotomous. Rather, Whyville should be seen as a world with many social groups embracing different practices. Figuring out who she wanted to be and how she wanted to participate was part of Zoe/bluwave's developmental task as a player.

Conclusion

In this chapter we began to look at the multiple and changing "identities" of a girl player called Zoe/bluwave in one virtual space and some of the interactions (or lack thereof) between her "identities" in Whyville and her "identities" in the club. More than a decade ago, Sherry Turkle (1995) challenged researchers to look at experiences in cyberspace (or in our case, virtual worlds) as "serious play" and to reflect on the multiple identities we take on in those spaces:

> "Without a deep understanding of the many selves that we express in the virtual we cannot use our experiences there to enrich the real. If we cultivate our awareness of what stands behind our screen personae, we are more likely to succeed in using virtual experience for personal transformation." (p. 269)

Our case study does not fully meet the challenge Turkle posed because it did not facilitate Zoe's reflection of her selves or identities in the virtual world. But we hope it illuminates potential areas where such reflection and critical discussion about perception based on appearance or language, conflicts between social worlds could be encouraged, especially with the understudied and growing population of younger participants in virtual worlds.

Acknowledgments

The data collection for this case study was supported by a grant of the National Science Foundation (NSF-0411814) and the analyses and writings in part by a grant of the MacArthur Foundation to the second author. The views expressed are those of the author and do not necessarily represent the views of NSF, MacArthur Foundation, the University of Pennsylvania, or the University of California, Los Angeles. We wish to thank Stanton Wortham, James Bowers, and the editors of this volume for comments on previous versions of this chapter. Special thanks also to Michael Giang taught us how to use SPSS to sort through logfiles and Cameron Aroz and Tina Tom who assisted in reducing the clicks and chat to first minute-by-minute and finally daily summaries.

References

Barton, A., Tan, E., & Rivet, A. (2008). Creating hybrid spaces for engaging school science: How urban girls position themselves with authority by merging their social worlds with the world of school science. *AERJ*, 45, 68–103.

Beach, R., Thein, A., & Parks, D. (2007). *High school students' competing social worlds: Negotiating identities and allegiances through responding to multicultural literature.* Mahwah, NJ: Erlbaum.

Black, R. W. (2006). Language, culture, and identity in online fanfiction. *E-Learning*, 3(2), 170–184. Retrieved April 28, 2008, from http://www.wwwords.co.uk/elea/content/pdfs/3/issue3_2.asp#6.

Boellstorff, T. (2008). *Coming of age in second life: An anthropologist explores the virtually human.* Princeton, NJ: Princeton University Press.

boyd, d. (2007). Why youth (heart) social network sites: The role of networked publics in teenage social life. In D. Buckingham (Ed.), *Youth, Identity, and Digital Media* (MacArthur Foundation Series on Digital Learning; pp. 119–142). Cambridge, MA: MIT Press.

Bradley, K. (2005). Internet lives: Social context and moral domain in adolescent development. *New Directions for Youth Development*, (108), 57–76.

Bruckman, A. (2000). Situated support for learning: Storm's weekend with Rachael. *The Journal of the Learning Sciences*, 9(3), 329–372.

Cassell, J. & Cramer, M. (in press). High tech or high risk: Moral panics about girls online. In T. McPherson (Ed.), *Innovative uses and unexpected outcomes* (MacArthur Foundation Series on Digital Media and Learning).

Cassell, J. & Jenkins, H. (Eds.). (1998). *From Barbie to Mortal Kombat: Gender and games.* Cambridge, MA: MIT Press.

Clarke, J. & Dede, C. (2007). MUVEs as a powerful means to study situated learning. In C. Chinn, G. Erkins, & S. Puntambekar (Eds.), *The Proceedings of CSCL 2007: Of mice, minds and society.* New Brunswick, NJ: Publisher.

Corsaro, W. (2005). *The sociology of childhood.* (2nd Edition). London: Pine Forge Press.

Ducheneaut, N., Yee, N., Nickell, E., & Moore, R. (2006). Building an MMO with mass appeal: A look at gameplay in World of Warcraft. *Games and Culture*, 1, 281–317.

Erikson, E. H. (1968). Identity: Youth and crisis. Norton: New York.

Feldon, D. F. & Kafai, Y. B. (2008). Mixed methods for mixed reality: Overcoming methodological challenges to understand user activity in a massive multi-user virtual environment. *Educational Technology Research and Development*, 56, 1042–1629.

Fields, D. A., Giang, M. & Kafai, Y. B. (2008, March). *Girl gamers in virtual worlds: Portraits of participation and positionings in a tween gaming club.* Paper presented at the annual meeting of the American Educational Research Association, New York.

Fields, D. A. & Kafai, Y. B. (2007). Stealing from Grandma or generating knowledge: Contestations and effects of cheats in a tween virtual world. In A. Baba (Ed.) *Situated Play: Proceedings of the Digital Games Research Association (DIGRA)* (pp. 194–202). Tokyo, Japan: University of Tokyo

Fields, D. F. & Kafai, Y. B. (2010). Knowing and throwing mudballs, hearts, pies, and flowers: A connective ethnography of gaming practices. *Games and Culture*, 5(1), 88–115.

Fields, D. A. & Kafai, Y. B. (2009). A connective ethnography of peer knowledge sharing and diffusion in a tween virtual world. *International Journal of Computer Supported Collaborative Learning*, 4(1), 47–68.

Gee, J. P. (1999). *An introduction to discourse analysis: Theory and method.* London: Routledge.

Gee, J. P. (2000/2001). Identity as an analytic lens for research in education. *Review of Research in Education*, 25, 99–125.

Giang, M. T., Kafai, Y. B., Fields, D. A., & Searle, K. A. (in press). Social interactions in virtual worlds: Patterns and participation of tween relationship play. In J. Fromme & A. Unger (Eds.), *Computer games/player/game cultures: A handbook on the state and perspectives of digital games studies.* New York, NY: Springer-Verlag.

Goodwin, M. H. (2006). *Hidden lives of girls: Games of stance, status and exclusion.* Oxford: Blackwell Publishing.

Holland, D., Lachicotte, W., Skinner, D., & Cain, C. (2001). *Identity and agency in cultural worlds.* Cambridge, MA: Harvard University Press.

Jenkins, H., Purushotma, R., Clinton, K. Weigel, M., & Robison, A. J. (2007). *Confronting the challenges of participatory culture: Media education for the 21st century.* Retrieved July 27, 2007, from http://projectnml.org/.

Kafai, Y. B. (2008) Gender play in a tween gaming club. In Y. B. Kafai, C. Heeter, J. Denner & J. Sun (Eds.), *Beyond Barbie and Mortal Kombat* (pp. 111–124). Cambridge, MA: MIT Press.

Kafai, Y. B., Cook, M. S., & Fields, D. A. (2007). "Blacks deserve bodies too!" Design and discussion about diversity and race in a tween online world. In A. Baba (Ed.), *Situated play: Proceedings of the Digital Games Research Association (DIGRA)* (pp. 269–277). Tokyo, Japan: University of Tokyo.

Kafai, Y., Feldon, D., Fields, D. A., Giang, M., & Quintero, M. (2007). *Life in the time of Whypox: A virtual epidemic as a community event.* In C. Steinfeld, B. Pentland, M. Ackerman, & N. Contractor (Eds.) *Communities and Technologies*, Berlin: Spring Verlag, 171–190.

Kafai, Y. B., Fields, D. A., & Cook, M. S. (2007). Your second selves: Resources, agency and constraints in avatar design in a tween online world. In Akira Baba (Ed.) *Situated Play: Proceedings of the Digital Games Research Association (DIGRA)*, Tokyo, Japan: The University of Tokyo, 31–39.

Kafai, Y. B., Fields, D. A., & Searle, K. (2010). Multi-modal investigations of relationship play in virtual worlds. *International Journal of Gaming and Computer-Mediated Simulations*, 2(1), 40–48.

Kafai, Y. B. & Giang, M. (2007). Virtual playgrounds. In T. Willoughby & E. Wood (Eds.), *Children's learning in a digital world* (pp. 196–217). Oxford: Blackwell Publishing.

Kafai, Y. B., Heeter, C., Denner, J., & Sun, J. Y. (2008). (Eds.) *Beyond Barbie and Mortal Kombat.* Cambridge, MA: MIT Press.

Kraut, R., Olson, J., Banaji, M., Bruckman, A., Cohen, J., & Couper, M. (2004). Psychological research online: Report of Board of Scientific Affairs' Advisory Group on the Conduct of Research on the Internet. *American Psychologist*, 59(4), 1–13.

Lam, W. S. E. (2000). Second language literacy and the design of the self: A case study of a teenager writing on the Internet. *TESOL Quarterly*, 34(3), 457–483.

Lave, J. & Wenger, E. (1991). *Situated learning and legitimate peripheral participation*. Cambridge: Cambridge University Press.

Leander, K. M. (2002). Locating La Tanya: The situated production of identity artifacts in classroom interaction. *Research in the Teaching of English*, 37, 198–250.

Leander, K. M. & Lovvorn, J. F. (2006). Literacy networks: Following the circulation of texts, bodies, and objects in the schooling and online gaming of one youth. *Cognition and Instruction*, 24(3), 291–340.

Nakamura, L. (2002). *Cybertypes: Race, ethnicity, and identity on the Internet*. New York: Routledge.

Nardi, B. A., Ly, S., & Harris, J. (2007). Learning conversation in World of Warcraft. *Proceedings, HICSS*.

Opie, I. & Opie, P. (1985). *The singing game*. Oxford: Oxford University Press.

Phaire, C. B., Cady, D., Hommel, M., Jarrett, K., Robbins, T, & Chamberlain, B. (2008, July). *Games and learning in practice: An educator panel on implementing curricula*. Symposium presented at the annual conference of Games + Learning + Society 4.0, Madison, WI.

Piaget, J. & Inhelder, B. (1969). *The Psychology of the child*. New York: Basic Books.

Shrier, K. (2005). *Revolutionizing history education: Using augmented reality games to teach history*. Unpublished master's thesis. Massachusetts Institute of Technology.

Squire, K. (2004). *Replaying history: Learning world history through playing Civilization III*. Unpublished PhD dissertation, Indiana University.

Steinkuehler, C. A. (2006). Massively multiplayer online video gaming as participation in a discourse. *Mind, Culture, and Activity*, 13(1), 38–52.

Sutton-Smith, B. (1986). *Toys as culture*. New York: Gardener Press.

Taylor, T. L. (2006). *Play between worlds*. Cambridge, MA: MIT Press.

Thorne, B. (1993). *Gender play: Boys and girls in school*. Brunswick, NJ: Rutgers University Press.

Turkle, S. (1986). *The second self: Computers and the human spirit*. Cambridge, MA: MIT Press.

Turkle, S. (1995). *Life on the screen*: Identity in the age of the Internet. New York: Simon & Schuster.

Vadeboncoeur, J. A., Hirst, E., & Kostogriz, A. (2006). Spatializing sociocultural research: A reading of mediation and meaning as third spaces. *Mind, Culture, and Activity*, 13(3), 163–175.

Wenger, E. (1998). *Communities of practice: Learning, meaning, and identity*. Cambridge: Cambridge University Press.

Williams, D., Yee, N., & Caplan, S. (2008). Who plays, how much, and why? Debunking the stereotypical gamer profile. *Journal of Computer Mediated Communication*, 13(4), 993–1028.

Wortham, S. (2004). From good student to outcast: The emergence of a classroom identity. *Ethos*, 32(2), 164–187.

Wortham, S. (2006). *Learning identity: The joint emergence of social identification and academic learning*. Cambridge: Cambridge University Press.

Index

LEARNING IN DOING: SOCIAL, COGNITIVE, AND
COMPUTATIONAL PERSPECTIVES

The Learning in Doing series was founded in 1987 by Roy Pea and John Seely Brown.